Regent's Study
General Editor: Pat

Faith in the Centre
Christianity and Culture

LEIGH ROAD
BAPTIST CHURCH
ESSEX

Regent's Study Guides

Faith in the Centre
Christianity and Culture

Edited by
Paul S. Fiddes

Regent's Park College, Oxford
with
Smyth & Helwys Publishing, Inc.
Macon, Georgia

Faith in the Centre

Paul S. Fiddes

© 2001
Published by Regent's Park College, Oxford OX1 2LB, UK
in association with Smyth & Helwys Publishing, 6316 Peake Road,
Macon, GA 31210, USA

The paper used in this publication meets the minimum
requirements of American National Standard for Information
Sciences—Permanence of Paper for Printed Library Materials.
ANSI Z39.48–1984 (alk. paper)

Faith in the centre : Christianity and culture / edited by Paul S. Fiddes.
    p. cm. — (Regent's study guides; 9)
    Includes bibliographical references and index.

    ISBN (UK)0-9518104-8-0 (pbk.)
    ISBN (USA)1-57312-363-3 (pbk.)

    1. Christianity and culture. I. Fiddes, Paul S. II. Series.

BR115.C8 F3 2001
261—dc21

2001034469

Contents

Editor's Note and Acknowledgements

Because this book is a Study Guide, I have added sub-headings through-out the chapters in order to guide readers through the arguments. This should also make clear the aim of the book as a whole: it is not merely a collection of pieces on a similar theme, but explores the relation between Christianity and Culture in an *integrated* way, each chapter complementing or expanding others. My introduction should also offer some guidance to the way that the chapters relate to each other. The responsibility for the sub-headings remains, however, mine rather than that of the separate authors.

I have not attempted to standardize different authors' practices in using personal pronouns for God. Some avoid, and some retain, the traditional form 'he/his'; I hope it will be understood that where the convention of a masculine pronoun is employed, there is no implication that God is being conceived as male.

Excerpts from 'Sweeney Agonistes' and *Four Quartets* in *The Complete Poems and Plays of T.S. Eliot* © 1969 by Esme Valerie Eliot, are reprinted by kind permission of Faber and Faber Ltd.
An excerpt from 'Little Gidding' in *Four Quartets* © 1942 by T. S. Eliot and renewed 1969 by Esme Valerie Eliot, is reprinted by kind permission of Harcourt, Inc.
Excerpts from 'Sweeney Agonistes' in *Collected Poems 1909-1962*, © 1930 and renewed 1958 by T. S. Eliot, are reprinted by kind permission of Harcourt, Inc.

The poem 'Lobgesang' from Stefan George, *Gedichte* © 1983 by Ernst Klett, Stuttgart, is reprinted by kind permission of the publishers.

An excerpt from a poem by Anne Ridler, in *Collected Poems* © 1994 Anne Ridler, is used by kind permission of the author and Carcanet Press, Manchester.

The Contributors

Mark Atherton is a Fellow of the Centre for the Study of Christianity and Culture at Regent's Park College, Oxford.

Oliver Davies is Reader in Philosophical Theology at the University of Wales, Lampeter, and a Fellow of the Centre for the Study of Christianity and Culture at Regent's Park College, Oxford.

Paul S. Fiddes is Principal of Regent's Park College, Oxford, and a University Research Lecturer in Theology, University of Oxford.

Frances Kennett is a Fellow of the Centre for the Study of Christianity and Culture at Regent's Park College, Oxford.

Alan Kreider was formerly Director of the Centre for the Study of Christianity and Culture at Regent's Park College, Oxford, and is now Associate Professor of Church History in the Mennonite Biblical Seminary, Indiana.

Larry J. Kreitzer is Fellow and Tutor in New Testament at Regent's Park College, Oxford, and a University Research Lecturer in Theology, University of Oxford.

Jean Lamb is an artist, and a minister in the Church of England serving a parish in Sneinton, Nottingham.

Marjorie Reeves is a Fellow of the British Academy, and an Honorary Fellow of both St Anne's College and St Hugh's College, Oxford.

Jane Shaw is Dean, and Fellow and Tutor in Ecclesiastical History, at Regent's Park College, Oxford.

Julian Thompson is Fellow and Tutor in English Literature at Regent's Park College, Oxford.

Nicholas Wood is Fellow and Tutor in Religion and Culture at Regent's Park College, Oxford, and Director of the Centre for the Study of Christianity and Culture in the college.

1

Introduction: The Making of a Christian Mind

PAUL S. FIDDES

1. 'The Christian Mind'

Nearly forty years ago, a book appeared whose title at least has remained influential ever since. It was called *The Christian Mind*, and its author, Harry Blamires, coined the expression as a counterpart to the way that we often speak of 'the modern mind' and 'the scientific mind'. He did so, however, with a deep sense of irony, observing that 'I have posited a Christian mind, chiefly for the purpose of showing that it does not exist.'[1] He was deploring what he felt to be the loss of the Christian frame of reference in his time, and he writes with a note of despair. Part of the purpose of the present book is to see whether, four decades later, there is more cause for hope.

By 'the Christian mind', and its loss, Blamires meant two things. First, the expression denotes a 'thinking Christianly' about human culture – about politics, social affairs, industry, education and the arts, 'or indeed about any of the vital fields of human activity generally regarded as the domain of secularism'.[2] In his day, Blamires detected a profound lack of such thinking, both theologically and morally; instead he found a captivity to the mind-set of a secular world-view. With a 'failure of intellectual morale', Christian people were compartmentalizing their Christian beliefs within the life of the church and private devotion, and were adopting a merely secular and materialistic approach when they engaged in the wider life of the world.

Second, a 'Christian mind' according to Blamires is not an individualistic reality; it means a 'community of discourse'. He certainly accepted that there were Christian writers and thinkers who were trying to apply their faith within such areas as politics and social studies, but they remained individual efforts. There was no 'field of discourse' or 'collectively accepted set of notions and attitudes' such as the phrase 'scientific mind' denotes. He could find no ongoing conversation, no 'living dialogue' about a Christian view of the world and its activities, either within the church or in society. There was 'no public pool of discourse fed by Christianly committed thought on the world we live in.'[3] He concludes that 'we have become afraid of our own convictions'.[4]

Where are we, forty years on? We are not in a captivity to secularism, as that phase has largely passed in western society, and it was never really present in the east anyway. Secularists remain as a 'globally élite culture',[5] often disproportionately powerful in the mechanisms of society and the media, but the prevailing mind is not 'modernist' but 'postmodern'. A good deal will be said in this book about the label 'postmodern', which remains useful despite its corruption into jargon and cliché. It denotes a reaction against any overarching theories about the world, whether they are scientific, political or religious. This mood is not marked by a tight, rational world-view – such as, for example, the secular thesis about life – but by tolerance towards a multitude of views and scepticism towards any coherence. It is profoundly relativist, and has room for 'new age' movements of spirituality. It presents its own kind of challenge to the Christian story.

There certainly seems to be more evidence of a 'field of discourse' about a Christian approach to culture than there was in Blamires' day, at least within the Christian community. Some of this may actually have been in response to the challenge that he threw down, though it must be said that most developments along this line have not closely followed his own deeply conservative and traditionalist view of what Christian theology and morality are, and neither does this present book. The *notion* of a 'Christian mind' has thus proved more useful than the exact content Blamires gave to it. Such a mind has been cultivated within the influential 'Gospel and Culture' movement initiated by the late Bishop Lesslie Newbigin, with its stress on the creation of 'public truth'; this has precisely developed a confidence in witnessing to Christian truth in the midst of the many conversations in the market place of our society, and a willingness for it to be tested in the same way as all truth.[6] A Christian mind is also fostered in a corporate way within the many new postgraduate courses in 'Applied Theology' that have developed in recent years, aiming to bring Christian belief and practice into interaction with the whole range of human experience within society and its structures.[7]

In addition to movements and courses, quite a number of 'Centres' and 'Institutes' have been created which focus on the relationship between faith and society, between Christian belief and culture, and these have provided communities of discourse which draw people into the ongoing dialogue that Blamires wanted to see happening.[8] One of these communities is the 'Centre for the Study of Christianity and Culture' (founded in 1994) at Regent's Park College in the University of Oxford, and the chapters in this book are based on lectures originally given in the Centre. They begin with the inaugural lecture of Dr Alan Kreider as the first Director of the Centre in 1996, and they end with a piece by the present Director, Dr Nicholas Wood.

This Centre in Oxford has some aspects that make it rather different from others, and which attempt to respond to the challenge of Blamires to create a 'field of discourse'. It is not a free-standing institute, but deeply embedded in the whole life of the college of which it is a part, and which contains a mixture of undergraduates, postgraduate students and some on a track towards ordination as Christian ministers. It operates therefore as a 'Centre' in two senses. It is in a real sense the centre of the college, acting as a point of focus for the college with its overall aim of encouraging a Christian world-view in all its students, whatever academic subject they are studying (whether, for example, theology, philosophy, law, English literature or geography) and whatever career or profession in society they intend to enter. The Centre thus aims to create a common discourse within a community of learning, enabling students to make links, in a spirit of open enquiry, between faith and various academic fields. Five of the chapters of this book are written by Fellows of the college involved in teaching variously for degrees in theology, world religions, history and English Literature.

At the same time, the Centre acts as a centre in another sense, providing a central meeting-place into which to draw people who are outside the college, whether in the wider community of the University or at work in various vocations in society. Major lecture series on the novel, poetry, music and art in modern society have drawn in distinguished practitioners in these fields to offer contributions or to be part of the discussion. Series on the place of the media, the danger of global warming, the culture of economics and the ethics of technology have given academics and managers in these fields an opportunity to discuss their daily work in the context of a Christian world-view. Other series have aimed to place the life of the Christian church within the wider life of society, exploring the nonconformist tradition in Britain, the nature of the Black Church, or the Celtic tradition within Christianity. Thus the circle of discourse is widened beyond the college to draw others in to be part of the dialogue. Two of the chapters in the present book are written by those who have come from outside the college to take part in public lecture series; such persons are, however, the major contributors to six other volumes, published or in preparation, which are the result of the work of the Centre.[9]

Holding together these two senses of a 'centre' is the group of Fellows of the Centre, pursuing their own research in diverse areas of faith and culture, and forming a community of support and intellectual stimulation for each other. They form their own circle of discourse in interaction with the other circles I have mentioned. They also *model* the way that a Christian mind can be created, which is especially important for young undergraduate students in college who do not sometimes have sufficient experience and maturity to break out of a compartmentalizing between personal faith and academic study. Three of the chapters of the present book are written by Fellows of the Centre.

I have described this particular experiment in developing a Christian mind, partly because it is the one with which I am most familiar and with which I have been involved since it was only the gleam of an idea, and partly to offer it as a case-study in response to Harry Blamires' challenge. If we take up the first aspect of the Christian mind identified by Blamires, then we need to ask how deeply theology – or talk about the triune God – has penetrated the studies of society and culture in which we are engaged. This remains a provoking question, and we need constantly to measure our work against the critique of Blamires that 'a good deal of what has been written in the attempt to bridge the gaps comes into the category of what I would call secular thinking trimmed with pious platitudes.'[10] The chapters which follow do try to take seriously such theological themes as creation and fall, the story of redemption in Jesus, the presence of God in the world, the nature of incarnation and the need for the self-revelation of God at the basis of human language and culture.

The second aspect of the Christian mind, its actualization as a common discourse, remains a perplexing challenge. From our experience of our Centre so far, it seems possible to achieve – at least to some extent – the creation of a Christian field of discourse within the academic community, across many different disciplines of study; it is also possible to foster a Christian mind within various professional groups, or circles of creative artists. This is hugely encouraging, and makes the situation look more hopeful than it appeared to Harry Blamires in 1963. However, it seems more difficult to create a field of discourse like this either within the Christian church as a whole, or within the varied membership of a local congregation. This is a challenge that the Centre intends to face more seriously in the next phase of its life, through a number of projects. Even more problematic is the interaction of Christian discourse with *public discourse* as a whole – that is, the mind-set which is shaped by advertising, television soap operas, tabloid newspapers, the internet, sports events, fashion and the rock and pop music scene. Some of the following chapters consider, in various historic periods up to the present, the relation between the common discourse of society and the Christian story and its symbols. There is clearly a particular problem facing Christian communication in a post-modern age, one which seems even more troubling than the predominantly secular mind that Blamires found himself confronting, and the last section of this introduction returns to the issue of a loss of a symbolic horizon.

2. Christianity among the cultures

The chapter by Alan Kreider following this introduction meets the challenge to take Christian theology and ethics seriously in thinking about culture and society. He concentrates on the Christian virtue of telling the truth and its rooting in the story of Jesus, considering its effect on public life and its place in mediation between groups in conflict. Here he returns to Richard Niebuhr's classic study, *Christ and Culture*, and recalls that Niebuhr prefers to think of this relation through the category of 'Christ

the transformer of culture.'[11] Alan Kreider asks, however, where in practice we might actually see this happening, and focuses on the
transformation that comes when Christian disciples follow Jesus as truth-
teller.

In identifying this point where the Christian mind takes effect, he is
also making several criticisms of Niebuhr's approach. Niebuhr tends to
separate out Christ from culture, as 'culturally rootless, abstracted from
particularity of place and time'. Christ, urges Alan Kreider, was thoroughly immersed in a Jewish culture of his time as 'the leader of a first
century renewal movement', and his command to tell the truth was a challenge to the many faces of culture that he confronted – whether varieties
of Judaism, Hellenism or the Roman occupation. Moreover, Niebuhr
treats 'culture' as something monolithic, whereas it has always been
'made up of… a multi-voiced chorus'. True as this was in the time of
Jesus, we are living in an even more multicultural environment, and different kinds of culture call for Christians to make varying responses to
them. This in turn calls for a criterion, and this can only be found – Alan
Kreider argues – in the story of the Christ who transformed cultures from
within a culture.

In his chapter, Alan Kreider works out the general principle of truthful speech through the particular instance of a prohibition of swearing
oaths (Matthew 5:34-7), and thereby demonstrates the cultural context of
all ethics. He also shows his own cultural identity within the Mennonite
(Anabaptist) tradition by his very selecting of this issue of a refusal to
take oaths. He affirms that the Christian approach to culture should not be
'against culture' in the sense of hostility to it, but his own tradition leads
him to stress an essentially counter-cultural stance; the historic refusal to
swear oaths, we may observe, inevitably made the Mennonite movement
an alternative culture. Christians who practise the teaching of Jesus will,
he thus asserts, create 'second cultures' within the cultures in which they
are 'committed participants'. While Christians must engage with the cultures 'humbly, repentantly, attentively', if these are to be transformed they
have to be placed under the critique of the story of the life, death and resurrection of Jesus. Other contributors to this book (especially myself and
Nicholas Wood) will return to the question of a relation between critique
and engagement.

This chapter has set the scene of Christianity as a culture among the cultures, and Jane Shaw now points out in her chapter that it is one of the tasks of the historian to chart the story of this interaction through the ages. Historians use a range of methods to investigate the past, and 'cultural history' studies the various meanings given to events by those who shared in them. As an example she draws on her own specialist study of the meanings given to the healings that were claimed to have happened in the dissenting churches of mid-seventeenth century England. This approach relies on an understanding of 'culture' as the web of meanings in which human life is suspended, a definition (by Clifford Geertz) to which Alan Kreider gives qualified approval, and one with which other contributors are also working. Cultural historians will have a special interest, therefore, in exploring the way that Christianity as a cultural system has both shaped and been shaped by its relation to other cultures.

Jane Shaw is urging Christian historians of the church to enter courageously into the wider discourse of cultural history, where they have customarily limited themselves to studies of church institutions and the development of Christian doctrine. Cultural studies, exposing the meanings found in events by marginal or overlooked groups in society, can enable us to look at moments in the Christian tradition 'with fresh eyes'. Sainthood in the Middle Ages, for instance, seems to have meant something different to women than to men. She is also proposing, conversely, that the Christian mind can have an effect on cultural study itself. Cultural studies as a discipline tends to assume that the world is a secular place, she observes, and misses the impact that religious belief, worship and mission has on culture. If she were responding to Blamires' complaint, she would perhaps say that the Christian mind not only *can* feed into the discourse of cultural studies, but *must* for the sake of the discipline itself.

Writing as a historian, Jane Shaw comments that her task is a limited one. Historians can chart the relation between Christianity as a culture and other cultures, but it is the job of the theologian, she suggests, to think about such matters as the relation between culture and *revelation*. To this I turn myself in the next chapter, while considering the particular challenge which our present culture presents to faith.

3. The challenge of 'postmodern' culture

If culture is the pattern of meanings that we give to all the events in our lives, then one significant way in which we express this pattern is in stories. Culture can be understood to a large extent as the stories people tell about themselves. These need not be only verbal; notes of music and shapes in visual art can also present story-like patterns. Writing as a painter and sculptor, Jean Lamb suggests in her chapter later on that forms found in nature, though distinct in themselves, can build together into narratives of a life-cycle. The relation between Christianity and culture can thus be re-expressed as the relation between the Christian story and the many stories of which cultures are made up. To use Blamires' terms, it is about the relation of Christian discourse to the many discourses in our society. In his early play, *Sweeney Agonistes*, Eliot makes such an attempt to allow stories to interact at every level, although in my view (and that of most critics) his experiment is a startling failure.

I suggest that, in the present situation of a culture that might be called postmodern, the question 'how can we tell the Christian story in the face of other stories?' breaks down into three subsidiary questions. Faced by a multiplicity of cultures and a 'pick and mix' spirituality, the first question is: how can all stories be judged by this one story? Faced by a 'crisis in representation', in which stories seem only to be about themselves and their own inner world, the second question is: to what does this story refer? Faced by a rejection of all large-scale stories that claim to interpret the whole of reality, the third question is: how can we tell a universal story?

The first question picks up Alan Kreider's claim that only the story of Jesus can offer a criterion for the appropriate response to different cultures. But how can this be the case if Christianity itself is a culture? My own answer does not neglect the critique of human cultures by the story of Jesus, especially in its opposition to the myth of redemptive violence, but I do place more emphasis than Alan Kreider on listening for the voice of God's Spirit through (but not *as*) other cultures. We hear this word because in all cultures – including postmodern ones – there is a human response to the self-revelation of God, and it is precisely this that enables us to tell the story of Jesus in a way that will 'out-tell' other stories. It is telling, and not judging, to which we are called. Kreider writes movingly about the need to listen to others when engaged in the process of conflict-mediation, and it is this listening that I want to transfer from individuals to whole cultures; it is this that will mark the 'repentant and attentive' engagement with cultures that Kreider also urges.

In his concluding chapter, Nicholas Wood deals with this same question of a balance between being counter-cultural on the one hand, and expecting an illumination of the gospel *through* culture on the other. He observes that the inculturation of the Christian gospel has always transformed and elevated 'that which is capable of carrying gospel for a new generation', and that this has resulted in turn in 'the expansion of the horizons of the gospel itself'. His concern is to ask how this can happen in the new situation of a postmodern culture, where many worlds overlap and interweave in a kind of 'space-time compression'. The process of mutual fertilization between gospel and culture seems more complicated in a culture where history is seen as 'an endless reserve of equal events' and where different worlds can be entered 'with little danger of genuine encounter.' He affirms that Christianity is all about God's willing engagement with the world, and so inculturation must be possible, characterized by both continuity and discontinuity with culture. The tension can be held together, he believes, by some form of fulfilment theology, since the movement from promise (in a culture) to fulfilment (in Christ) is not unbroken but has unexpected leaps within it. In discerning this process, which has more of poetry about it than rationality, the local congregation plays a strategic part as 'a hermeneutic of the gospel'.

In my own chapter I underline that telling the Christian story confidently in the face of other stories requires a theology of revelation, and Nicholas Wood's proposal is similarly based in the conviction that we live in the presence of a self-unveiling God. The story to which the Christian church bears witness has emerged from encounters with a self-revealing God at decisive moments in history, and the same God opens God's self to all peoples in all cultures, whatever response is actually made to the divine offer. Only this perspective will enable us to hold together a critique of culture and a listening to culture. This meets, I think, the demand of Harry Blamires that we should be creating a common discourse with a solid theological foundation (though perhaps it is not a theology that he himself would have espoused).

My replies to the second and third questions raised by our present culture about telling the Christian story flow from the first. To the question, 'what does this story refer to?' we may answer that it is not about observing God but engaging in the life of God. The question, 'how can we tell a universal story?' must be answered 'humbly and non-coercively, in tune with the nature of the story itself.' The two chapters which follow mine elaborate, in fact, on these two questions, beginning with the last one.

4. The relation of story to history

In her chapter, Marjorie Reeves reflects further on the way that the meanings which make up culture are expressed in stories. It is, she affirms, Great Stories from the past that nourish the human spirit. Working through the power of memory, they can liberate us from a world in which we are trapped in the demands of the 'instant' moment. Though we must examine carefully what we mean by 'history', and not all Great Stories are based in history, Marjorie Reeves believes that the historical root of many stories is essential to their effect; this is especially the case with the Christian story. Here she has some sympathy with the insight of medieval typology that a story offers a multiplicity of meanings to enrich the reader just because there is some encounter with God in history lying at its origin. In the nineteenth century, she observes, the greatest challenge to the truth of the 'Great Stories' arose from the question of their historicity. Today, in a postmodern culture, the challenge is different, and perhaps more dangerous. It is, as we have already seen, the relativizing of all stories, and the denial that any stories have universal relevance. Marjorie Reeves summarizes this mood as asserting that there are only 'a multiplicity of transient voices, each trapped within its own cultural frontiers'.

She thus returns to the issue I have already raised as the third question in my chapter: what truth can there be in a story which claims to be a metanarrative or large-scale story applicable to all cultures? Reeves replies that recognition of its authority requires a leap of faith, but that this is based precisely in the particularities of history. A particular encounter with God at one time and place is handed down in the memory and universalized in a story. The concept of incarnation affirms that truth must always be embodied in a *specific* situation, and this for Christians is supremely the case with 'the life, word and death of that most particular of human beings, Jesus of Nazareth.' This event seals 'the authority of the particular', which gives rise to and validates the universalized form of the story.

Once again we see the need for a robust theology of revelation, or the affirmation that 'the universal Creator God has chosen to reveal himself continuously to his people through particularity.' Arising out of this particularity, abiding truths are mediated to us through 'concrete story, reinterpreted by every changing culture'. In support of this, Marjorie Reeves cites the unexpected public success of a recent exhibition at the National Gallery: 'Seeing Salvation. Images of Christ.'

In considering the power of story and image from history, we need of course to ask whose history it is. Jane Shaw has already drawn attention to the value of cultural history in alerting us to perspectives on history from the marginalized and oppressed groups in society. Later in the book, Frances Kennett offers a study of the Mexican woman poet and nun, Sor Juana, and describes her as finding her own voice through 'creating her own personal history, and a specific female history'. Well aware of the use of history by the centres of power of her time (the church and the court), she did not abandon history, and especially the Christian story with which she kept faith in her life and her poetry; but, as Frances Kennett puts it, 'she scanned history for the benefit of her female contemporaries... in an attempt to define another space of discourse in her own salon....' Her view of Mary, for example, was rather different from the idealized figure produced by a male establishment. If story rooted in history is to have a liberating effect in the present, then the roots need to be examined by those who are other than the dominant social forces. This will create a Christian mind, a discourse among the oppressed, which can contribute to the common discourse in society, even in disturbing ways.

In giving an account of the work of Sor Juana, Frances Kennett reflects on her own role as a female interpreter of this remarkable woman. She is in sympathy with those feminist writers who are interested in women as subjects, creators of their own fully human identity, rather than with more 'postmodern' critics who have lost interest in the subject (and the author of a text) altogether as a mere creation of language and social structure. 'It is ironic today, she comments, 'that at the same time as women begin to assert themselves, in postmodernist theory the very notion of a "subject" begins to unravel.' Nevertheless, she finds positive gain in the criticism of the role of the subject as controlling a world of objects around; undermining the *absolute subject* has enabled 'a move beyond oppositional and dualist thinking'. I believe that she would agree with Jean Lamb that the postmodern mood has been useful in so far as it has mounted an attack on the self-centred and dominating ego of the artist, cultivated in the Renaissance and fostered in the Enlightenment. Beyond this critique, perhaps what is needed is a notion of co-creativity, a sharing with God in the creation of a subject who shows the same self-giving nature as God.

These considerations about the subject, and so an author, lead us into the second of the sub-questions I suggested are posed by postmodern culture: what does a text – and so a story – refer to? Does it refer beyond itself to the world, to its author, or even to God? This is the area explored in more detail by Oliver Davies in his chapter on the relation between theology and poetry.

5. The relation of the story to the world

The chapter by Oliver Davies is quite a technical one – more specialist than one might perhaps expect to find within the covers of a 'Study Guide'. But this piece is both important and exciting. As well as dealing with the question of what a written text might be all about, Oliver Davies is meeting head-on a challenge laid down by Blamires: that is, the demand that a Christian mind should take a view of culture which is thoroughly Christian, rather than capitulating to a non-Christian world-view. From within the specialised world of cultural studies and the philosophy of religion, we can follow here the work of a scholar who is determined to think Christianly about the world.

In this chapter he makes a comparison between the way that theology (or talk about God) uses words, and the way that words are used in poetry, and he finds interesting similarities between the two enterprises. Words in both theology and poetry are used in a strange way, set apart from ordinary speaking; they carry multiple meanings; they seem to come from outside the author by a kind of inspiration, and this gives them a liberating power. Words in both theology and poetry create a new world, a 'second world' which pictures new possibilities and helps us to live our lives in fresh ways. Words in both areas open up a space which has its own kind of truth. It is no wonder that poets are often seen as God-like creators, and that poetry has come to replace religion for many people in the modern world.

But Oliver Davies also finds important differences between poetry and theology, or between the role of the poet and the theologian, and these are connected with the question of what words refer to. He accepts that the words of any human text, whether a poem or a story, only relate to the world around in an indirect way. This is part of the strangeness of poetic language; it certainly reflects in some way the experience of living in the world, but it essentially opens out a *new kind of experience* for its readers which enables them to return to the realm of the everyday to change the world, hopefully for the better. A piece of creative writing thus releases the self into a 'broader context', and enables the self to touch a more primary kind of reality. But this is not the same, he asserts, as what happens in theology. Here there are words that have been seized hold of by the self-revealing God, so that the new world to which they point is nothing less than participation in the triune fellowship of God. Words are 'strange' in theology because they are answerable to God. A poem opens out new possibilities within the world; words used by God for revelation open up new possibilities which come from beyond the world.[12] A poet is 'inspired', but a Christian believer is indwelt by the Spirit of God. In human art, the self is lost for the sake of creative language; in theology, the self loses itself for the sake of serving another, as God has given God's own self for us in Christ. In literary texts there is an unending play of meaning which arises from the overflowing nature of words themselves; in theology there is never-ending meaning to be gained because we are exploring the depths of the personal mystery of God.

Perhaps the greatest difference is in the respective relations of theology and poetry to history, and here Oliver Davies echoes some of the thoughts of Marjorie Reeves. The poem offers a new world, he affirms, which stands *in contrast* to 'the realm of ordinary perception and existence'. It uses metaphor with some reference to the ordinary world, but it is a minimal connection. The Christian story, however, is rooted in history. That is, it refers to historical events that have been transformed in a paradoxical way by the presence and revelation of God. Because these events have been transformed by the renewing action of God they *can only be spoken about* with the help of metaphor, and so in a historical faith everyday events and metaphor 'converge' rather than sliding apart.

In this account, Oliver Davies confirms and extends my own kind of proposal – that the Christian story, used by God as a vehicle of self-revelation, refers to God in the sense of enabling engagement in God. He also takes issue with the extreme of postmodern literary criticism, which finds *no* reference in any literary text to what lies either beyond or 'in front of' the text, since for metaphor to work at all it needs to be grounded in the familiar; nevertheless, he finds the reference to the everyday world to be reflected or oblique. Above all, he has clarified in a thoroughly theological way the difference between words which are merely human and those which are captured by God's act of revelation. The question, it seems to me, is *what* human words can be so used by God: are they restricted either to scripture or to the speech within the church that we call theology? My own chapter about the relation between Christianity and culture suggests that any words in any culture *can* become a place of encounter with the living God, although Christians have reasons for thinking that scriptural witness to Christ has a unique place within this range of words. Given the difference between a human work of art and speech enabled by revelation, the question is whether there is any limit to the first becoming the second. Using Oliver Davies' labels, while theology is not simply poetry, is it possible for poetry to *become* 'theology' in any sense? I suggest that there is in fact nothing to prevent the common discourse of a culture becoming a means of hearing the divine Word – though not of course becoming the Word.

6. A community of discourse

The chapters in the first section of the book, together with the last two chapters, concern – at least in parts of their content – the relation of

Christianity to a culture that can be called postmodern, and it is to this situation that I intend to return at the end of this introduction. Four chapters, however, deal with the interaction between Christianity and earlier cultures: the context for the accounts of the creative work of Hildegard of Bingen and Sor Juana are the medieval world and the period of the Counter-Reformation respectively; in studies of the novelist Kingsley Amis and an episode of 'Star Trek', their subjects are located in later modernism. Now, in each of these periods, public discourse in some way already contains an awareness of the Christian story, even in the modern examples that seem secular on the surface. Christian discourse, inside and outside the church, depends on this awareness and trades upon it.

These examples remind us that until recently in the west the Christian culture has been interacting with a range of cultures that have themselves been influenced by the Christian tradition. They present examples of mutual shaping, and while a historian would be preoccupied in tracing this story (as Jane Shaw describes the historical task), for a theologian they offer clues to the way that the Spirit of God might be at work to disclose the creative and redemptive presence of God in the midst of the cultures.

As Mark Atherton shows, the context in which Hildegard was writing music, theology and poetry was the unified culture of Christendom. The view of the cosmos was of integration into a comprehensive hierarchy, and in doctrinal formulation unity was at a premium. Hildegard's strategy as a Christian artist was not to disrupt this unity in an obvious way, but to subvert it and renew it. The unity was newly structured by her as a musical harmony encompassing the whole of creation, 'the sacred sound through which all creation resounds'; also, Hildegard presents the unity of creation in a new way as something which she actually 'sees' as happening in front of her (spiritual) eyes. Both the music and the vision, moreover, are rooted in her own experience as a woman in the religious life, in the liturgy and singing among other women in her convent. Unity is not denied, but re-visioned, and out of this comes a prophetic voice of protest for justice on behalf of those who are excluded from the benefits of the unity, or pushed to its edges.

Sor Juana is writing at a time when society is still profoundly shaped by the church, but when the unified vision has broken into multiple forms

of Christian and political authority, held together by a system of checks
and balances and finding expression in the exuberance of the baroque
style. Frances Kennett describes this setting vividly, and shows how Sor
Juana makes use of the diverse and competing forces around her, creating
her own identity and her own history as a woman to mingle with them.
She makes clear that Sor Juana does not isolate herself from the stories of
her Christian culture, but adds her own to them and tells them in her way.
In doing so she not only gives voice to women within a male world, but
also expresses 'the fears and thoughts of the poorest elements of society
as a sub-text in her conventional work for the court and church hierarchy.'

By the time that Kingsley Amis is writing, in the mid-twentieth century, society is exhibiting the secularization that Blamires found making
its creeping entrance into the Christian church. In Amis' novels, representing that culture, there is nevertheless a memory of the Christian story,
and the secular outlook is in fact largely formed in reaction against it.
This is a kind of dialogue, though not a friendly one, that Blamires seems
to have overlooked. In his chapter, Julian Thompson presents Amis as
remaining in conversation with Christianity throughout his creative life,
though in two modes. In the first he demonstrates what often been called
'protest atheism', partly refusing to believe at all in the omnipotent, all-
determining God of classical Christian thought, and partly angry with this
'non-existing' God for the mess he has made of the state of the world,
thus implying at least a kind of half-belief. To this Amis adds, secondly,
another kind of half-belief: a wistfulness for the stability of traditional
Christian institutions in a world that is changing in a way of which Amis
does not approve.

We should not assume, too easily and quickly, that we can build on
these two elements and undermine 'protest atheism' by correcting – as we
should – our notion of God from a tyrannical director of events to a humble God who limits the divine self and suffers in order to give created
persons freedom.[13] It seems that Amis is at least vaguely aware of the
alternative model of a God who allows a free 'run of the play', but objects
that the incarnation in Christ thus 'made so little difference to anything'.[14]
The Christian apologist has to show that the humility, and indeed the suffering of God, does make a difference to everything, and has the power to
overcome evil.[15]

While in the examples of Hildegard and Sor Juana we see Christian communicators relating to the culture around them, and join imaginatively with them in their venture, in this case we as readers are the practitioners of the Christian mind entering a conversation with two key features of a secular culture – protest atheism and nostalgic wistfulness for belief. With Amis it becomes apparent that the second aspect, a 'hunger to be more serious', contains a protest from within the culture itself against certain of its prevalent trends, notably materialism and superstition.

A third aspect of a culture undergoing secularization is exemplified in science fiction such as the television series *Star Trek*: here there is still sufficient memory of the Christian story to use it in building new myths.[16] Indeed, Kingsley Amis himself was aware of the theological echoes in science fiction, commenting on this phenomenon in his study of the genre, *New Maps of Hell* (1960). In his chapter about one episode of *Star Trek*, 'Bread and Circuses' (1968), Larry Kreitzer analyses a complex example of the interaction of Christianity with several cultures. In a story about religious martyrs being thrown to wild animals in the arena, the Christian faith is related both to its early days in Ancient Rome and to a mythical modern 'Rome' set on another planet, in which the deadly games are now televised. Further, the story acts as a commentary (as science fiction usually does) on the culture of the present age which has created it. Three cultures and their religions thus interweave with Christianity and with each other, their mutual involvement depending on a play of words between a religion of the 'Sun' and a religion of the 'Son' (Christ). The making of the myth thus requires a general memory of the overcoming of the brutal might of the Roman Empire by faith in 'the Son', and perhaps also (as Kreitzer suggests) a more detailed memory of parts of the Gospel story as told by Luke.

This case-study demonstrates the truth of Marjorie Reeves' claim that stories rooted in history have a power to affect us in the present. Here, however, the main point I want to make is that this episode and the series in which it is set shows at the least an unease with trends of its own culture, and might even be said to voice a protest against it. Its focus on the so-called 'Prime Directive' of Starfleet (not to interfere with the natural historical development of other cultures), its attack on imperialism and its stress on the 'brotherhood of man' (*sic*) could be seen as critical of tendencies in American culture of its time. Its optimism about the future ('wouldn't it be something to watch, to be part of?') *could* be seen as an uncritical espousal of the American dream, not yet troubled by postmodern nightmares; or, as Larry Kreitzer inclines to think, it could be seen as a prophetic voice calling for hope at a time of loss of confidence – such hope as, we may add, Christian theologians were also invoking at that time.[17]

These aspects of a secular culture – protest atheism (especially over human suffering), a nostalgia for belief and a new myth-making – are still present in remnant in our own time, among the multiple voices of a postmodern culture.[18] We must pay them attention as we 'read' a culture, in Paul Tillich's terminology,[19] discerning both the prevailing trend of a culture and the internal voices of protest and dissent against it. But, as I have already indicated, in our period of culture we can no longer rely on the memory of the Christian story and symbols that marked the earlier period of secularization.

7. Renewing the images

We are living in a culture that the poet Seamus Heaney has characterized as one in which there is a loss of 'religious voltage' from our language, 'a big lightening, an emptying out' of religious reference.[20] People do not know the great stories of the past, and the images of Christian, Jewish and classical literature no longer resonate in the public arena. There no longer seems the possibility of having a 'common discourse' in which a Christian mind about the world can be formed and communicated; it seems that any community of discourse will have to be a minority one. A word like 'wood' or 'tree', for example, could easily in the past have acquired a rich overload of meaning, and be brought into a context of other words in which multiple meaning would emerge. Let us consider here a brief medieval lyric:[21]

> Now goth sonne under wod:
> Me reweth, Marye, thy fair rode.
> Now goth sonne under Tre:
> Me reweth, Marye, thy sone and thee.

The poet sees the sun going down at evening behind a wood, or forest, and in his mind this scene merges with the 'wood' of the cross, the 'tree' of redemption, and with the Gospel story of the darkening of the sun at the moment of crucifixion. 'A particular moment at nightfall... can bring to mind the sunset of Good Friday.'[22] There is a play on words between 'sun' and 'son' ('sonne' and 'sone'), since in the passion story the life of the *son* is extinguished at the same moment as the light of the *sun*. The beauty of the scene reminds the poet of the fairness of Mary's face ('rode'), at the same time as pitying the darkening of that face in sorrow at the death of her son. Somewhere in the background is also an echo of the tree in the Garden of Eden that became the tree of death for the descendants of Adam. The compression and intensity of meaning is difficult to catch in a modern translation, but the following might serve as a rough paraphrase:

> Behind the wood sinks the sun to its place:
> I pity, Mary, thy fair face;
> Now goes the sun down, behind the tree:
> I pity, Mary, thy son and thee.

It seems impossible for such a poem to have its effect now without first providing the reader with at least a short course in biblical studies and Christian tradition. The episode of 'Star Trek' on which Larry Kreitzer comments also relies on the longstanding play of words between 'sun' and 'son',[23] but this lyric makes even greater demands on a familiarity with story and symbol. It is no wonder that poets such as David Jones were driven to desperation as they considered the fragmenting of culture and the loss of a common language.[24] We are living at a time of 'cultural bereavement', as the artist Jean Lamb points out in her chapter in this book, and Rowan Williams speaks aptly of a situation of 'lost icons'.[25] While forty years ago Harry Blamires lamented a lack of common discourse in which to explore a Christian mind about the world, it now seems in our post-modern culture that the very *possibility* of such a discourse is ruled out.

So it seems. But I suggest that we should not despair, or abandon the hope that Christian images can be renewed and stories re-told. There is perhaps a sign of hope in a recent television advertisement – for Foster's lager – in which a wide-eyed and frantic woman gasps to her husband that 'I've just seen the four horsemen of the apocalypse', and he replies nonchalantly, sipping his beer, 'Never mind: it's not the end of the world.' The advertisers are relying on at least a slight acquaintance with the symbol of the four horsemen of the Book of Revelation, a symbol revived in our time through such new forms as the film *Apocalypse Now*, and Terry Pratchett's comic-fantasy novel *Good Omens*, in which the terrible Four make their appearance as Hell's Angels on motorbikes.[26]

The chapters gathered together in the present book point the direction towards such a renewal in culture through a Christian mind. In the first place, I suggest that we should take courage to *tell* the Christian story, and the complex of stories that make up the Christian heritage.[27] We need to recapture the art of story-telling using the forms and media of our culture, a striking recent example being the collaboration between the Heartland Campaign and the magazine *Vogue* in re-telling the story of the Prodigal Son (in this case the Prodigal Daughter) through a lavish six-page fashion spread and a window display in Fenwicks' Bond Street store.[28] At the beginning of the modern phase of secularization in the 1940s, Dietrich Bonhoeffer called for a period of public silence by the church, a self-discipline which would give it time to listen penitently to others, and in which it would wait for God to renew the language of proclamation and give it the gospel-words that were lacking in a 'world come of age'.[29] It may well be that our culture is the one in which such words are now being given.

But this telling of the story is only possible, in the second place, if we do *listen* to the witness of the cultures around us. I make this point in my own chapter, and Nicholas Wood expands on it in the form of 'fulfilment theology'. If such a listening is to be more than opportunist and modish, we need a theology of revelation in which we have confidence that God is continuing to disclose God's own self in the world, and that culture is a response to this self-unveiling; then the symbols and stories which emerge from our cultural context will not only be seen as *fulfilled* in the story of Jesus, but will enable us to understand this story better as they interact with it.

Third, Jean Lamb urges as an artist and as a woman Christian minister that we should pay attention to the given forms that can be found in the natural world. She calls them 'found forms', and she is notably drawn to the forms to be found in the material of wood, making the same kind of connections with the wood and 'tree' of the cross as does the medieval poet. The cross, she remarks, is 'a man-made perversion of the tree'. Broken and needing redemption though these 'found forms' are in a fallen world, through exploring them we can submit ourselves to the creative Spirit of God. Lamb observes, as we have already seen, that the ego of the artist which strives to be dominant has been exposed to critique through the postmodern attack on the subject. This might be a healthy voice of protest within the culture, but the actual result has been a kind of funeral of the self and a loss of hope. There is a more hopeful disruption of the self-glorifying ego in submission to the art of the Creator. Through found forms we can find the Creator's intention in the world, and can 'allow God to work out the image of salvation for us in the world today'.

This artistic method shows, we notice, confidence in the presence of a self-disclosing God here and now; it is no mere tracing of signs of God in creation in a static way ('natural theology'), but an expectation that God can be met through forms in nature, and that it is *God* who will make images of salvation live. Thus through the natural world, as through human culture, images and stories can be found to renew the tradition with which we have been entrusted. In a time when the common stories and symbols have been largely lost, the only hope is in a God who will, in self-disclosure and in the midst of the cultures, seize hold of the language[30] in a new way.

The cover of this book, a design by Gustav Klimt, *'Tree of Life'* (painted between 1905-9),[31] sums up the main themes of this introduction and the chapters which follow. It depicts a 'found form', the tree, which evokes key symbols in the biblical story of salvation – the tree in Eden, the cross of Calvary, and the tree of life in the Book of Revelation whose leaves are 'for the healing of the nations' (Rev. 22: 2). This tree is embedded in human culture, as its glittering mosaic surface and elaborate twining branches show; its style embraces eastern art forms as well as western. Under its branches and around its trunk we have an impression of a throng of human persons, and the tree itself has a kind of human (perhaps female) shape. It is, as Klimt declares, the 'tree of life', and life includes death as the perching of the black bird in the branches makes clear. Yet death is subordinate to life, cross cannot suppress resurrection, as the vitality and colour of the tree are undimmed.

The tree of life stands in the centre of the garden (Genesis 2:9). Our hope in Oxford is that our Centre – for the Study of Christianity and Culture – will enable many to put faith in the centre of the world of human cultures today.

Notes to Chapter 1

¹ Harry Blamires, *The Christian Mind* (London: SPCK, 1963), pp. vii, 3. For an updated critique, see Blamires, *The Post-Christian Mind* (London: SPCK, 2001).

² Blamires, *The Christian Mind*, p. 41.

³ Ibid., p. 13.

⁴ Ibid., p. 84.

⁵ So Peter L. Berger in Berger (ed.), *The Desecularization of the World* (Grand Rapids: Eerdmans, 1999), p.10.

⁶ See Lesslie Newbigin, *Truth to Tell. The Gospel as Public Truth* (Grand Rapids: Eerdmans, 1991); also, *Gospel and Culture: a guide to study of the issues raised in Good News in our Times* (Board of Mission of General Synod of Church of England, 1991).

⁷ See the useful discussion of the nature of 'applied' or 'practical' theology' in James Woodward and Stephen Pattison, *The Blackwell Reader in Pastoral and Practical Theology* (Oxford: Blackwell, 2000), pp. 4-7.

⁸ Some examples are: The Institute for Contemporary Christianity (London); The Centre for Christian Communication (St John's College, Durham); Theology and the Arts (Ridley Hall, Cambridge); The William Temple Foundation (Manchester Business School); Centre for the Study of Christianity and Contemporary Society (University of Stirling); Centre for Faith and Culture (Plater College, Oxford); The Centre for Christianity and Public Life (University of Edinburgh).

⁹ Books based on the lecture series of the Centre are being published mainly by the University of Wales Press, Cardiff, in the series *Religion, Culture and Society*, Series Editors Oliver Davies and Gavin Flood. Already published are: Jane Shaw and Alan Kreider (eds), *Culture and the Nonconformist Tradition* (1999); Paul S. Fiddes (ed.), *The Novel, Spirituality and Modern Culture. Eight*

Novelists Write about their Craft and their Context (2000). In preparation are four further volumes on: *Celts and Christians*; *The Culture of Economics in the Modern World*; *Composing Music for Worship in the New Millennium*; and *Metaphor, Faith and Tradition. Poetry and Contemporary Culture*.

[10] Blamires, *The Christian Mind*, p. 41.

[11] H. Richard Niebuhr, *Christ and Culture* (London: Faber and Faber, 1952), pp. 192-6.

[12] In this affirmation, Davies offers a marked contrast to those who urge that in a secular age we should develop a notion of 'theology as art' that concentrates on the immanence of the divine rather than the transcendent: see Beverley Clack, 'The Theologian as Artist: Exploring the Future of Religion', in Liam Geron (ed.), *English Literature, Theology and the Curriculum* (London: Cassell, 1999), pp. 313-26.

[13] An example of this strategy is Jürgen Moltmann, *The Crucified God*, transl. R. A. Wilson and J. Bowden (London: SCM Press, 1974), pp. 219-27, claiming that the suffering of God 'takes metaphysical rebellion up' into the very life of God.

[14] See below, chapter by Julian Thompson, p.198.

[15] See my attempts to express this in *Participating in God. A Pastoral Doctrine of the Trinity* (London: Darton, Longman and Todd, 2000), pp. 206-10.

[16] See William B. Tyrell, 'Star Trek as Myth and Television as Mythmaker', *Journal of Popular Culture* 10 (1977), pp. 711-19.

[17] Jürgen Moltmann published his *Theology of Hope* in 1964 (transl. J. W. Leitch [London: SCM Press, 1967]); Gerhard Sauter published his *Zukunft und Verheissung* ('Future and Promise') in 1965 (Zürich, Theologischer Verlag).

[18] John Drane describes the persistence of the secular mind in a postmodern culture in his book *The McDonaldization of the Church. Spirituality, Creativity and the Future of the Church* (London: Darton, Longman and Todd, 2000), pp. 85-88.

[19] For this method, see my chapter below, pp. 83-86.

[20] Seamus Heaney as interviewed by Jeremy Hooker, in a BBC Radio 3 programme, 'Daring the Depths', 15 November 1991, produced by Michael Symmons Roberts; cited by Roberts in his lecture 'Freeing the Waters. Poetry in a Parched Culture' given in the Centre for the Study of Christianity and Culture, November 2000, and to be shortly published. Cf. Seamus Heaney, *The Redress of Poetry. Oxford Lectures* (London: Faber and Faber, 1996), pp. 3-9.

[21] Printed in R. T. Davies (ed.), *Medieval English Lyrics. A Critical Anthology* (London: Faber and Faber, 1971), p. 54. The lines are quoted in the early thirteenth-century prose work, St Edmund's *Speculum Ecclesiae*.

[22] Peter Dronke, *The Medieval Lyric* (London: Hutchinson, 1968), pp. 64-5.

[23] See for example, the hymn by Walter of Châtillon, 'Sol eclypsim patitur/ dum sol verus moritur ('the sun suffers an eclipse as the true sun dies'), cit. Dronke, *Medieval Lyric*, p. 64; also the Christmas hymn by Charles Wesley, 'Hark! the herald-angels sing' with its lines 'Hail the Sun of righteousness!/ Light, and life to all He brings,/Risen with healing in his wings' (cf. Malachi 4:2).

[24] David Jones comments on the 'Break' with past tradition, but remains hopeful about the resonance of symbols, in *Anathemata* ([1952]; London: Faber and Faber, 1972), pp. 15-17. He is, however, despairing in such later poems as 'A, a, a, Domine Deus'.

[25] Rowan Williams, *Lost Icons. Reflections on Cultural Bereavement* (Edinburgh: T. & T. Clark, 2000), pp. 160-71.

[26] Terry Pratchett and Neil Gaiman, *Good Omens* (London: Corgi Books, 1991), pp. 257-63.

[27] See my chapter below, pp. 87-89.

[28] 'A New Spirit', *Vogue*, May 1999; captions by Rachel Fiddes. The promotions' director of *Vogue* commented that the parable was 'an incredibly contemporary story for the materialistic post-Thatcher generation'; see the report by Martin Wroe and Margaret Driscoll, 'Bible Story comes back into Vogue', The Sunday Times, 18 April 1999.

[29] Dietrich Bonhoeffer, *Letters and Papers from Prison*, Enlarged Edition, edited by Eberhard Bethge, transl. J. Bowden and others (London: SCM Press, 1971), p. 300.

[30] This is Karl Barth's expression: see Barth, *Church Dogmatics*, transl. and ed. G.W. Bromiley and T.F. Torrance, Volume I, Part One (Edinburgh: T. & T. Clark, 1975), p. 430.

[31] *Tree of Life* was a working design for Gustav Klimt's *Stoclet Frieze*, and is tempera, water-colour, gold paint, crayon and gold and silver leaf on paper.

Part I
Faith and Culture

2
Christ, Culture, and Truth-telling

ALAN KREIDER

1. Mediation and the transforming of cultures

Allow me to introduce you to my grand-niece, Hannah. Hannah is nine years old, and she goes to a multicultural school in a medium-sized American city. Last autumn, when the school year was beginning, Hannah's teacher told the children, 'I'm going to need some help from you so the class can function as a community.' The teacher produced a list of jobs for everyone – librarians, paper-passers, newsletter writers, chalk-board monitors, to name just a few. Also on the list was the job of 'mediator,' which she described as a problem solver. Hannah found that intriguing because, she reports, 'I knew that I wanted to help people.' She also knew that people at her church talked about mediation and that her uncle works as a mediator. So Hannah applied for the job of mediator and, along with another girl, was accepted. Someone then came to her school and taught her and her friend what a mediator does.

But Hannah and the other mediator soon discovered that mediation involved work. Children in her class had real conflicts. When one of these erupted, Hannah and her friend would ask the children in conflict to fill in forms describing the problem. Then the two mediators would call the parties together. Hannah and her friend would tell the children about rules of good conflict: to the best of their ability they must tell the truth, saying how *they* saw the conflict; they must listen well; and they must use 'I' language ('I feel so angry when you do that') and not 'you' language ('You make me so angry'). Sometimes, Hannah reports,

we cannot manage the problems. Then the teacher helps. Sometimes the kids yell at each other. That makes it hard. Sometimes they won't listen to each other or they call each other a liar. That makes it hard, too. But usually we are able to resolve the conflict when the kids listen to each other.

One day at home Hannah had a surprise. She and her sister Adrienne had a big disagreement with their mother. They were angry at her because she let their little sister do something she would not allow *them* to do. Mom was being unreasonable. Everyone was shouting at each other, and Hannah and Adie were crying. Suddenly Hannah remembered. 'Stop. Stop. Everybody stop. We'll never get anywhere like this. Now, Mom, you sit down there, and we'll sit over here. First, Mom, you tell us your side of this and we'll listen. We'll be sure we understand what you're saying. When you're done, you will listen to us. And then somehow we'll work it out.' And Hannah's mother reports that they did work it out, though in a different way – a better way – than either she or the girls had thought possible.[1]

It may seem a long way from Hannah to Richard Niebuhr. Certainly his *Christ and Culture*, and not the story of an American nine-year-old, is the obvious place to begin thinking about Christ, culture, and truth-telling.[2] *Christ and Culture* is a great book; it has shaped the thought patterns of two generations of Christian intellectuals in the West. Niebuhr's typology of five responses of Christians to culture – Christ against culture, the Christ of culture, Christ above culture, Christ and culture in paradox, and Christ transforming culture – has been widely persuasive. Numerous writers have adopted these categories as a conceptual framework. And perhaps it is not surprising that Niebuhr's preferred category, 'Christ transforming culture,' has been the dominant theme of these writers. Christians, Niebuhr and his disciples alike believed, should not accommodate themselves to culture; still less should they be against culture. Their task is to transform culture.

But Hannah's story suggests some problems with Niebuhr's approach.[3] The first is Niebuhr's reference to *culture* and not to *cultures*; Niebuhr generally tended to view culture as a monolithic phenomenon. One is either against culture as a whole, or for culture as a whole. If someone, like the stereotypable Tertullian, is critical of serving in the army but writes brilliant Latin prose, Niebuhr simply views the person as inconsistent.[4]

But what about Hannah? What is her culture? She is an American, shaped by peer pressure and the catechetical powers of television; but she is also the daughter of Mennonite parents and a regular part of a Mennonite church community – and hence she is shaped both by her societal culture and by her family and church culture. Hannah, her family, and her church community are in some respects typically American; in other respects they are culturally distinctive.

Hannah and her Mennonite community stand in tension with Niebuhr's categories. In 1951 Niebuhr could still assume that the western 'civilization' commonly called Christendom was culturally cohesive. This civilization, which assumed itself to be built upon Christian values, was a comprehensive 'culture.'[5] In each 'nation' this culture coincided with the entire populace. Insofar as Niebuhr speaks of the church, he does so in terms of its equivalence with the prevailing culture. And mission, which he does not mention, would by implication be the activity through which the church's messengers bring good news to those 'in foreign parts.'

Forty-five years after Niebuhr wrote, we are more aware of the crisis of Christendom than he was. We cannot any longer easily equate the adjective 'Christian' with the adjectives 'English' or 'American.' We also know about 'multiculturalism' in ways that Niebuhr could not have known. It was the fate of his grandchildren to discover the cultural function of hyphens: African-Americans, Bengali-Britons, Croatian-Canadians. So the culture of any given country is made up of many cultures; and some of these, such as the Amish or Orthodox Jews, seek relatively more cultural *Lebensraum* than others. But these separatist groups are not against culture. They have developed distinctive cultures of their own which often cause people, conscious of the despair and anomie inherent in their own cultures, to stop and ponder. A sign of this is the recently published *Riddle of Amish Culture*.[6] Why, we wonder, do the Amish choose to live like that? A national culture is not monolithic; it is made up of cultures in multi-voiced chorus. One is not 'against culture' simply because he or she gains primary self-identity from one of the less numerically strong cultural groupings – even if that minority culture is one of the Christian churches.

A second problem is that Niebuhr assumed that culture is basically beneficent. Culture was not perfect, to be sure; otherwise there would be no need to transform it. Niebuhr understood that 'human nature is fallen or perverted, and that this perversion not only appears in culture but is transmitted by it.'[7] But his tone in discussing culture is upbeat; and his comfortable view of culture is indicated by his lack of attention to areas of what we might call 'perennial perversion,' evident in many cultures, which Christ might want to transform.

Is a more nuanced approach possible? What would Hannah say? Hannah is a mediator. She knows that there are conflicts of interest in her culture, verbal violence, and physical mayhem. But we are not interested in Hannah's story because she deals with playground fights – these are a standard component of many cultures. Instead, what fascinates us about Hannah is what we are not used to: a self-consciously mediatorial approach, especially on the part of a nine-year-old. Culture (in the form of family squabbles) may be worse in some places than others, and at worst it is a perversion. What is it, in contrast, that produces the transforming mind of a mediator?

Niebuhr's definitions of culture do not help answer this question. At times Niebuhr used anthropological definitions. He quoted Malinowski: 'Culture is the "artificial, secondary environment" which man superimposes on the natural. It comprises language, habits, ideas, beliefs, customs, social organization, inherited artifacts, technical processes, and values.'[8] This is a descriptive, value-free definition, encompassing all of humanity. How, given that definition, could anyone be against culture? At other times Niebuhr used 'culture' to denote the national cultures of the Christian West: culture is 'the prevailing culture.'[9] About that, Anglican bishops as well as Rastafarians express critical thoughts.

This indeed is the point. All culture – whether that of the orthodox Jews or of the 'prevailing culture' – is both 'human' and 'inhuman,' both 'graced' and 'disgraced.'[10] Anthropologist Clifford Geertz has likened the human being to 'an animal suspended in a web of significance he himself has spun.'[11] We might query this: all of us cultural beings are in webs that others have spun, over many centuries; at times we may feel ourselves captives in these webs, disempowered by them. But with that proviso the web is a helpful metaphor. It helps us to function in necessary ways – to move about, to capture our food, even to create beauty. But the web can also be in disrepair; it can be dysfunctional, not conducive to the *shalom* of spiders.[12]

At every point cultures thus call for discernment. There is, I believe, no single appropriate response to the question of Christ and culture. In each of the cultures in which Christians take part, we will ask: should we flow with this, accepting the stream of cultural continuity, which is what most of us do most of the time? Should we as much as possible oppose dominant cultures, seeking somehow to opt out of them or subvert them, which is what Jesuit Daniel Berrigan and his friends have long done in the States? Should we seek to engage ourselves to change and transform them? Or simultaneously and selectively, in various areas of our life, should we flow with cultures, subvert them, and change them? How do we decide? What criteria do we use?

Here we come to a third problem with Niebuhr's scheme: the place of Christ in it. Who is the Christ who transforms culture? Is it the Jesus of first-century Galilee and Judaea? But his teachings – on worry, enemies, the oath – are, we read, 'incompatible with the duties of life in society'; taking them seriously can lead one into a 'thoroughgoing opposition to the institutions of culture.'[13] What about Niebuhr's Christ? He is culturally rootless, abstracted from particularity of place and time. Although he functions as a 'focusing point' for humanity, the focus is curiously blurred.[14]

2. Christ the criterion of culture: the call to truth-telling

What if we started at a different point, with the Jesus who was the leader of a first-century Jewish renewal movement, with the one whom his followers proclaimed to be Lord and Messiah? This Jesus, as he appears in each of the four gospel narratives, was an eminently cultural figure. He was born into one of several first-century Jewish cultures. In many ways he affirmed that culture and swam in its stream. He also came into contact with other cultures: the many faces of Hellenism and the cultures of the Roman occupying forces. As Jesus encountered these cultures, he did not query everything. But he manifested the prophet's discerning eye for current manifestations of the perennial perversions: 'You know that [in the Gentile cultures] those whom they recognize as their rulers lord it over them.... But it is not so among you; but whoever wishes to become great among you must be your servant' (Mark 10:42-43). Jesus set out to form a movement that, through its catechesis and common life, would live in his tradition and would thereby challenge and transform cultures.

That this way of being cultural would not be readily acceptable to 'the prevailing culture' is indicated by the cross. The cross reminds us that it is glib and unhelpful to invoke triumphalistically the 'transformation of culture.' Christ transforms culture by indirect, at times harrowing, means. And yet immense potential for cultural transformation resides in the words and way, the death and resurrection of Jesus. What Niebuhr says of Augustine, I would therefore say of Jesus: 'He himself is an example of

what conversion of culture means.'[15] As such he is both the ultimate criterion by which to measure all cultures and the source of 'good news' by
which they may be challenged and changed. It is from Jesus Christ, I
believe, that Hannah's vision of being a mediator ultimately comes.

Hence my proposal. In thinking about Christ, culture, and truth-
telling – in Oxford, in an era in which public discourse is full of duplicity
that does not intend to mislead, and in which church-attendance has
become the activity of specific cultures in multicultural Britain – I propose that a way forward can come from the Matthaean Jesus, from a
famous passage in the Sermon on the Mount, where he links truth-telling,
remarkably, with oath-taking:

> I say to you, Do not swear at all.... Let your word be 'Yes, Yes' or 'No,
> No'; anything more than this comes from the evil one. (Matt. 5:34-37)

What did Jesus mean by this teaching? In Matthew's gospel there is,
along with elaborations, a compact teaching of two injunctions and a
warning. First, whereas the rabbis had grown increasingly severe in their
critique of oath-taking, Jesus intensified this critique: he prohibited oath-
taking altogether for his disciples. If obedient to him they will 'not swear
at all.' Second, he called them to truth-telling. Their words will be 'yes,
yes,' or 'no, no.' This, according to Paul Minear, is a 'command for trans-
parently honest speech.'[16] Note the warning: this teaching is very
important. The Jesus of Matthew's Gospel says that 'anything more than
this comes from the evil one.'[17] If this seems a harsh judgement, Adolf
Schlatter commented that Jesus tended to see as Satanic things that no one
else saw as such, whether it was the will to power or the 'veiling of
truth.'[18]

3. Truth and the refusal to swear oaths

Some commentators on Matthew 5:34-37 are convinced that disciples of
Jesus today should invariably tell the truth and always avoid oaths. But a
larger number of scholars find this problematic: it ignores other biblical
teaching, in both Testaments;[19] it 'jumps the gun' eschatologically; it is
legalistic, literalistic, and above all impractical. As Robert Guelich put it,
'In a society built around the use of oaths to guarantee one's honesty, setting them aside would be as impossible as prosecuting anger or lust.'[20]

But is it impossible to conceive of society without the use of the oath? This impossibility has been the common assumption of western Christendom. Yet Christians have not always thought like this. Early Christianity arose against a background in which there was widespread criticism of oath-swearing. Rabbis, at times severely, cautioned against the use of oaths; and Stoic philosophers sought to limit their incidence.[21] Nevertheless, in both Jewish and Hellenistic worlds oath-taking was a part of life, a means of lightly or solemnly in the presence of God asserting one's veracity in everyday dealings, and – in the empire and city states – of ensuring social cohesion. In fourth-century Athens, the oath is 'the bond that maintains democracies.'[22] And, in cases where even under oath truth was not told, the oath embodied 'the provisional curse': if my sworn word is not true, said the younger Pliny, 'Let the divine vengeance fall upon my own head, and my whole family.'[23]

In this milieu, the early Christian movement appears to have intensified the rabbis' hesitations. No patristic scholar has yet studied the attitude of the early Christians to the oath,[24] but my own gleanings in the patristic writings indicate that most early Christian writers who wrote about the subject – including Justin, Irenaeus, and Cyprian – reported it to be Christian practice never to swear oaths but rather to tell the truth.[25] They did so on the basis of the assumption that the teachings of Jesus were good news: they believed alternative living in face of the perennial perversions was possible.[26]

The repudiation of oaths was in part a response to imperial regulations which required all citizens to manifest their loyalty and imperial conformity. Christians under persecution, from Polycarp onwards, frequently showed themselves unwilling to swear 'by the genius of the emperor.'[27] But it was not only the emperor's genius that impeded them from swearing. For some, such as Cyprian, it was simply the word of Jesus, which he passed on as one of 120 principles of conduct which he taught to new converts: 'That we must not swear,' without qualification.[28] Others appended a rationale which they derived from Jesus. The martyr Apollonius stated, 'We have been ordered by him never to swear and in all things to tell the truth... for from deceit comes distrust, and through distrust in turn comes the oath.'[29] Christians refrained from the oath, wrote Clement of Alexandria, because they were 'addicted to truth.'[30]

Some Christians did not consistently repudiate oath-taking. Both Tertullian and Origen seem to have wavered between a principled refusal of all oath-taking and a flexible willingness, from case to case, to allow swearing in certain circumstances.[31] A reluctance by some Christians to follow their leaders' demanding teachings is also discernible in some cases.[32]

In the fourth and fifth centuries things changed. As the emperors were converted and Christianity became at first legal and then compulsory, the arguments of Christian writers shifted. Not rapidly, however. Basil of Caesarea developed the theme that 'Swearing is absolutely forbidden.'[33] Gregory of Nazianzus penned a dialogue that rejected the various arguments for oath-taking that some Christians were now advancing.[34] In the Latin West Hilary of Poitiers and, as late as the sixth century, Caesarius of Arles demonstrated that Christian leaders continued to reject oath-taking.[35]

The writings of John Chrysostom, however, reveal the changes under way. He himself, in late fourth-century Antioch, passionately instructed Christians, in both catechism and sermons, not to swear at all. If they wished their words to carry special weight, they should say, 'Believe me.'[36] But they were swearing anyway. Some were engaging in 'frivolous cursing and swearing.'[37] Others, to give additional solemnity to their oaths, were placing their hands on the Gospels or even going to local synagogues where the 'oaths that were taken there were more awesome.'[38] A rationale began to be advanced by some of John's flock: 'I take an oath in a just cause.'[39] From the *Apostolic Constitutions* we probably get a fair picture of the Syrian church – one that teaches 'thou shalt not swear at all' so 'our word might be firmer than an oath' but also recognizes sometimes oaths 'cannot be avoided.'[40]

Why did oaths seem unavoidable? Partly, it seems, because of the pressure of new Christians, more thoroughly instructed by their catechists in doctrine than in behaviour, who continued to comport themselves in conventional ways. Partly also because of the behaviour and legislation of the imperial government. Under Christian emperors, Christians were not compelled to swear by the *genius* of the emperor. Instead, by Chrysostom's time soldiers in the legions – whether Christian or not – were required to swear fidelity to the empire 'by God, by Christ and the Holy Spirit, and by the *majesty* of the emperor.'[41] In the lawcourts, as early as 334, litigants were required to give evidence that was 'bound by the sanctity of an oath.'[42] In 395 they were urged to invoke God as witness.[43] By the sixth century, the Justinian Code reported that the law courts could not function without the oath: 'Judges would not be able to decide the cases brought to their tribunal except in the presence of the holy gospels.'[44]

It is in this setting of proliferating oath-taking that Augustine wrote. He was profoundly committed to truth-telling,[45] and also aware of the earlier Christian tradition which claimed that 'a Christian isn't allowed to swear.'[46] And he was aware of the Christians' capacity for self-deception and deadly-dangerous habit. To avoid perjury, which led to God's vengeance ('the stench of a dead soul'), Augustine counselled the believers in Hippo not to swear at all, because 'if you don't swear at all, you can never swear a lie.'[47] However, Augustine's hermeneutic is more complex than Justin Martyr's – in the Old Testament God had sworn and commanded the Israelites to swear; and in the New Testament, he was convinced, on several occasions Paul had sworn. Therefore Christians could, reluctantly, carefully, after due soul-searching, take oaths, if two conditions were met: (a) if there was 'great necessity,' which includes the oaths that are 'demanded of you'; and (b) if it was for some greater good, for example enabling people to believe 'what it is to their benefit to believe.'[48]

Necessity and the benefit of others – these were arguments that were to have a successful future in Christian Europe. They were infinitely elastic; they also enabled the guardians of the benefit of others, i.e. the powerholders in state and church, to rationalize each expansion of the oath.[49] All of this took place in the presence and name of God, whose authority permeated and sanctioned the authorities and power relationships on earth. Gradually, as institutions developed, Christian civilization in the West – Christendom – became an edifice of oaths.

In Christendom oaths were omnipresent. Oaths of fealty bound underlings to lords. Centralizing monarchs such as Charlemagne or William the Conqueror used loyalty oaths to expand their authority and to bind entire populations to them.[50] Monarchs at their coronations swore oaths to govern well. Oaths, more slowly than one might expect, also entered the church, as bishops swore to be obedient to the pope and to be doctrinally orthodox; local incumbents and churchwardens also swore, as did students upon matriculating and graduates upon graduating.[51] In continental towns on a specified day (the *Schwörtag*) all the adult males would gather in a central *Platz* to swear their loyalty to the town.[52] In late medieval London, 'All the rites of passage in City life – apprenticeship, freedom, holding office – were sanctioned by the taking of oaths...'[53] Private and public contracts were secured by oaths, and in courts of law the truth of testimony was undergirded by compulsory oaths.

Now, in all this oath-taking, there was little to compel truthfulness. Monarchs, of course, had tried and true methods of punishing unfaithful subjects: *force majeure*. But until the sixteenth century, at least in England, perjury was not a crime; it was a sin, and its punishment was God's business – actualizing the provisional curse. The 'great danger in swearing' didn't come from the law; it came from the offended God, who would punish the perjurer posthumously and very possibly gruesomely in this life. To remind oath-takers of the solemnity of their oaths, sacred objects proliferated upon which oaths were taken – the Gospels, relics, crucifixes. One of these, the eleventh-century *Red Book of Derby*, was filled with retributive power: those 'who should swear untruly upon this book should run mad.'[54]

When the Reformation broke out in the sixteenth century, the magisterial Reformers were determined to abolish these 'oaths by creatures.' But oath-taking in the name of God remained laudable and necessary. For Luther it was one of the accepted means by which Christians 'succour the need of the neighbour.'[55] Luther's colleague Melanchthon contended that 'government and justice are constituted upon the oath.'[56] Zwingli's successor Heinrich Bullinger agreed: the oath is 'the bond, which holds together the whole body of the common good and of just government.'[57] In the following century in England, the dimensions of this were spelled out by Puritan divine Daniel Featly:

> Oaths are necessary for the execution of the magistrate's office and the preservation of human society. For without such oaths the commonwealth hath no surety upon public officers and ministers: nor kings upon their subjects; nor lords upon their tenants; neither can men's titles be cleared in causes civil, nor justice done in causes criminal; nor dangerous plots and conspiracies be discovered against the state.[58]

These affirmations are resounding, and one is struck by how similar they are – at the height of Christendom – to what Lycurgus had said in Athens three centuries before Christ. Why were the Reformers so vociferous? It was not that they were content with the way the oath was functioning in Christendom. As English Reformer Thomas Becon surveyed the realm, he found an epidemic of cursing and what he termed 'customable swearing.' And in the law courts he found perjury: 'O incomparable vice!'[59] But these perversions, one suspects, were perennial and had been present for centuries. The novelties which the Reformers and their successors faced were two. New movements of popular protest had emerged which viewed oaths as instruments of oppression,[60] and new dissenting traditions had arisen which thoughtfully and articulately repudiated the use of the oath altogether. To those charged with maintaining civil order, these movements seemed infinitely dangerous.

One of these movements, the Anabaptists, developed their views on the oaths unevenly and gradually.[61] But by 1560 they, in many countries, were pretty well united that all of life should be governed by the rule of truth-telling. As Menno Simons, a second-generation Anabaptist leader, put it in a representative passage: 'if you fear the Lord and... are asked to swear,... continue in the Lord's Word which has forbidden you so plainly to swear, and let your yea and nay be your oath as was commanded, whether life or death be your lot....'[62] As the Anabaptists discovered, one could perjure oneself with no great danger; but when one refused to swear one could be burned for heresy.

A century later in England the Quakers came to conclusions similar to those of the Anabaptists. William Penn asserted a Quaker understanding of how oath-refusal interlocked with a commitment to truth-telling:

> ... if Christians ought never to lie, it is most certain that they need never to swear; for swearing is built upon lying; take away lying, and there remains no more ground for swearing; truth-speaking comes in the room thereof.[63]

The Quakers' oath-refusal rarely led to their execution, but in the second half of the seventeenth century it led to repeated imprisonments. Occasionally, given the capacities of George Fox for prophetic gesture, this could lead to something approaching street-theatre. In 1664, in Lancaster, a judge handed Fox a Bible and ordered the oath to be read to him in the presence of a jury. Would he now swear? Fox responded:

> Ye have given me a book here to kiss and to swear on, and this book which ye have given me to kiss, says, 'Kiss the Son'; and the Son says in this book, 'Swear not at all'; and so says also the apostle James. Now,

I say as the book says, and yet ye imprison me; how chance ye do not imprison the book for saying so? How comes it that the book is at liberty amongst you, which bids me not swear, and yet ye imprison men for doing as the book bids me? Why don't ye imprison the book?

As Fox raised the book, pointing to Matthew 5, a court official snatched the Bible from his hands, and the judge said, 'Nay, but we will imprison George Fox.'[64]

Arguments such as Penn's and actions such as Fox's unleashed vigorous debate about oaths in late Stuart England. This debate was made the more poignant as many loyal citizens realized that throughout the political and religious turbulence of the previous half century they had repeatedly sworn loyalty to the sovereigns of the moment – and thus they had repeatedly perjured themselves.[65] The debate has since continued sporadically in most western countries. In many places the impact of the Enlightenment and the French Revolution led to a reconsideration of oath-taking.[66] In England debate on oaths flared up in the 1830s and 1880s;[67] in Germany it reached a peak of intensity in the 1960s in light of the loyalty oath which many Germans had sworn to Adolf Hitler.[68]

As the centuries have gone by, the pattern of oath-taking has changed. In England, for example, the number of areas in which oaths are deemed appropriate has dwindled: contracts are no longer validated by oaths; and undergraduates, unlike their medieval predecessors, no longer swear to observe their college statutes. The character of oaths has also changed: after lengthy debate, in 1911 the clause 'So help me God' was removed from the oath formula; no longer do witnesses explicitly invite God to strike them dead if their testimony is untrue. As early as 1696 Quakers were allowed to give testimony upon affirmation in civil cases; in 1869 the right of affirmation was opened to all who wished; and in 1888, after a fierce struggle, the last stronghold of compulsory oath-taking – the House of Commons – was breached and Members of Parliament could be admitted to the house upon affirmation. Meanwhile, perjury has emerged as a civil crime, punishable by fines and imprisonment for false evidence under either oath or affirmation.[69]

It is totally possible, in England today, to live without swearing oaths. The oath remains a common feature of English legal life, but it is no longer a bond that holds society together. In its current form, in these last days of Christendom, the oath still requires witnesses to swear 'by Almighty God.' But these words, according to many observers, mean nothing to most people who say them. And the notable thing is that they do not necessarily lead to truth-telling in court. Some have argued that this is because the oath places witnesses under undue pressure and does not assist them to recall events accurately.[70] In contrast, a recent study has argued that the oath does not put witnesses under enough pressure, and the study advocates legislation which would make perjury a crime, not against the state but against the victim. '[T]he incidence of perjury is widespread, and... is frequently committed without shame,'[71] which is no surprise to anyone who followed the recent trial of O. J. Simpson. It is unclear whether this widespread perjury is a result of a loss of Christianity's place in society. One cannot do a scientific comparative study of lying under oath across the centuries, but one cannot help observing that throughout the history of the Christian West people in every period complained about the prevalence of perjury.[72] Whatever else the oath may do, it does not seem to have led to truth-telling in court.

What about truth-telling more widely, in the course of daily life? Speaking only of the Anglo-Saxon world, we are living in an era whose verbal images assume the power of deception: 'cover-up', 'spin-doctor', 'fiddling.' U. K. insurance companies in 1994 lost an estimated £600 million in bogus or exaggerated claims.[73] In many professions, according to Sissela Bok, 'deception is taken for granted,' and is hard to change: 'existing deceptive practices and competitive stresses make it difficult not to conform.'[74] Of course, one can justify these in terms of some greater good. But she is concerned at the social cost when truth-telling becomes abnormal. We can pillory our politicians, but don't they reflect the morality of their constituents? Is it possible to be a person of truth-telling in a society in which lying is a way of life?

I believe that it is hard but possible. And God, I believe, has given us a mechanism for cultivating truthful living: the Church, not as an institution but as people committed to one another in Christ in face-to-face relationships. The Church is not commonly taken seriously in ethical thinking, at least in the Christendom tradition. In his other writings, unlike *Christ and Culture*, Richard Niebuhr allows a place between the individual and the 'culture' for the church as an ethically creative subculture.[75] And, whereas Sissela Bok does list a number of such groupings, significantly missing from her list is the church.[76] Christians, she must assume, may gather for worship, but their worship will not change the way they live.

4. The church as a 'second culture'

It might do us good, in post-Christendom, to listen to the experiences of eastern Europeans of the 1980s. One of them, Czech dissident Ivan Jirons, for example, spoke of the creative potential of what he called a 'second culture.' Jirons at first had in mind groups that gathered in basements to play rock and roll, but Vaclav Havel came to use the term 'second culture' for the various groups devoted to social change which sprang up in the late Iron Curtain Age.[77] Walter Sawatzky has shown how instrumental these groups, whose only power was truthfulness, were in bringing about the past decade's monumental changes.[78]

What if the church were to conceive of itself as a 'second culture' devoted to social change? If it did, it would be in the grand biblical tradition: of Abraham, who left the dominant culture of Ur to pioneer a culture with new foundations; of Israel, whose alternative politics stood as a 'light to the nations' to teach them by example how to live; of Jesus' disciples, who were 'a city set upon a hill'; of the early Christians, who spread less by what they said than by 'the remarkable and admittedly extraordinary constitution of their own commonwealth.'[79] The church in its early years grew because it fascinated people, because its culture embodied ways of living that were good news to those who observed them.[80] Might something similar be possible in our day?

It might be if we were to see Jesus not only as the Son of God or as the 'focusing point for humanity,'[81] but as the normal human being. Jesus' words and ways point to real life. It is not always clear what living in his way means, but the Jesus who emerges in each of the four Gospels challenges every era's assumptions about what is normal – in areas of wealth and power, violence, sex, and truth. He grappled with the perennial perversions which passed as the 'normal practice' of his day. And he called his followers to band together through his love and pardon to continue his struggle to bring normality to humanity. To appropriate this reality God's people must teach it by story, memory, and ritual.[82] Granted, they will never realize it in full; they will always remain marked by their sin, trapped by abnormality. But when people respond to Jesus with a faith-filled belief that his way can be lived, surprising things can happen. In their common life they develop new skills and disciplines which change them so that, in their public life, they function differently; they become re-reflexed. New solutions to intractable problems spring to mind. And the church, so functioning, becomes the laboratory of God's future.

The experience of 'second cultural' living has been the lot of Quakers and Anabaptist/Mennonites since their origins. Of course, these nonconformist groups have always been – and are – far from exemplary. Their very differing histories have been marked by infidelity and pain; yet they may at times point the way for other Christians in post-Christendom, in which Christians are a 'second culture' in a world they cannot dominate. A sample of this is their Jesus-based resistance to oath-taking and their espousal of its positive correlative – the development of skills and disciplines in truth-telling. Significantly, Hannah, our nine-year-old mediator, belongs to a Mennonite culture as well as to an American culture, and the teacher who began the mediation program in her school is also Mennonite. But this vision is not uncongenial to Catholics or Anglicans in post-Christendom. The Bishop of London, shortly after his enthronement, articulated something similar:

> ... at the top of the agenda of every human society is going to be the question of how we relate, how we live together peacefully; and the church as *a school of relating...* is very well-placed to make a contribution.[83]

A transformation of cultures thus begins in the church as a 'school of relating.' The church though cannot stop and revel in its new understandings and skills. It is always discovering how to live in its missionary engagement with people in the structures and pain that we share with them. But the church will not prosper in mission until it has something distinctive to offer. For that reason it, following Jesus, must learn the everyday practices of normal living.[84] Of the many examples of normal living that I could cite, I shall now look at just two, which constitute a 'no' and a 'yes.'

5. Contributing to culture with a 'no' and a 'yes'

The 'no' is to the oath, following Jesus' first injunction, 'Do not swear at all' (Matt. 5:34). To some this may seem an irrelevance – in a situation in which swearing itself has become devoid of meaning, why not swear? Others may find this unnecessarily rigid, in light of biblical evidence that seems unclear or contradictory. Still others, such as Romano Guardini, wish to combat the demise of the oath. Why capitulate to yet another attempt to strip away the sacral dimension of life?[85]

While registering their concerns, I nevertheless believe that our Christian contribution to culture would be stronger if we said 'no' to the oath, for four reasons.

1. The first reason is to reaffirm the conviction that it is Christ who is able to transform culture. Christians across the centuries have discovered endless ways of removing the imaginative radicalism from his message; the result has been Christendom, in which Jesus' words must appear to be 'against culture.' A 'second culture' church in post-Christendom has the opportunity of agreeing with Jesus instead of arguing with him. If it stopped sanding down the jagged edges of Jesus' utterances and started saying 'yes' to them and asking how they might be lived, the church's cultural impact would be transformed.[86]

2. A second reason is to construct boundary rituals. Communities which know that they do not represent the views of a majority of people in a society retain their cohesion, and their sense of identity, by developing 'powerful practices.'[87] These remind one, suddenly, 'I'm one of them. This ritual may not seem all that important, but it's important to me. I observe it because it bonds me with a distinctive people, Jesus' disciples, who stand for things that I care about.' So when we affirm instead of swearing, we are identifying ourselves visibly as members of a community who are committed to truthfulness, not only in court but all the time.

3. A third reason to say 'no' is to change culture. Consider the withering of the oath in modern Western societies. In comparison to the sixteenth century, it has been limited to comparatively few areas. Its wording has progressively been changed: in the U. K. the conditional curse 'So help me God' was removed from the oath formula in 1911. The oath has also been supplemented by the affirmation, which since 1869 has had equal force in British law.[88] In this process of oath reform observe how Christian nonconformists such as the Quakers have worked in alliance with freethinkers.[89] Might the withering of the oath, like the ending of slavery and the struggle for racial and gender equality, be an example of Christ transforming culture?[90]

4. The fourth reason to refuse to swear an oath, and the most pressing one, is to reassert the Christian concern for truth-telling. When Jesus repudiated the oath, his main concern was to call a halt to two-level truth-telling, to the 'differentiation between the words which have to be true, and those which don't have to be true.'[91] The oath is a solemn expression of this two-level approach, but so, less solemnly, are other common expressions. We are used to hearing real estate agents say, 'Well, to be quite honest,' and we may start wondering what they have been the rest of the time. Newt Gingrich, as Speaker of the U. S. House of Representatives, often said 'frankly' when under pressure and having to be evasive.[92] In contrast, Jesus invites his followers to give up all formulas of two-tier truth-telling because he wants them to be truthful people, telling the truth all of the time. It is not only our words under oath that will 'take God's name in vain' (Exod. 20:7); God's name – God's character as God of truth – is taken in vain every time we bend the truth. Jesus reminds us that we will need to give account, not only of our words under oath, but of all our words (Matt. 12:36-37).

Our 'no' is thus to oath-taking; our corresponding 'yes' will be to truth-telling, following Jesus' second injunction: 'Let your word be "Yes, Yes" or "No, No" ' (Matt. 5:37). Many Christian traditions have affirmed a clear commitment to truth-telling. The *Quaker Faith and Practice* does this by means of queries: 'Are you honest and truthful in all you say and do? Do you maintain strict integrity in business transactions and in your dealings with individuals and organizations?'[93] But the stories that a tradition tells may indicate this is not always easy.

Menno Simons, one of the Mennonite tradition's founders, was often pursued by authorities who wanted to try him for heresy and burn him. Once he was travelling by coach – on the roof because all the seats inside had already been taken – when it was halted by armed men on horseback. 'Is Menno Simons in there?' they shouted. Menno looked inside and asked, 'Is Menno Simons in there?' The passengers said no. So he turned to the militiamen and said, 'They say he isn't in there.' The armed men rode off and Menno survived.[94] Was this white lie in keeping with the new *Mennonite Confession of Faith*, which reads: 'We commit ourselves to tell the truth, to give a simple yes or no...'?[95]

A typical way to respond to this incident, and to approach the question of truth-telling in general, would be to concentrate on quandaries, on ethical dilemmas; and these continue to trouble all thoughtful Christians. A recent Quaker training document poses the issue on the basis of immense international experience: 'Can concern for our neighbour give rise to situations where love has priority over truthfulness?'[96] The danger has always been that dissimulation, like oath-taking, can become endlessly self-justifying. How can this reflexive, self-justifying dissimulation be curbed? Sissela Bok has proposed three demanding criteria – one might call them 'quandary limitation devices' – which anyone must meet who considers telling an untruth.[97]

However, the truly challenging question is not how we respond to quandaries or under what circumstances we are allowed to lie. It is rather 'How do we become truthful persons, persons capable of truth-telling?' To become truthful people we must also ask questions like this: How, in the midst of a macro-culture in which dissimulation often appears to rule, can one develop 'second cultures' in which people can tell the truth and live the truth? How can truth-telling become a way of life?[98]

6. Three commitments of a 'second culture' of truth

To make 'living the truth' happen, a truthful 'second culture' must make three commitments that grow out of the teaching and way of Jesus. The first is a commitment to be truthful: 'yes, yes; no, no.' This involves an inner intention to speak without deception. This does not mean that we will engage in promiscuous self-disclosure, or that we will always say everything we think or know. There is ample room, in the truthful life, for silence, discretion, the keeping of confidences and even the pleasantries that lubricate social interchange. (When people ask you, at 7:45 a.m., 'How are you?' they are not necessarily asking for a doctor's report!) But this does mean that we are committed to making the words that we utter true words. This can require conversion, a specific decision no longer to flatter, or to say the convenient word, or to save face, or to make excuses, or to cover and hide to make things look better. This conversion is hard, but it is a conversion to life. There is inner freedom for those who discover that they don't have to be duplicitous.[99]

But truthful words are only one part of being truthful: truthful speech must be backed up by a congruent life.[100] Jesus' words about hypocrisy, especially on the part of religious leaders, were severe. But Jesus himself holds out the model that indicates that integrity and wholeness are God's design for normal living: 'I am the way, the truth, and the life' (John 14:6). Truth in Jesus' Hebrew thought entailed words that are non-deceitful, but it went much deeper than that: it involved a 'being-true and a living-true that calls for 'doing the truth" (John 3:21).[101] If there is a lack of congruency between the 'truth' that one speaks and the 'truth' that one does and is, people sense the dissonance.

In addition to being truthful, a truthful 'second culture' requires a second commitment – a commitment to listening. 'Those that have ears to hear,' said Jesus, 'let them listen' (Matt. 11:15; 13:9, 43). James underlined this for members of his community: 'let everyone be quick to listen, slow to speak....' (James 1:19). Despite our commitment to say only things that are true, we discover as we mature that our perspectives are limited, our 'truths' are imperfect. We learn that our understandings are enriched, but also limited, by our experience and place in society: we are limited by our socialization in class and economic interests, and by our national and religious allegiances; we may even be conditioned by our culture to speak in what Deborah Tannen has called 'genderlects.'[102] Our problems are compounded by the unconscious burdens that we carry, the unassimilated realities that lurk in our psyches. We see, but through a glass darkly. We are complex people, and we can become simple and whole only in the companionship of others. For this reason, point-making conversation, which (to misquote Clausewitz) is the continuation of war by other means, will not lead us to the larger truth that we all deeply seek. That truth will come as we learn to become people of intentional presence to others. According to Quaker mediator Adam Curle, we can 'listen deeply,' not rehearsing our own next comment but generally internalizing what the other is saying. When we do that, he observes, 'we will often find that the right words are given to us.'[103] As we speak and listen truly, we will thus discover an eschatological dimension to truth-telling.[104]

Truth-telling of this sort nurtures relationships and builds common life. And the common life is rooted in a truthful second culture's third commitment: a commitment to good process. Good process involves at least two disciplines. The first of these is *direct speech*. Jesus was insistent upon direct speech: when one of his friends had problems with another of his friends, there was one thing that that disciple should not do – go to a third friend (Matt. 5:23; 18:15). What group psychologists call 'triangling'[105] was ruled out of Jesus' community. Subsequent writers have underscored the point. Early in their history, the Society of Brothers emphasized it as their first law: 'there must never be talk, either open or hidden, against a brother or a sister, against their individual characteristics – under no circumstances behind their back.'[106] In Finkenwalde Dietrich Bonhoeffer came to a similar position.[107] This commitment to direct speech requires vulnerability – Jesus urges his friends to seek out, directly, even the brother or sister 'who has something against you' (Matt. 5:23).[108] In such encounters Christians can offer each other wisdom as well as forgiveness; in the words of the 1780 Covenant of the New Road Baptist Church, Oxford, they may 'watch over and admonish one another.'[109] The New Testament has several terms for these direct, truth-telling encounters. One, from 1 John 1:6-7, which became a central commitment of the East African Revival, is 'walking in the light.' A second, from the epistle to the Ephesians, is 'speaking the truth in love.' Loving truthfulness enables Christians to become community, 'body,' 'members of one another.' So 'let us put away falsehood' (Eph. 4:15-16, 25)! Through the discipline of direct speech, congregations are offered the destiny of developing cultures, not of superficiality and opacity but of transparency and trust.

The second discipline of good process is *handling conflict interactively*. The Matthean Jesus, in a famous passage (18:15-20), instructed his followers about how to cope with sin and broken relationships ('If another member of the church sins against you'), and also of dealing with moral discernment and decision-making ('binding and loosing'). The process that Jesus offers his friends is deliberate, sensitive to the frailties of people, and community-building. It is instructive to note, in the narratives of the earliest Christian communities in the Book of Acts, how often appears a similar concern for process (Acts 6:1-6; 11:1-18; 15:1-29).[110] From these we can observe that, from the beginning, conflict among Christians was not only normal – as the Apostle Paul stated, it was a necessary means by which truth emerges.[111]

Of course much of Christian history has been marked by bad process. As we seek to recover from this history, the learnings of the non oath-taking groups, the Quakers and Mennonites, may at times point the way. From their early days, the Quakers were concerned with procedure: their 'threshing' meetings were occasions for listening to differing viewpoints, within a framework of agreed agenda and procedural rules. Before long the recognizable patterns of Quaker decision-making had emerged in the meetings for business; these patterns have been characterized as 'learning to listen – not going to the meeting with the mind made up,' silent worship when conflict arises, participation by all, and decision by consensus.[112]

Anabaptist origins also hold out helpful models of group decision-making – including the process leading up to the 'Brotherly Union' at Schleitheim in 1527. Subsequent Anabaptist groups were often untrue to their origins, fractious, divisive, conflict-shy. But within the past twenty years Mennonites, helped not least by David Augsburger's writings, have been learning the art of *Caring Enough to Confront*.[113] Recent Mennonite thinkers have learned much from social psychologists and communications theorists who have helped them to give practical expression to biblical and traditional Mennonite communal values. The results of their work, for example in the *Mediation and Facilitation Training Manual*, are helpful to all groups who expect God to speak through any member and who believe that good process leads to wise decisions that build community.[114]

7. Christian engagement with cultures

All of this may seem laudable but essentially churchy, intramural, and otherworldly. And it may remain that: one cannot underestimate the capacity of Christians to act as if the rest of the world were simply not there! Yet I restate my thesis: Christians will transform cultures when they learn to live the teachings of Jesus, practising and refining these in 'second cultures,' so that they can offer their learnings as gifts to the other cultures in which they are committed participants. It is not that only Christians will come as purveyors of superior insight. Christians, especially those who believe that Jesus' teachings provide insight into process, often discover that secular westerners, or members of non-Christian religious traditions such as Mahatma Gandhi, have come to truths that are correlative to those of Jesus – and that they may be, to our shame, farther along in the practice of these than most Christians. As Christians we must engage with the cultures humbly, repentantly, attentively. Nevertheless, the approaches of Jesus to truth-telling offer useful paradigms for the behaviour of all groups.

This is always challenging and never straightforward. Take truth-telling in business, for example. From the Quaker movement's earliest days, an approach of transparent truth-telling appeared to be good for

Quaker businessmen.[115] A ballad written about Pennsylvania farmer-preacher Cyrus Bomberger makes the same point about businessmen in the Anabaptist/Pietist tradition:[116]

> He's a full measure man
> He won't tell you a lie
> When Cyrus rolls his wagons to the scales
> Just wave him right on by
> Level on the level, signed with the shake of a hand
> Unaffected, well-connected
> Simple, honest man

How attractive and yet how quaint this sounds. How does it apply to a world in which Quaker-inspired firms like Rowntrees have been taken over by Nestlés, in which significant decisions are taken by faceless people in Switzerland or cyberspace? How do Christians committed to truth-telling respond to a business environment whose closest analogies come from the game of poker, in which bluffing is basic?[117] Can Christians function with truthful congruency in large businesses? When they are there, can they at times see things that elude others? Is there any mileage in John H. Yoder's recent suggestion that 'Paul's solidarity models of deliberation [as in 1 Cor. 14] correlate with the reasons that the Japanese can make better cars than Detroit'?[118]

Similar questions of truthfulness and congruency, attentive listening and good process, arise in all areas – in academic administration and in local government, in the arts and in medicine, even in non-profit organizations. Quakers and Mennonites, among other groups, have wrestled with them in their global relief and development programs with results that are not always clearcut.[119] Two administrators of the Mennonite Central Committee recently reflected that they and their colleagues try to mingle 'transparency' with 'congruency', honesty with discretion. Given these goals they operate by 'instinct,' and keep track of their history with 'narratives.' So they ponder decisions and experiences. In apartheid South Africa, when Mennonites were allowed to work in the tribal homelands but banned, because their commitment to non-violence seemed subversive, from working in the Republic, they applied for transit visas and said that they were 'visiting friends' – without mentioning that their friends were at the office of the South Africa Council of Churches. Was that in keeping with 'transparency'? A concern for honesty also led the Mennonite Central Committee to refuse to smuggle Bibles into the former Soviet Union.[120]

A commitment to truthfulness can lead to a distinctive style which holds out unique possibilities. An English Quaker theologian, Eva Pinthus, for many years annually visited the German Democratic Republic. She was allowed to travel with exceptional freedom as she encouraged Quaker groups and built bridges between the various Christian traditions. She recently reflected: 'Telling truth in the political context is not black or white, but on the other hand Friends are trusted because they are known for their integrity.... [In] the context of working in East Germany before the wall came down, I don't think I ever had to tell a downright lie, but I did not necessarily tell all the Truth. A smile and silence was often my answer, or a shrug of the shoulder.'[121]

Let us now return to the place we began, mediation. We are living in a world divided not by competing ideologies and power blocs but by conflicting communal identities. Nation-states no longer seem to be the world's fundamental political units; it is now clear that they are full of cultures, many of which cross political borders. People of different religions and races and national heritages live as uncomfortable neighbours who can, under certain circumstances, emerge as enemies who violate and kill one another. At times these situations are ones of evident injustice and call God's people to solidarity and advocacy. Especially in such a multicultural world, the sensitivities and disciplines of the mediator are important. When should Christians advocate? When should they mediate?[122]

A recent book, *Religion, the Missing Dimension in Statecraft*, provides case studies of both advocacy and mediation. It analyzes the contribution of many groups and traditions to international and intercultural peacemaking in recent decades: advocacy from Evangelical Protestants in the former German Democratic Republic, in which 'the Sermon on the Mount got the better of city hall' and from Filipino Catholics in 1986 in the bloodless anti-Marcos revolution. It also tells stories of Moravians, working with Baptists and a Mennonite 'technical assistant,' bringing reconciliation in revolutionary Nicaragua between the Sandinista government and the Miskito Indians; and of Quakers in the late 1960s working tirelessly to assist communication and healing between the warring factions in the Nigerian/Biafran conflict.[123]

Mediation is a newer ministry than advocacy. It is a humble ministry – Adam Curle has described it as 'a lot of persuasion, clarification, message carrying, defusing, honest brokering, encouraging, and liaison.'[124] It can be dangerous: while the Mennonite 'technical assistant' John Paul Lederach was assisting the parties towards a solution, anonymous people phoned him with threats to kidnap his family – some people have a vested interest in prolonging hostilities.[125] The ministry of mediation is Christian: it grows out of the teachings of Jesus, and because it is about reconciliation it is also at the heart of the Christian gospel. Quakers and Mennonites have taken a special institutional interest in this area – both are at work around the world mediating and training mediators, and both are making low-profile but strategic contributions to the peace process in Northern Ireland.[126] But mediation as well as advocacy is classically Christian, and both require the disciplines and commitments of truth-telling.

Hannah comes from a Mennonite home; she attends a Mennonite church. But the vision of helping others by being truthful, by listening well, and by enabling them to have conflict that is productive and not destructive is a vision that is open to all Christians. As Hannahs proliferate, as more and more Christians catch this vision, they will fascinate people as they challenge the perennial perversions. Imagine the ripples of change that will spread not only through the churches but also throughout our many cultures, even through our cities and our universities. Richard Niebuhr would recognize it: that when we learn from Christ to be truthtellers, we learn one way in which Christ transforms culture.

Notes to Chapter 2

This chapter is an expanded version of the inaugural lecture of Alan Kreider as Director of the Centre for the Study of Christianity and Culture, given at Regent's Park College, Oxford, 6 March 1996. In its present form it was first printed in the Conrad Grebel Review (University of Waterloo, Canada), 15, no. 3 (1997), pp. 207-33, and we gratefully acknowledge permission to reproduce it here.

[1] Conversations, 30 December 1995 and 3 March 1996; Hannah Gerig to Alan Kreider, 29 January 1996.

[2] H. Richard Niebuhr, *Christ and Culture* (New York: Harper & Brothers, 1951).

[3] For recent evaluations of Niebuhr's *Christ and Culture*, see Walter Brueggemann, 'Rethinking Church Models Through Scripture,' in his *A Social Reading of the Old Testament: Prophetic Approaches to Israel's Communal Life*, ed. Patrick D. Miller (Minneapolis: Fortress Press, 1994), pp. 263-75; Charles Scriven, *The Transformation of Culture: Christian Social Ethics after H. Richard Niebuhr* (Scottdale, Pa.: Herald Press, 1988); Brian J. Walsh, 'The Transformation of Culture: A Review Essay,' *The Conrad Grebel Review*, 7 (1989), pp. 253-67; Duane K. Friesen, 'An Anabaptist Theology of Culture for a New Century,' *The Conrad Grebel Review* 13 (1995), pp. 33-53; John Howard Yoder, 'How Richard Niebuhr Reasons,' in Glen H. Stassen, D. M. Yeager, and J. H. Yoder, *Authentic Transformation: A New Vision of Christ and Culture* (Nashville: Abingdon, 1996), pp. 31-90.

[4] Niebuhr, *Christ and Culture*, pp. 69-70.

[5] Niebuhr often used the terms 'culture,' 'civilization,' and 'nation' interchangeably.

[6] Donald B. Kraybill, *The Riddle of Amish Culture* (Baltimore: Johns Hopkins University Press, 1989).

[7] Niebuhr, *Christ and Culture*, p. 45.

[8] Ibid., p. 33.

[9] Ibid., p. 45.

[10] John Francis Kavenaugh, S.J., *Following Christ in a Consumer Society: The Spirituality of Cultural Resistance* (Maryknoll, N.Y.: Orbis Books, 1981), pp. 16-17.

[11] Clifford Geertz, *The Interpretation of Cultures: Selected Essays* (New York: Basic Books, 1973), p. 5.

[12] A helpful biblical insight into the study of culture may come from scholars who have worked with the Pauline concept of the 'principalities and powers.' These are God-designed and God-ordained for the sustenance and service of the created order; they are creationally good. But they have, according to Paul, become rebellious, exalting themselves as lords instead of functioning as servants. The result is variable, depending upon the extent of their usurpation. At worst, the result is the asphyxiation of humanity and the destruction of creation. A systemic interlocking of various structures and cultures leads to what several biblical writers call 'the world'–hence the Christian call to overcome it (e.g., 1 John 5:4). Wink calls this 'the domination system.' See Hendrik Berkhof, *Christ and the Powers* (Scottdale, Pa.: Herald Press, 1962); Walter Wink, *Engaging the Powers: Discernment and Resistance in a World of Domination* (Minneapolis: Fortress Press, 1992).

[13] Niebuhr, *Christ and Culture*, pp. 9, 60.

[14] Ibid., p. 29.

[15] Ibid., p. 208.

[16] Paul S. Minear, 'Yes or No: The Demand for Honesty in the Early Church,' *Novum Testamentum* 5 (1971), p. 2.

[17] James, who introduced his summary with 'above all,' urges oath-avoidance and truth-telling 'so that you may not fall under condemnation' (James 5:12).

[18] Adolf Schlatter, *Der Evangelist Matthäus*, 2nd ed. (Stuttgart: Calwer Vereinsbuchhandlung, 1933), p. 183.

[19] Biblical texts which authorize, or have been seen to authorize, the use of oaths, include Gen. 24:2-3; Lev. 19:12; Deut. 6:13; Ps. 110:4; Jer. 4:2; Rom. 1:9; 2 Cor. 1:23; 11:31; Gal. 1:20; Phil. 1:8; Heb. 6:16.

[20] Robert Guelich, *The Sermon on the Mount* (Dallas: Word Publishing, 1982), p. 218.

[21] Ulrich Luz, *Matthew 1-7: A Commentary*, trans. W. C. Linss (Minneapolis: Augsburg Fortress, 1989), 314-15.

[22] Lycurgus, *Against Leocrates,* 79. Cf. Cicero, *De Officiis* 3:104; 3:107.

[23] Ashley Montagu, *The Anatomy of Swearing* (London: Rapp and Whiting, 1968), p. 59; Pliny, *Panegyricus* 64:3.

[24] Paolo Prodi, 'Der Eid in der europäischen Verfassungsgeschichte, Zur Einführung,' in idem, ed., *Glaube und Eid: Treuformeln, Glaubensbekenntnisse und Sozialdiziplinierung zwischen Mittelalter und Neuzeit* (Munich: R. Oldenbourg Verlag, 1993), p. xi, has commented on 'the not yet researched problem of the refusal of the oath in the first centuries of Christianity.' The fullest collection of texts is that of William Penn, *A Treatise of Oaths: Containing Several Weighty Reasons Why People called Quakers Refuse to Swear*, in *Select Works of William Penn*, 4th ed., vol. 2 (London: William Phillips, 1825), pp. 29-127. The most helpful treatment by a contemporary scholar is that of Ulrich Luz, *Matthew 1-7* (see note 21), pp. 318-21. Cf. Robert M. Grant, 'Sacrifices and Oaths as Required of Early Christians,' in *Kyriakon: Festschrift Johannes Quasten*, ed. Patrick Granfield and Josef Jungmann, vol. 1 (Münster: Aschendorff, 1970), pp.15-17; Alan Kreider, 'Oaths,' in Everett Ferguson, ed., *Encyclopedia of Early Christianity*, rev. ed., vol. 2 (New York: Garland, 1997), pp. 823-24.

[25] Justin, *1 Apol.* 16; Irenaeus, *Adversus Haereses* 2:32.1; Cyprian, *De Mortalitate* 4.

[26] Karlmann Beyschlag, 'Zur Geschichte der Bergpredigt in der Alten Kirche,' *Zeitschrift für Theologie und Kirche* 74 (1977), p. 297.

[27] *Martyrdom of Polycarp* 9 (Herbert Musurillo, ed., *The Acts of the Christian Martyrs* [Oxford: Clarendon Press, 1972], pp. 8-9).

[28] Cyprian, *Ad Quirinum* 3:12.

[29] *Acta Apollonii* (Musurillo, *Acts of the Christian Martyrs*, p. 93). See also *Acts of Phileas* (AD 307) 3 (Musurillo, pp. 331-35).

[30] *Stromata* 7.8. See also *Stromata* 5.14; *Paedagogus* 3.11.

[31] Cf. two passages from early Tertullian (*De Idololatria* 11, which forbids swearing, and *Apol.* 32, which appears to allow it); several passages in Origen (*De Principiis*, 4:19 and *Exh. Mart* 7), which forbid swearing; and *Hom. Jer* 5:12, which concedes that 'it is necessary to begin by swearing the entire truth, with discernment and justice,' so that later, having progressed, one might become worthy of 'no longer swearing at all.' See also *Contra Celsum* 8:65.

[32] Pseudo-Clement, *Hom.* 3:55; Eusebius, *H.E.* 6:9.

[33] Basil of Caesarea, *Epp.* 22:1; 199:29; 207:4; 217:81-82.

[34] *Patrologia Graeca* (ed. J. P. Migne) 37, cols 789-814.

[35] Hilary of Poitiers, *On Matthew* 4.23; 4.34; Caesarius of Arles, *Sermon* 14:3. Cf. Benedict, *Rule* 4.

[36] John Chrysostom, *Baptismal Instructions* 1:39-43; *Hom. on Matthew* 17:5; *Sermons on the Statues* 8:6.

[37] John Chrysostom, *Hom. on the Statues* 3:47.

[38] Idem, *Hom. against the Jews* 1:3.

[39] Idem, *Hom. on Genesis* 15:17.

[40] *Apostolic Constitutions*, 4:36; 5:12; 6:23; 7:3. Cf. the *Didascalia Apostolorum* of a century earlier, 5:12.

[41] Vegetius, *Epitoma Rei Militaris* 2:5.

[42] *Codex Theodosianus* 11:39.3. Already in the second decade of the fourth century, the imperial tribune Marcellinus sent by Constantine to adjudicate the Donatist dispute in North Africa swore to give judgment 'by the wonderful mystery of the Trinity, by the sacrament of the Lord's incarnation, and by the health of the prince' (F.X. Kraus, ed., *Real-Enzyklopädie der Christlichen Alterthümer*, vol. 1 [Freiburg-im-Breisgau: Herder'sche Verlagshandlung, 1882], p. 396).

[43] *Codex Theodosianus* 2:9.3.

[44] *Codex Iustinianus* 2:59.1-2.

[45] Augustine, *De Mendacio* 25; *Contra Mendacium* 36-37.

[46] Idem, *Sermon* 180:6, 11.

[47] Ibid., 180:3.

[48] Idem, *De Serm. Mont.* 1:17.51; *Sermon* 180:10.

[49] André Holenstein, 'Seelenheil und Untertanenpflicht: Zur gesellschaftlichen Funktion und theoretischen Begründung des Eides in der ständischen Gesellschaft,' in Peter Blickle (ed.), *Der Fluch und der Eid* (*Zeitschrift für historische Forschung*, Beiheft 15 [Berlin: Duncker und Humblot, 1993]), p. 11.

[50] Alfred Haverkamp, *Herrschaftsformen der Frühstaufer in Reichsitalien*, vol. 2 (Stuttgart: Anton Hiersemann, 1971), p. 327.

[51] Theodor Gottlob, *Der kirchliche Amtseid der Bischöfe*, Kanonistische Studien und Texte, 9 (Bonn: Ludwig Röhrscheid Verlag, 1936).

[52] Wilhelm Ebel, *Der Bürgereid als Geltungsgrund und Gestaltungsprinzip des deutschen mittelalterlichen Stadtsrecht* (Weimar: Hermann Böhlaus Nachfolger, 1958), pp. 11-46.

[53] Susan Brigden, *London and the Reformation* (Oxford: Clarendon Press, 1989), p. 27.

[54] Keith Thomas, *Religion and the Decline of Magic* (London: Weidenfeld and Nicolson, 1971), p. 44.

[55] Sermon to the people of Wittenberg, 1518, in *D. Martin Luthers Auslegung der Bergpredigt*, ed. Erwin Mühlhaupt (Göttingen: Vandenhoeck und Ruprecht, 1961), p.102.

[56] Philip Melanchthon, *Verlegung etlicher unchristlicher Artikel* (1536), in *Werke*, ed. R. Stupperich, vol. 1 (1950), p. 311.

[57] Heinrich Bullinger, *Der Widertöufferen ursprung*, 2nd ed. (Zürich, 1561), fol 181b, cited by Heinold Fast, 'Die Eidesverweigerung bei den Mennoniten,' in *Eid, Gewissen, Treupflicht*, ed. Hidburg Bethke (Frankfurt-am-Main: Stimme Verlag, 1965), p. 141.

[58] Daniel Featly, *The Dippers Dipt* (London, 1646), p. 142.

[59] Thomas Becon, 'The Invective Against Swearing,' in Becon, *Works*, ed. John Ayre, Parker Society, vol. 1 (Cambridge: Cambridge University Press, 1843), pp. 362, 368, 388.

[60] For an example, see Peter Blickle, 'Huldigungseid und Herrschaftsstruktur im Hattgau (Elsaß),' *Jahrbuch für Westdeutsche Landesgeschichte* 6 (1980), p. 119. I owe this reference to John D. Roth.

[61] Edmund Pries, 'Anabaptist Oath Refusal: Basel, Bern and Strasbourg, 1525-1538' (Ph.D. diss., University of Waterloo, 1995); *idem*, 'Oath Refusal in Zurich from 1525 to 1527: The Erratic Emergence of Anabaptist Practice,' in *Anabaptism Revisited: Essays on Anabaptist/Mennonite Studies in Honor of*

C.J. *Dyck*, ed. Walter Klaassen (Scottdale, Pa.: Herald Press, 1992), pp. 65-84; Walter Klaassen, 'The Nature of the Anabaptist Protest.' *Mennonite Quarterly Review* 45 (1971), pp. 308-309.

[62] Menno Simons, *Confession of the Distressed Christians* (1552), in *Complete Works*, ed. L. Verduin and J.C. Wenger (Scottdale, Pa.: Herald Press, 1956), pp. 519-20.

[63] William Penn, *A Treatise of Oaths: Containing Several Weighty Reasons Why People called Quakers Refuse to Swear* (1675), in *Select Works*, vol. 2 (1825), p. 44.

[64] George Fox, *Journal* (Everyman Edition), p. 231. Fox could not have known this, but John Chrysostom almost thirteen hundred years earlier had visualized the scene: 'But thou, if thou heedest nothing else, reverence at least that book, which thou reachest forth in putting an oath; and open the Gospel, which thou takest in hand when thou biddest swear; and when thou hearest what Christ declares concerning oaths, shudder and desist' (*Homilies on the Statues* 15.14).

[65] Christopher Hill, *Society and Puritanism in Pre-Revolutionary England* (New York: Schocken Books, 1967), p. 415.

[66] Helen Silving, 'The Oath,' *Yale Law Journal* 68 (1959), pp.1350-53.

[67] James Endell Tyler, *Oaths: Their Origin, Nature, and History* (London: John W. Parker, 1834); Moncure D. Conway, *The Oath and Its Ethics* (London: F.G. Hickson, 1881); 'Tertullian,' *The Affirmation Bill: Reasons Why it Cannot Be Permitted to Become the Law of the Land Considered and Stated* (London: David Bogue, [1883]); R. W. Dale, *Oath or Affirmation: A Sermon* (Birmingham: Hudson and Son, [1883]).

[68] Heinrich Fausel, 'Zur Frage des Treueids im Totalstaat,' *Evangelische Theologie*, 25 (1965): 84-95; Bethke, (ed.), *Eid, Gewissen, Treupflicht*; Gottfried Niemeier, (ed.), *Ich Schwöre: Theologische und juristische Studien zur Eidesfrage* (Munich: Chr. Kaiser Verlag, 1968).

[69] Beginning with an act of 1540 (32 Henry 8 c. 9) and culminating in the Perjury Act of 1911 (1 & 2 George 5 c. 6).

[70] Helen Silving, ' The Oath', p. 389; cf. Robert C. Sorenson, 'The Effectiveness of the Oath to Obtain a Witness,' *Journal of Criminal Law* 47 (1956-1957), p. 292.

[71] *False Witness: A Report by Justice*, by a Committee chaired by Muir Hunter, Q.C. (London: Stevens & Sons, 1973), pp.1-2.

[72] Benjamin P. Moore, 'The Passing of the Oath,' *American Law Review* 37 (1903), pp. 558, 564.

[73] Paul Vallely, 'The Whole Truth: Who Needs It?' The *Independent*, 23 May 1995, p. 17.

[74] Sissela Bok, *Lying: Moral Choice in Public and Private Life* (Hassocks, Sussex: Harvester Press, 1978), p. xvii.

[75] H. Richard Niebuhr, 'The Responsibility of the Church for Society,' in *The Gospel, the Church and the World*, ed. Kenneth Scott Latourette (New York: Harper and Brothers, 1946), pp.130-32: the church is a 'social pioneer' which gives a 'radical demonstration' in faith in God so that eventually all nations may be blessed.

[76] Bok, *Lying*, pp. 243-45.

[77] Vaclav Havel, 'The Power of the Powerless' (1978), in *Living in Truth*, ed. Jan Vladislav (London: Faber and Faber, 1987), p. 101.

[78] Walter Sawatzky, 'Truth Telling in Eastern Europe: The Liberation and the Burden,' *Journal of Church and State*, 33 (1991), pp. 701-729.

[79] Gen. 11:31; 12:4; Isa. 49:6; Matt. 5:14; *Epistle to Diognetus* 5:4.

[80] Alan Kreider, *Worship and Evangelism in Pre-Christendom*, Alcuin/GROW Joint Liturgical Studies, 32 (Cambridge, England: Grove Books, 1995).

[81] Niebuhr, *Christ and Culture*, p. 29.

[82] On the importance of ritual in developing a communal self-consciousness, see Friesen, 'An Anabaptist Theology of Culture,' p. 38.

[83] Richard Chartres, in The *Independent*, 6 September 1995, p. 5 (italics mine). Cf. Stanley Hauerwas, who has advocated the church as 'a community where the truth is lived and spoken' (*Christian Existence Today: Essays on Church, World, and Living Between* [Durham, N.C.: Labyrinth Press, 1988], p.102).

[84] Stanley Hauerwas, *In Good Company: The Church as Polis* (Notre Dame, Ind.: Notre Dame University Press, 1995), p. 8.

[85] Romano Guardini, *Das Ende der Neuzeit: Ein Versuch qur Orientierung*, 7th ed. (Würzburg, 1950), p.103; for a conservative Calvinist perspective, see David G. Hagopian, 'So Help Me God: A Biblical View of Oaths,' *Antithesis*, 1 (1990), pp. 42-7.

[86] This might, as Stuart Murray has noted ('Oathtaking in Vain,' *Third Way*, March 1990, p.12), have evangelistic impact. Most people today are unaccustomed to looking to the churches in late twentieth-century English society for either *glasnost* or gospel; they expect rather a reiteration of old ideas and a justification of old ways. By the same token, Christian political action is often devoted to defending Christendom practices that are being undermined by what

may be measures of justifiable secularization. If Christians today, because they are being re-reflexed by Jesus, represented new approaches, and if they were willing to abandon Christian privileges in the name of Christ, people might be drawn in new ways to a living faith in Christ.

[87] James W. McClendon, Jr., *Systematic Theology: Ethics* (Nashville: Abingdon Press, 1986), p.173.

[88] See Robin Spon-Smith, *The Law Society's Guide to Oaths and Affirmations* (London: The Law Society, 1993), for current formulas.

[89] A sample of this is the collaboration between Quaker MP John Bright and atheist would-be MP Charles Bradlaugh in 1880 (*Report from the Select Committee on the Parliamentary Oath*, in *Reports from Committees*, 12 ([London: House of Commons, 1880], p. 21).

[90] John Howard Yoder, 'Against the Death Penalty,' in H.W. House and J.H. Yoder, *The Death Penalty Debate* (Dallas: Word Publishing, 1991), pp.149-54.

[91] Schlatter, *Evangelist Matthäus*, p.181; Dietrich Bonhoeffer, *The Cost of Discipleship*, trans. R.H. Fuller (London: SCM Press, 1959), p. 123: 'Since they always speak the whole truth and nothing but the truth, there is no need for an oath, which would only throw doubt on the veracity of all their other statements.'

[92] The *Independent on Sunday, Sunday Review*, 7 January 1996, p. 4.

[93] *Quaker Faith and Practice*, Advice 37.

[94] *Mennonite Encyclopedia*, V (Scottdale, Pa.: Herald Press, 1990), p. 555. The five volumes of the *Mennonite Encyclopedia* have a six-page entry on the 'Oath' (*ME*, IV, 2-8) but no entry on 'Truth.'

[95] *Mennonite Confession of Faith* (Scottdale, Pa.: Herald Press, 1995), Article 20.

[96] 'Integrity and Truthfulness in Quaker Work,' training document for Quaker Peace and Service workers (1993), p. 1.

[97] Bok, Lying, pp. 31, 90-106. The three criteria are: 1) last resort–'one must first seek truthful alternatives'; 2) moral evaluation–one must weigh the moral arguments for and against a lie that one is considering, while attempting imaginatively to enter into the perspective of those deceived; 3) the 'test of publicity'–what might 'a public of reasonable persons' say about the lie?

[98] This is a longstanding concern of Stanley Hauerwas. See his *Truthfulness and Tragedy* (Notre Dame, Ind.: Notre Dame University Press, 1977), p. 8, for an early formulation.

[99] J. Daniel Hess, *Integrity: Let Your Yea be Yea* (Scottdale, Pa.: Herald Press, 1978).

[100] McClendon, *Systematic Theology: Ethics*, p. 355.

[101] Pinchas Lapide, *The Sermon on the Mount: Utopia or Program for Action?* (Maryknoll, N.Y.: Orbis Books, 1986), p. 74.

[102] Deborah Tannen, *You Just Don't Understand: Women and Men in Conversation* (New York: Ballantine Books, 1990).

[103] Adam Curle, *True Justice: Quaker Peace Makers and Peace Making* (London: Quaker Home Service, 1981), pp. 59, 61. Curle relates this to Jesus' promise of the Holy Spirit's guidance to people under pressure (Matt. 10:20); one could also relate it to the Johannine Jesus' promise that the Holy Spirit will 'guide you into all the truth' (John 16:13).

[104] On this anticipatory perspective on the possibility of ideal speech, see Charles Elliott's reflection on Jürgen Habermas, in his *Memory and Salvation* (London: Darton Longman & Todd, 1995), pp.188-9.

[105] Edwin H. Freedman, *From Generation to Generation: Family Process in Church and Synagogue* (New York: The Guildford Press, 1985), pp. 75-8.

[106] 'The First Law of Sannerz,' in *God's Revolution: The Witness of Eberhard Arnold*, ed. Hutterian Society of Brothers and John H. Yoder (New York: Paulist Press, 1984), p.130.

[107] Dietrich Bonhoeffer, *Life Together*, trans. John W. Doberstein (London: SCM Press, 1954), pp. 70-2.

[108] For this reason, direct speech presupposes communities in which there is both trust and a relative parity of power among the members. Where these are lacking, gossip is inevitable and, as Patricia Meyer Spacks has argued, can have 'special value as a resource for the oppressed and dispossessed.' See her *Gossip* (New York: Knopf, 1985), p.15.

[109] See Daniel Turner, *A Sermon... Preached at Oxford November 17, 1780, on the Occasion of the Re-establishment of a Christian Church of Protestant Dissenters in that City* (Oxford, 1780), p. 21. Cf. the North American Mennonite baptismal commitment to 'give and receive counsel.'

[110] See, for example, the instructive comments on Acts 15:1-28 of J. Nelson Kraybill, 'Conflict and Church Decision Making,' *Anabaptism Today*, 11 February 1996, p. 16.

[111] '... there have to be factions (*haireseis*) among you, for only so will it become clear who among you are genuine' (1 Cor. 11:19).

[112] John Punshon, *Portrait in Grey: A Short History of the Quakers* (London: Quaker Home Service, 1984), pp. 60, 77; Michael J. Sheeran, *Beyond Majority Rule: Voteless Decisions in the Religious Society of Friends* (Philadelphia: Philadelphia Yearly Meeting, 1993).

[113] David W. Augsburger, *Caring Enough to Confront: the Love-Fight* (Scottdale, Pa.: Herald Press, 1973). This book has sold widely, and has been followed by other *Caring Enough* books which have helped many Christians grow as truth-telling people.

[114] Jim Stutzman and Carolyn Schrock-Shenk, (eds.), *Mediation and Facilitation Training Manual*, 3rd ed. (Akron, Pa.: Mennonite Conciliation Service, 1995), esp. pp.183-241. See also Ralph Lebold, 'Decision-making,' in *Mennonite Encyclopedia*, V, pp. 219-21, with literature cited there.

[115] George Fox, *Journal*, vol. 1, p.186; Frederick B. Tolles, *Meeting House and Counting House: The Quaker Merchants of Colonial Philadelphia, 1682–1763* (Chapel Hill: University of North Carolina Press, 1948), p. 59; Isabel Grubb, *Quakerism and Industry before 1800* (London: Williams and Norgate, 1930), pp. 65, 117.

[116] *Brethren Encyclopedia*, vol. 1 (Philadelphia: The Brethren Encyclopedia, Inc., 1978), p. 158. The ballad was written by Andy Murray of Juniata College, Pennsylvania, and recorded on A. Murray and T. Murray, *Goodbye Still Night* (record album, 1978). I owe this reference to Donald B. Kraybill.

[117] Albert Z. Carr, 'Is Business Bluffing Ethical?' *Harvard Business Review*, Jan/Feb 1968, pp.143-53. Cf. Richard C. Chewring, John W. Eby and Shirley J. Roels, *Business Through the Eyes of Faith* (Leicester, Inter-Varsity Press, 1990), pp. 235-41. I owe these references to Delmar Good. For Quaker reflections on this issue, see John Cockroft, *et al.*, *Questions of Integrity: A Quaker Perspective* (London: London Yearly Meeting, 1993).

[118] John H. Yoder, 'Sacrament as Social Process: Christ the Transformer of Culture,' *Theology Today* 48 (1991), p. 41.

[119] See 'Integrity and Truthfulness in Quaker Work,' a training document for Quaker Peace and Service workers (1993).

[120] Bob and Judy Zimmerman Herr to Alan Kreider, 13 February 1996.

[121] Eva Pinthus to Alan Kreider, 22 January 1996.

[122] For recent attempts to struggle with this dilemma, see Larry A. Dunn, 'Deciding when to stand between,' *Gospel Herald*, 2 January 1996, pp. 6-8.

[123] Douglas Johnston and Cynthia Sampson, eds., *Religion, the Missing Dimension in Statecraft* (New York: Oxford University Press, 1994), pp. 141, 72.

[124] Quoted by Cynthia Sampson, ' 'To Make Real the Bond Between Us All': Quaker Conciliation During the Nigerian Civil War,' in Johnston and Sampson, *Religion*, p. 99.

[125] Bruce Nicholls, 'Religious Conciliation Between the Sandinistas and the East Coast Indians of Nicaragua,' in Johnston and Sampson, *Religion*, p. 71.

[126] For example, the low-key work, over many years, of the Quaker House, Belfast (*Quaker Experience of Political Mediation*, rev. ed. [London: Quaker Peace & Service, 1992], pp. xxxiii-xxviii). The peaceful resolution of the July 1995 Loyalist/Nationalist crisis about marching routes in Portadown, County Armagh, was facilitated by two mediators (one Catholic, one Presbyterian) of the 'little-known Mediation Network' (*Portadown Times*, 12 July 1995); both mediators were trained by Mennonites.

3
Looking with Fresh Eyes: Christianity and Cultural History

JANE SHAW

1. Methods in the study of history

What understanding might an historian have of the interaction between Christianity and culture, and what distinctive contribution can an historian make to the study of Christianity and culture? These are not questions which historians of Christianity (ecclesiastical or church historians) have asked much until recently. Ecclesiastical historians have traditionally focused on the institutions which made up the church, the ministers or priests and prominent lay people who peopled them, and the theological ideas which those clerics (and lay people) held. They have, therefore, generally studied the Church somewhat in isolation from the wider culture. This has sometimes been exacerbated by the fact that many ecclesiastical historians write the histories of their own denominations with little reference to other Christian traditions, let alone the wider cultural context.

Historians using other sorts of methodologies have expanded the horizon of the history of Christianity in the following ways. *Intellectual historians* writing about religion have tried to broaden the picture by relating theological ideas to philosophy, literature and other intellectual currents, but their work is limited to the domain of élite ideas. *Social historians* have broadened the scope of church history by looking at Christianity *in* society, asking questions about the social structures of the churches and the social position of the people who were members of them (their age, gender, social status, profession or trade, and so on). Social historians have been influenced by both sociologists of religion, such as Durkheim and Weber, and the Annales School as it developed in France in the 1930s and 40s. They therefore look at the ways in which religion interacts with and reflects the *structures* of society, be those economic, geographic, or demographic. Relying in this way on the social sciences, they often take certain structures as given, and thereby sometimes come to see Christianity not so much as a theological system but rather as a social structure.

There are limits to all of these methodologies, at least for the study of Christianity and culture: let me illustrate this by looking at the ways in which ecclesiastical, intellectual and social historians might approach a particular example before turning to examine the perspectives of a *cultural historian* of Christianity. The example is taken from the period of the Civil War and the Interregnum, in mid-seventeenth century England, when there began to occur, amongst a number of the new sects and independent churches which were then flourishing, events which were interpreted and publicly proclaimed as miracles. The Baptists, Quakers, and Ranters experienced miraculous healings, survival after long periods of fasting and even, on occasion, claims to raise the dead. The Baptists, for example, became interested in healing miracles and, in particular, the use of healing oil, with the result that a number of churches and ministers became involved in this healing ministry. Prominent early Baptists in London, such as William Kiffin, Vavasour Powell and Hanserd Knollys, began to practise such healing, for themselves and in their churches.[1]

Ecclesiastical (or church) historians would primarily be interested in the churches and ministers involved in these healing miracles. They would ask how these incidents of miracles contribute to our understanding of early Baptist church life. What does the involvement of Kiffin, Powell and Knollys in such healing miracles tell us about the development of their churches, for example? What does the use of a biblical text – James 5: 14-15 – as the basis for such a religious practice tell us about the authority of the Bible for early Baptists? Were such healing miracles incorporated into the worship of these churches, and if so, how? The ecclesiastical historians' questions would, therefore, be focused on the significance of these events for the growth of the Baptist churches in the areas of theology, religious practice and ministry.

Intellectual historians would probably pay little attention to such incidents, considering them to be inconsequential to larger theological issues. If they had any interest in miracles at all, in this period, it would be in the intellectual debate about miracles which occurred between theologians, clerics, philosophers and other gentlemen of letters in the early eighteenth century.

Social historians would be interested in compiling sociological data about these miraculous events: the number of such miraculous healings; the times and places where they occurred; the number of people involved and their social status, gender, age and so forth. For example, they might consider whether it was significant that such prominent early Baptists as Powell, Kiffin and Knollys were so actively involved in these events. If they wanted to relate these incidents to broader social concerns, they might ask how they could be tied into a general folk belief in magic and supernatural healing. And they would most likely ask how economic and demographic factors were influencing the sects and independent churches at this time, in order to provide some sort of sociological explanation for the renewed occurrence of miraculous healings.

Cultural historians might well be interested in all of the above, but primarily they would be interested in the *meanings* given to those healings, (and to the events surrounding them), both by the participants and by others in the wider culture. Why, for example, were these healings claimed as miracles? Such a question takes us both into the realm of theology and into an exploration of the events of the times; in this case, the political context might be particularly significant, as this was a time of great political upheaval. A cultural historian might ask why such events were claimed as miracles, some one hundred years after the Protestant Reformation in England had apparently abolished a belief in miracles as well as the general means by which they occurred (relics, shrines, pilgrimages). Wondrous events continued to occur in seventeenth century England but they were not explained in the theological language of the miraculous. Rather, they were interpreted in terms of providence; that is, God's omnipotence and judgement in the world, a safer doctrine for the Puritans who associated miracles with the threats and trappings of the Papists. Why then would these ministers and church members interpret certain events as miracles rather than as providence? The claims of the (often more radical) independent churches to experience miracles might be seen as something of a theological and political statement against the dominant Puritan groups who had taken control in the Civil War.

Another layer of meanings is added when we remember that within the structures of the Anglican Church – which had been abolished along with the monarchy in the Civil War – the one figure who was legitimately allowed to perform healing miracles was the monarch, who could touch for 'the king's evil'. This was a practice initiated by Edward the Confessor (and formalized into a liturgy by Henry VII) in which the king touched those who were suffering from scrofula: the monarch's healing powers in this respect were attributed to the sacred nature of kingship. The independent ministers' claims to perform healing miracles can thus be seen as part of a far broader political challenge to the divine right of kings which resulted in the execution of the king, the abolition of the established church and an upturning of social and political hierarchies; the claim made by these ministers that they were exercising some kind of holy healing power was, then, a potential challenge to kingly authority and a statement about certain social hierarchies.

These lines of inquiry lead us to understand the ways in which religious practices (in this case certain events claimed as miraculous) and theological beliefs (in this case a belief in miracles, alongside the doctrine of providence) are not 'purely religious' but are both shaped by, and in turn shape, the wider culture. Events and ideas claimed as distinctly Christian are necessarily a part of the political, social, and intellectual context in which a church, Christian group or Christian person is located. The implications of this, and of Christianity's being a distinctly historical religion, rooted in a particular historical event, will be discussed shortly. But before we can proceed in that direction, some discussion of culture and cultural history is needed.

2. Culture and cultural history

Cultural history might simply be defined as a history of meanings. This definition comes rather immediately out of cultural anthropology as it has developed in the last twenty or thirty years. The anthropologist, Clifford Geertz, defines culture as a web of meanings in which the human is suspended.[2] Anthropologists thus come to define culture as the meanings given to *everything* about a particular people. This is helpful to historians, as William Bouwsma points out, because 'it is centrally concerned with the construction and symbolic expression of meaning in every dimension of human activity.' It is a point which has been taken up by later followers of the Annales school who have written on the history of 'mentalités', and have shown that social and economic structures are not 'natural' structures outside of culture, but, rather, that social and economic relations and structures are themselves culturally produced and explained. As an example, we might point here to the ways in which Charles Dickens illustrates both the meanings given to utilitarianism, in terms of education, family and way of life, and its cultural (as well as economic) effects, in his portrait of the Gradgrind family and their neighbours in his mid-nineteenth century novel, *Hard Times*.

Furthermore, as the example of Dickens' novel highlights, if the human being is 'an animal suspended in a web of significance he himself has spun' (Geertz), then, as Bouwsma points out, 'he spins these webs primarily from – or with the help of – language.'[3] Language is the basis of culture, and so it is most frequently through the stories people tell about their lives and experiences, and all that surrounds them, that we can come to understand what meanings they give to those things. This point has especially been emphasized by the French poststructuralist theorists, and their Anglo-American followers, in recent years, and cultural historians have increasingly drawn on this work.[4]

3. Christianity as a culture among the cultures

How can such an anthropological understanding of culture help a historian of Christianity? Geertz would define religion quite simply as a cultural system which produces and reflects ideas and meanings at all levels of society. This suggests that religion is not merely cultural but also a system; thus, any analysis of religion must involve looking not only at the history of religious meanings (i.e. religious culture) but also at the systems by and through which those religious meanings are produced and disseminated. The cultural historian must look at a religion's interaction with other aspects of culture (or other sub-cultures) to understand it fully. In this sense, we can see Christianity as a cultural system, both shaping and shaped by the broader cultural context. Some examples are necessary to illustrate these points.

The work of nineteenth century British and European missionaries, in places such as Africa, was necessarily influenced by both the culture they came from and the new cultures they encountered; in turn their work influenced the cultures they encountered and the cultures back home. Their home cultures necessarily informed their motives for mission: while many surely had strong ideals about what they were doing, their missionary work was deeply intertwined with the political imperialism by which European countries 'scrambled for Africa' to build their empires and exercise control not only over the peoples they colonized but also over each other. They certainly brought their own cultural presuppositions and attempted to impose them. For example, Victorian Christian ideas about the proper roles for women and men, and the separation of private and public spheres along gendered lines, was brought to many an African tribe – especially (and ironically, perhaps), by white women missionaries who could reach into the home in a way in which the European men could not. The 'domestication' of various African tribes in this way undoubtedly contributed to the aims of the political imperialists, even if it was carried out with 'purely' Christian motives.

And yet, once the missionaries encountered the native peoples whom they hoped to convert, those cultures frequently made an important impact on them. Many of them faced the following question: how much would members of certain African tribes need to change their own cultural ways, including their indigenous religious values and customs, in order to be Christian? The example of John Colenso, (Anglican) Bishop of Natal, working in Africa in the 1850s and 60s, provides an interesting case. He provoked criticism for defending polygamy along biblical lines : he did not insist, as other missionaries did, that men give up their several wives when they were baptized. He also argued that the people of Africa were already redeemed and just needed further education, and he used a Zulu term for God. The cultures which the white missionaries encountered did not only affect them, but they also began to influence the world back home.

If we can understand that Christian cultures necessarily 'mingle' with other cultural systems, then we can begin to understand in a fresh way the dilemmas Christians have faced throughout their history in seeking a single 'true' or 'pure' Christianity, and the reason why this quest can never arrive at a certain destination. The Protestant reformers of the sixteenth century were, at least in part, rebelling against the superstitions which they felt the Roman Catholic Church had allowed to flourish, and were seeking a 'pure' or 'true' Christianity. With some historical hindsight we can see not only the abuses in the Roman Catholic church which the Protestants saw but also the strengths of a medieval Christian culture which had strong roots in local religious customs and folk religious beliefs, and which emphasized the importance of kith and kin over the individual.[5] We can also see how the Protestants relied upon and interacted with other cultural forms for their own growth and identity, not least the printing press and the political support of princes and monarchs. The difference between the South American theologian Leonardo Boff and the current Pope about Liberation Theology provides a contemporary example of such a cultural clash within Christianity, where different cultural contexts produce very different understandings of the gospel.

The distinctive nature of Christianity is an important factor to consider at this point. Christianity is a historical religion. It is, unlike many of the other world religions, rooted in a particular historical event: namely, the Incarnation. This event occurred not in a sterile unit but in the mess of every day social and political life, at a particular time, in a particular region of the world, as the theologian Hans Küng points out in his book, *The Church*.[6] And because Christians (or most of them) believe in a trinitarian God, they also believe in the notion of the Holy Spirit, and thus in ongoing revelation – revelation which occurs in the cultures in which we are situated, not outside them. It happens on the streets, in the arts, in the laboratory, in the law courts and in the geographical landscapes which we inhabit. The task of articulating *how* Christian revelation and culture interact must, primarily, fall to the theologians, but the cultural historian can help to explain how Christianity comes to form a series of cultural systems and how those Christian cultures interact with other cultural contexts. In short, the historian can explain how and why Christianity is always culturally situated; the theologian can explain why this is vital to the very nature of Christianity. Let us thus turn to that fast-growing body of work known as 'cultural studies' to see both how it can help us in the study of Christianity and culture, and how such a study of Christianity and culture might enrich that essentially secular field of study.

4. Cultural studies today

The anthropological definition of culture with which I have been working up to this point – that is, as a web of meanings in which human beings are suspended – stands in opposition to some other understandings of the word. 'Culture' is, indeed, a much contested term. For example, it is often taken to mean 'high' or 'highbrow' culture: if a person is described as 'cultured', we immediately grasp that they have some considerable knowledge of certain visual arts, classical music, literature, (especially that of the Greeks and Romans), and so on. Most historians see the roots of this separation of 'high' culture from the rest of the population in the eighteenth century, when the middle classes were emerging and wanted to prove their social status by cultivating all that which was 'polite' rather than 'vulgar'.[7] This notion of culture has, not surprisingly, led to the use of the term 'popular culture' to define all that which falls beyond the élite or polite – folk tales, popular music, advertisements, horror movies and a host of other things.

Such an élite/popular split is, of course, problematic, not least because it is simplistic, but particularly because it carries within it *our* cultural assumptions about what constitutes 'élite' or 'popular'. This has sometimes led scholars to make serious mistakes, as Peter Brown pointed out in his book, *The Cult of the Saints*. He noted that historians writing on the fourth-century cult of the saints had continued to assume that the cult was necessarily a popular practice; in this they were following Gibbon's élite/popular split (which was based on David Hume's two-tier philosophy of religion) which associated such forms of active piety with the vulgar. Brown went back to the evidence and found that in fact the cult was associated with quite prominent Roman citizens.[8] To take another example, Lawrence Levine has written about the enormous popularity of, and familiarity with, Shakespeare at all levels of society in nineteenth-century America, which firmly contradicts our current notion that Shakespeare is 'high' culture.[9] This notion is simply confirmed, rather than contradicted, by current attempts to 'popularize' Shakespeare, such as the BBC's recent experiment, in the 1994 Shakespeare season, to bring Othello to the council housing estate.

Another definition of culture confines it to the humanities and arts; Raymond Williams defines culture in this sense as 'the works and practices of intellectual and especially artistic activity'.[10] While this has tended to mean the works produced by a rather élite section of the society, it has increasingly come to include the artistic and intellectual works of those formerly excluded: the example of the recent popularity and immense marketing of literature by Black female writers, especially, perhaps, that of Toni Morrison (which culminated in her winning the Nobel Prize for Literature) illustrates this point ably. Some would also want to see 'popular' culture and the mass media included in this definition: film, television, advertisements, radio, fashion, print journalism, and fiction of all kinds.

The artistic focus of this understanding of culture means that it is closely related to yet another notion of culture – that which sees a split between two cultures not along the lines of élite/popular, but along the lines of arts vs. sciences. C. P. Snow articulated this in his (in)famous attack on literary culture as backward.[11] He announced that the educated world was divided into two cultures, literary and scientific, between which there was neither communication nor understanding; in return, he was scathingly attacked by the Cambridge literary critic, F. R. Leavis.[12]

Given these varying definitions of 'culture', what then does cultural studies, as a field, study? Some engaged in cultural studies are primarily engaged in an analysis of those cultures which are not marked out as dominant or 'highbrow': youth cultures, working class cultures, postcolonial cultures, cultures marked out as 'feminine'. This work covers subjects as diverse as popular music, films and videos of all kinds, clothes and changing fashions, and Black, Asian and Hispanic literature, as well as the literature of white authors which has been neglected because of their authors' gender, sexuality or class. Others in the field of cultural studies look at rather traditional areas of study – philosophy, Western literature and so on – but from the perspective of the 'marginalized'. For example, Edward Said, in his recent work, *Culture and Imperialism*, looks at authors such as Jane Austen and Joseph Conrad and musicians such as Verdi to see how novels like *Mansfield Park* and *Heart of Darkness*, and operas such as *Aïda*, reflected western imperialism. He asks how western culture both reflected and reinforced that political endeavour.[13] This approach shows how artistic and literary culture is necessarily related to politics and society; it also examines 'high' culture to reveal the mechanisms by which it exercises itself as 'high'.

The intellectual underpinning of cultural studies is an understanding of the ways in which 'culture' in its many senses has material effects; by neglecting certain cultures as fields of study, or by treating 'culture' as a purely aesthetic realm, we have failed to understand how culture has affected our material circumstances and social practices. The work of cultural studies points, also, to the ways in which cultures are always partial and particular, never universal or apolitical. In all of these ways, cultural studies has been much affected by poststructuralist and postmodernist theorists.

For example, poststructuralism has focused on questions about subjectivity and identity, pointing to the ways in which we are subjects rather than selves: that is, we are both subjects of our own lives and *subjected* to the influences which shape us. To go back to the anthropological understanding of culture, we find ourselves suspended in a web of meanings and yet also have some role in spinning the threads of that web. The web of meanings both constructs us as humans and is constructed by us – and theorists such as Lacan and Derrida would claim that this happens primarily through language. This line of thinking takes us away from the notion that a human being is a purely free and rational agent or self, and into an understanding of the human as *culturally* constructed. Hence cultural studies works with the premise that to understand the human subject and society, we must understand the meanings we give to both our selves and to the structures which surround us – that is, culture in all its manifestations. One consequence is that characteristics we so often take as 'natural' – what it means, for example, to be a man or a woman, to be black or white – are seen to vary from culture to culture (as the work of cultural anthropologists and cultural historians shows us).

Not surprisingly, cultural studies has an overtly political spin, and some would want to speak of 'cultural politics'. For example, Chris Weedon and Glenn Jordan, in their recent work entitled *Cultural Politics*, write of 'culture as a key site in the political struggle to reproduce and transform power relations. Cultural politics focus on struggles over meanings, values, forms of subjectivity and identity'.[14] This involves understanding not only how cultures form us as particular sorts of sub-jects (marked by gender, class, race, and so forth), but also how, where and why certain cultures are dominant. Not all meanings hold equal weight in a given culture. We only have to look around us for a minute to see that not all cultures have equal status. This kind of analysis means that we must take into account the networks and lines of power in any given culture(s), and in this regard, cultural studies as a field has been much affected by Michel Foucault's work on power. Such insights have led, for example, to the phenomenon known as multiculturalism, and in sec-ondary and higher education this has led both to attempts to question the canon of literature studied and to bitter political arguments about what students should learn.[15]

5. Christianity and cultural studies

What, then, can we learn from this field of cultural studies in the study of Christianity and culture? First, and this is perhaps the most obvious thing, the subject matter of cultural studies may help us to perceive the worth in studying Christianity's interaction with aspects of culture which are not simply the domain of the élite. How, for example, have Christian stories been retold in film and popular fiction? How, in turn, have apparently sec-ular films reflected Christian values?[16]

Secondly, the emphasis in cultural studies on re-examining traditional areas of study in terms of neglected topics may help us to look at specific moments in the Christian tradition with fresh eyes. Two examples from recent cultural histories of Christianity may help illustrate the point. Peter Brown's work on Christianity and the body, in which he looks at many of the Church Fathers on the specific subject of the body and sexuality, owes a certain debt to both cultural anthropology and the work of Michel Foucault, and examines a much neglected (one might even say repressed) thread in early Christian history.[17] Caroline Walker Bynum's work on late medieval female saints shows the ways in which holiness meant some-thing rather different for women than for men. For men, it meant the renunciation of worldly goods (we think of St Francis), because they had the worldly goods to renounce. Women, who could not easily own prop-erty, showed their holiness by the means which were close to them, namely their bodies – for example, they fasted, living only on the Host. This makes sense of the seemingly peculiar religious practices – extreme physical mortification and self-starvation – of a saint such as Catherine of Sienna.[18] Similarly, the intellectual turn towards the study of marginalized cultures gives theologians the tools to makes sense of new theologies – liberation, feminist, and black theologies, for example – in their cultural context.

Thirdly, the emphasis, in cultural studies, upon the construction of identity or subjectivity within culture may give us new ways of studying the complexities of Christian identity. How have Christians shaped their identities in relation to the cultures in which they have found themselves? For example, Judith Stacey's recent book on evangelical families in Silicon Valley gives us a sense of how conservative Christians have shaped their identities in relation to their work in an area of fast-growing technology.[19]

Finally, the study of Christianity and culture can, potentially, contribute a great deal to the area of cultural studies. It is a field which – precisely because of its liberal origins and 'leftward' leanings – assumes that the world is essentially a secular place. Religion in general, and Christianity in particular, have been little studied by such cultural critics who have accepted the secularization thesis rather unquestioningly. For example, in a conference about cultural studies held in 1992 in Illinois, the papers from which event have been published in a large volume entitled *Cultural Studies*, only one paper covered the subject of religion. It was a paper on mid-nineteenth century Baptist missionaries, written by a cultural historian, Catherine Hall, who was interested in those missionaries in terms of their masculinity, ethnicity and relationship to imperialism, not their religion. There is a yawning gap between that paper and the work of Baptist historians writing on nineteenth-century mission from a denominational perspective. The study of Christianity and culture can help to close that gap by taking seriously both Christianity and a wide variety of cultures. It is also telling that the only academic from the field of religion who was involved in the conference – Cornel West – was on this occasion speaking on the subject of the black intellectual, rather than a specifically religious topic.

The intellectual flaw (and irony) of this general antipathy towards religion, displayed by those engaged in cultural studies, is that the secularization thesis is a story about the white, western world: whether it applies to the modern, western world can be deeply questioned; that it does not apply to other cultures is almost without question. Thus we have the situation that academics committed to the study of cultures marginalized by their ethnicity, class, gender and so on impose a certain set of very white and very western liberal values about religion (or lack of it) onto cultures which have Christianity at their heart. For example, African-American culture, and its growth in the last two or three hundred years, cannot be understood without a deep sense of the centrality of the Black Church to all aspects of Black culture. And yet, in a talk given in the mid 1990s at Harvard, Stuart Hall, a British black cultural critic, and for a long time the head of the Centre for Contemporary Cultural Studies at Birmingham, remarked that religion had nothing to do with understanding Black culture – much to the chagrin of the African-Americans in the audience. Similarly, much attention has been paid, by cultural critics such as Homi K. Bhaba, to postcolonial cultures, but it is hard to understand those cultures without paying a good deal of attention to the legacy not only of imperialism but also of nineteenth-century Christian missions It is telling that the average participant in the Anglican Church today is not white, male and British (as we might be led to think), but black, female, most certainly not British, and probably not a speaker of the English language. What can *this* tell us about both Anglican culture and identity in the early twenty-first century *and* the postcolonial legacy?

Clearly, then, culture is the field in which questions about identity, consciousness and social organization are played out – and these are questions which are vital to the practice and study of Christianity. How we pray, worship, understand salvation, read the Bible and put into practice the Gospel injunction to 'love thy neighbour as thyself', are all to be understood in relation to the wider culture, and are themselves cultural forms. The study of Christianity and culture therefore addresses questions which are at the heart of both the academic endeavour and the shaping of the Christian mind in the early twenty-first century.

Notes to Chapter 3

[1] For further details of these healing stories, see my forthcoming book *Miracles in Enlightenment England* (New Haven: Yale University Press, 2002).

[2] Clifford Geertz, *The Interpretation of Cultures* (New York, Basic Books, 1973).

[3] William J. Bouwsma, 'From History of Ideas to History of Meaning', in his *The Usable Past. Essays in European Cultural History* (Berkeley: University of California Press, 1990), pp. 344-5.

[4] See, for example, the essays in Lynn Hunt (ed.), *The New Cultural History* (Berkeley: University of California Press, 1989).

[5] See Keith Thomas, *Religion and the Decline of Magic* (Harmondsworth: Penguin, 1971) and John Bossy, *Christianity in the West 1400-1700* (Oxford University Press, 1985).

[6] Hans Küng, *The Church – Maintained in Truth. A Theological Meditation* (London: SCM Press, 1980).

[7] See, for example, Peter Burke's explanation of this in *Popular Culture in Early Modern Europe* (1978; revised reprint: Aldershot: Scolar Press, 1994).

[8] Peter Brown, *The Cult of the Saints. Its Rise and Function in Latin Christianity* (Chicago: Chicago University Press, 1981).

[9] Lawrence Levine, *Highbrow/Lowbrow. The Emergence of Cultural Hierarchy in America* (Cambridge, Mass.: Harvard University Press, 1988).

[10] Raymond Williams, *Keywords* (Oxford: Oxford University Press, 1976), p. 90.

[11] C. P. Snow, *The Two Cultures and the Scientific Revolution. Rede Lecture (London: Cambridge University Press, 1959)*; expanded as *The Two Cultures: and a Second Look* (Cambridge: Cambridge University Press, 1969).

[12] See F. R. Leavis and Michael Yudkin, *Two Cultures? The Significance of C. P. Snow* (London: Chatto and Windus, 1962).

[13] Edward Said, *Culture and Imperialism* (New York: Vintage Books, 1993).

[14] Glenn Jordan and Chris Weedon, *Cultural Politics. Class, Gender, Race and the Postmodern World* (Oxford: Blackwell, 1995), p. 19.

[15] See Henry Louis Gates Jnr., *Loose Canons: Notes on the Culture Wars* (New York and Oxford: Oxford University Press, 1992).

[16] See Larry J. Kreitzer's series of volumes on *Reversing the Hermeneutical Flow: The New Testament in Fiction and Film* (Sheffield: Sheffield Academic Press, 1993); *The Old Testament in Fiction and Film* (Sheffield: Sheffield Academic Press, 1994); *Pauline Images in Fiction and Film* (Sheffield: Sheffield Academic Press, 1999).

[17] Peter Brown, *The Body and Society. Men, Women and Sexual Renunciation in Early Christianity* (New York: Columbia University Press, 1988).

[18] Caroline Walker Bynum, *Holy Feast and Holy Fast. The Religious Significance of Food to Medieval Women* (Berkeley: University of California Press, 1989).

[19] Judith Stacey, *Brave New Families* (Berkeley: University of California Press, 1989).

4
The Story and the Stories: Revelation and the Challenge of Postmodern Culture

PAUL S. FIDDES

1. The stories people tell about themselves

'Death is life and life is death'. Would members of an audience hear this line from a play as a comment on the general awfulness of life, meaning no more than 'life is hell'? Or would they hear it as something more profound, perhaps an allusion to the 'dark night of the soul' as described by St John of the Cross? Would they hear it as a statement on life for the *masses* or for the *mystics*? Is it a sound-bite or a philosophy? Is it low culture or high culture?

The phrase actually comes from a rarely-performed fragment of a play by T. S. Eliot, *Sweeney Agonistes* (1924), and the character who utters it sees all the ambiguities when he complains:

I gotta use words when I talk to you
But if you understand or if you don't
That's nothing to me and nothing to you
We all gotta do what we gotta do
We're gona sit here and drink this booze....[1]

As my opening questions indicate, what Eliot was attempting was an experiment in communication across cultures. What he was trying to achieve was intriguing, although, I am going to suggest, ultimately unsuccessful. As he explains elsewhere, one character was meant to have a high sensitivity and intelligence, 'equal to the most sensitive and intelligent members of the audience', but his speeches were to be addressed to those persons in the play who were materialistic, 'literal-minded and visionless', in a way that would make sense to them. The audience too would be made up of both kinds of people, and so the same play would have a different impact on different hearers.[2]

The character thus described by Eliot was Sweeney, who was to operate on two cultural planes at once, as the very title *Sweeney Agonistes*
suggests. 'Sweeney' evokes echoes of Sweeney Todd, the murderous bar-
ber of popular folklore. Sweeney inhabits the world of the sleezy
night-club, the comic-book, the pub, the fortune-teller and the brothel.
But he is also Sweeney *Agonistes*. The *Agonist* was the hero in a Greek
melodrama, fighting for a cause against antagonists, the protagonist arguing a case against opponents, like *Samson Agonistes* in Milton's poem. So
Sweeney is a low-life character, whose name and situation recalls an
English poem, and who speaks in the tones of a tragic hero of Greek
drama and a mystical theologian. The play is headed by a quotation from
St John of the Cross: 'The soul cannot be possessed of the divine union,
until it has divested itself of love of created things.' Unfortunately, as critics point out,[3] it is not at all clear that what Sweeney means by 'life is
death' is any more than what it means to the 'literal minded and visionless' - whether on the stage or in the audience - that is, 'life is hell'.

Sweeney is, for all that, meant to illustrate Eliot's theory of culture. In
his book, *Notes Towards a Definition of Culture*, Eliot observes the different meanings of 'culture'. On the one hand it may mean the ethos of
what we usually call 'a cultured individual', enjoying the so-called high
culture of the ancient classics, the opera, Shakespeare and Wordsworth.
On the other hand, there is the anthropological sense, where it simply
means the whole way of life of a people, what people usually do, or as
Eliot puts it, 'all [their] characteristic activities and interests'.[4] The latter
include, he suggests:

> Derby Day, Henley Regatta, Cowes, the twelfth of August, a cup final,
> the dog races, the pin table, the dart board, Wensleydale cheese, boiled
> cabbage cut into sections, beetroot in vinegar, nineteenth-century Gothic
> churches and the music of Elgar.

He adds generously that 'the reader can make his own list.' Eliot
believes that we must hold both notions of culture together, high and low,
and that low culture on its own is a joyless thing. He thinks that the lives of
ordinary people depend in the end, for what makes life worth living, on the
great classics of culture, even if they participate in them unconsciously.

Sweeney is his attempt to show this symbiosis between the night-club and classical drama, between popular proverb and theology.[5]

I suggest, however, that we should modify the idea of culture in its widest sense as 'everything people usually do'. This would make it simply equivalent to 'human society', and I believe that there is a useful point of clarity in distinguishing between the two. I propose to use the word 'culture' in the general sense of the *meanings* that people give to 'everything they do',[6] and in particular to focus on the way that these meanings take form in 'the stories people tell about themselves'. We organize our activities and our interests in language. This does not have to be highly reflective, but what is distinctive of culture is the shape that we give to our experience so that we can understand it. Moreover, once this language exists, there is also a contrary movement of influence in which it shapes and constructs our experience itself. In choosing the word 'story' for this organizing function of language, I also intend to include music and art as well as words. That is, the pattern of notes in music, and the relationship of masses and colours to each other in visual art are also a kind of story, even where it is not translated into a pattern of words. My concern in this essay is, however, with the web of *words* which society spins to understand itself, and this includes all that can be called 'high' or 'low' or even 'middlebrow'.

Eliot's play *Sweeney Agonistes* does in fact witness to this telling of stories at every level of human reflection. Sweeney playfully promises to carry off Doris, a woman of uncertain (if not easy) virtue to his 'Cannibal Isle':

You'll be the missionary!
You'll be my little seven stone missionary!
I'll gobble you up. I'll be the cannibal.[7]

When she asks what they will do on this island without telephones, gramophones, or motor cars, he replies:

Birth, and copulation, and death.
That's all, that's all, that's all, that's all…

She reacts, 'I'd be bored', but does not realize – as Sweeney does – that this is all there is to the life she lives at the moment. Sweeney is able to put a story to this life: 'I've been born, and once is enough.' Another story he tells is more gruesome, though potentially more profound. He knew a man once, he says, who murdered a girl and kept her in disinfectant in his bath for a couple of months. This is not just a comic-book tale, befitting his name of Sweeney, but a story of the human experience of remorse, in which the guilty conscience is plunged into the dark night of non-being:

> He didn't know if he was alive
> and the girl was dead
> He didn't know if the girl was alive
> and he was dead
> He didn't know if they were both alive
> or both were dead...

The summary of this state of mind is the line I began with: 'Death is life and life is death'. Eliot apparently intends this story to be a parable of the dark night of the soul as described by St John of the Cross. He aims to draw the everyday, even sordid, stories of life into the great story of the soul and God. As the hapless murderer killed the one he loved and propelled himself into darkness, so we must leave behind all the things we love in the world to approach the darkness in which we meet God. But the analogy is surely too horrific to work; neither Eliot nor Sweeney seem sufficiently concerned about the girl. Though Eliot might protest that even the hell of guilt can be a place of encounter with God, the girl cannot be reduced to a mere symbol. The stories do not seem to belong together at all.

I believe we should pronounce Eliot's experiment a failure, though a brave attempt to let stories intersect at the different levels of the tabloid newspaper and the mystical treatise. I intend to return to this wreckage of a project at the end of my essay, but meanwhile to move on to consider more fully the Christian story at which Eliot hints (in his own way).

2. The Christian story

The story to which the Christian church bears witness has emerged from encounters with God at decisive points in history. The story is about God's project in creation, to make persons with whom to enjoy fellowship. God commits God's self to a particular people, beginning with Abraham, who are to be the bearers of the divine promises to the whole world. They fail to share in this mission to the world as God wants, and so the choice falls upon one person - Jesus Christ - who is obedient to God in life and death, and brings into human existence the transforming power of resurrection. The story begins with creation and ends with the new creation of the whole universe.

My purpose here is not to recount this story in its biblical detail, but to claim that the story is the result of revelation, without which we would not be able to tell it. I do *not* mean that the story itself has been revealed, as if it has been spoken to us from the clouds by a heavenly story-teller. I mean that it has been formed among people as they have reflected (with the help of God's Spirit) on events in history where they have met God in a special way.[8] In these momentous meetings God has revealed *God's very self* to them, opened up the divine life, unveiled the heart of divine love. Revelation is not a message but - as Karl Barth puts it - 'the person of God speaking'.[9] This is why scripture above all calls Jesus Christ the 'Word' of God; the word is not a set of propositions but a living person, and the written text witnesses to this Word.

The story then is the result of meeting this speaking God in many times and places. It is the pattern that the community of God's people places upon the meetings of God with Abraham in the plains of Ur, with Moses at the burning bush, with prophets in the temple sanctuary or out in the wilderness, with wise men in their schoolrooms, with people in the triumphant experience of exodus and in the despair of exile. Finally the story is shaped by meeting with God in the face of Jesus Christ, on the dusty roads of Galilee, at the humiliation of the cross in Jerusalem, and in unconfined fellowship meals with the risen Lord. The story is human response to revelation, inspired by the Spirit of God. The story is also the place where God's people can encounter God again even as they tell it;

the telling of the story is a rendez-vous with the God who desires to be open to us and draw us into the fellowship of God's own life.

As the church reflected upon this story it re-told it in a more doctrinal form, in the shape of the Trinity. The story was nothing less than God's mission from eternity; it was the story of the Father sending forth the Son from his being in an eternal joy of birth, sending the Son into the turmoil of human history at a particular moment in the person of Jesus, and the gathering into God of many sons and daughters through the persuasion of the Holy Spirit. The Trinity is the greatest story of all, the supreme meta-narrative.

The church of Christ therefore has a culture, which takes form in a structure of words. The story has come into being in a particular language, in particular places. As Lesslie Newbigin puts it,[10] the Christian community offers a 'plausibility structure' for explaining the world, as all cultures do. It has its own way of linking events together into a coherent whole, in which it finds hope for the future.

3. The Story and the Stories

But if this is the case, there is a basic question about the Story and the stories. How shall we relate the Christian story, which is the result of revelation, to the many stories that make up culture? If culture is the stories that people tell about themselves in order to understand where they have come from, where they are, and where they are going, how shall we tell the Christian story in the midst of the stories? Can we avoid some of the pitfalls that, with respect, T. S. Eliot seems to have fallen into with his Sweeney? Facing the particular challenge of our modern-day culture, I want to break this question down into three sub-questions.

a. How can all stories be judged by this one story?

First, there is the question as to how one story can act as a critique of the many stories. We might want to say that the Christian story operates as a kind of measure of culture. When H. R. Niebuhr enquires what the relation might be between Christ and Culture, and concludes that Christ is 'transformer of culture',[11] this implies that Christ judges all culture; but, as I have pointed out, the story of the Christ is itself a form of culture. How can one culture then stand out from among others as their yardstick or criterion?

Putting the question another way, how can we resist the view of the Christian story as just one private preference that people might make, in a culture which is not really secular at all, but which has rather made religion into a supermarket choice? The recent report of the Church of England, *Search for Faith*, laments the 'pick-and-mix' spirituality of today, in which people construct their own religion out of a mixture of cultural elements in a spiritual free market.[12] A person, for instance, may have her children baptized, marry in church and attend the festivals of Easter and Christmas, but to these she adds some astrology, Zen meditation and some use of crystals for communing with nature; she also arranges the furniture and plans the decoration in her house according to the art of *Feng Shui*, a practice which promises to promote health and wealth and which has attracted clients such as the Body Shop, Marks and Spencer and Queen's Park Rangers Football Club.

Unlike such do-it-yourself methods of individual spirituality, the Christian story is a coherent whole, offering a universal story embracing history and the cosmos; but how can it be brought into critique with culture, when it is itself culturally shaped? Actually, this very claim to wholeness prompts a question in our present culture, but before we come to this there is an even more basic challenge to be faced.

b. To what does this story refer?

A second question arising from the intellectual mood of our time is this: what on earth is this story all about? It may seem obvious to Christians that their story is about both God and the world, but there is in fact a crisis of confidence at the moment in what *any* written text or work of the visual arts refers to. There is what might be called a 'postmodern suspicion' about finding anything outside the story itself. A story, it is said, is not strictly about anything except itself. It is a self-contained world from which the outside world is absent, since the words of the story gain their meaning only from their relation to each other; even the author is excluded. We can *enter* this world, and wandering within it will have

some effect on the way we live and face the future, but it does not itself
directly refer to any reality than itself.

At the heart of every story is an absence, a silence, and in this way of
thinking, the greatest absentee is God. In his book *Real Presences*,
George Steiner refers to this crisis as a shattering of trust, a breaking of a
contract.[13] However slippery and fragile words might be, Western civilization has in the past lived with a trustfulness that there is some kind of
relationship between the word and the world. It is this contract of trust –
we might prefer to use Steiner's alternative term 'covenant' – that has
now broken down.

This 'crisis of representation' has befallen the academic and artistic
community, but it is not absent from popular culture. Television gives us
many examples of advertisements which scarcely refer to the product any
longer, but entice us instead into the inner world occupied by the persons
portrayed; there is the beautiful girl who finds freedom driving a car, or
the man whose stylish life apparently involves taking off his jeans and
washing them there and then in a launderette, and we exclaim in bewil-
derment: 'what was that advert all *about*?' In a culture where stories do
not reflect an external reality in any direct way, how shall we tell the
Christian story which points to the reality of God? Further, the claim that
the Christian story refers in a holistic way to the relationship between
God and creation leads to a third question.

c. How can we tell a universal story?

In a society which is suspicious of all large-scale stories, a comprehensive
story seems oppressive. Once again this characterizes the mood which is
frequently dubbed 'postmodern', and which has reacted against the
attempts of our modern age to provide all-encompassing explanations for
the world, whether they be scientific, economic, religious or political. It
suspects that these 'grand stories' or 'meta-narratives' are in fact ideologies which are designed to dominate people.[14] And the worst offenders are
religious explanations which appeal to revelation, which insist that they
must be believed because they have been disclosed by God: surely, it is
said, these above all are intended to keep people in a domination of fear
and to manipulate them.[15]

While the terminology of 'meta-narratives' belongs to the intellectual world, popular culture shows in its own way a turning away from comprehensive viewpoints and theories. There is not only the pick-and-mix spirituality I have already referred to, but the preference for single-issue social campaigns (recent examples in the UK were protests against the disposal of the Brent-Spa oil platform, the construction of the Newbury by-pass road and the extension of Manchester Airport) rather than allegiance to political parties with comprehensive programmes. There is the continual shifting of images on television, moving quickly from one visual impact to another so that the mind and eye cannot dwell on any one too long, even on the news. This is the culture, of the disposable image and sound-bite, into which we speak a story with universal claims.

In a moment I want to explore the path by which we have come to the point in our culture where these three questions arise: how can we *judge* any story? What is a story *about*? And how can we tell a *universal* story? The three questions, I suggest, have to be tackled in dealing with the overall question: how can we relate the Christian story to the many stories of culture? It is the Christian idea of revelation, I want to suggest, that offers a perspective within which these questions are best answered.

4. Reading the style of a culture

Perhaps the theologian who has thought most carefully in this century about culture and revelation is a contemporary of T. S. Eliot, Paul Tillich. Writing in the 1950s,[16] he suggested that if we gave our attention to the culture around us we would find three features. First there was the *predominant movement* of the culture, which he identified as the spirit of industry, or management of society through technology. Second, however, there could be discerned a *spirit of protest* against the main spirit; this he found to be a powerful expression of the human predicament of estrangement, an existential sense of being alienated from the works of our hands and from the very roots of our being, an anxiety about the threat of nonbeing. Third, this protest took the form of *prophetic voices*, raised on behalf of particular issues.

Tillich did not stop with analysis of culture, but went on to suggest the way that faith came into interaction with it. Christianity should meet culture, he believed, with the symbols of faith, and especially the picture of the Christ. Religion is about our ultimate concerns, what finally matters to us; with the help of revelation, it can give answers to the questions that culture raises when it is in quest of final meaning. So the Christian story *judges* the predominant spirit. It *answers* the questions raised by the spirit of protest, showing that the answer to a sense of alienation is the healing reality that has been revealed in Christ. With regard to the prophetic voices, it encourages them where they draw attention to what is of ultimate concern, but judges them when they begin to make idols of anything less – such as their own survival, for instance.

It appears then that Tillich sees revelation – especially the appearing of healing power in Christ – as an answer to the questions of culture. But he rightly asks why the protest movement in culture should raise these questions about ultimate meaning in the first place.[17] He believes that this is because we are already seized and held by the Spiritual Presence of God. It is because, at its roots, culture is linked to the depths of Being. God then is as much in the questions as in the answers; we only ask about ultimate reality because what is ultimately real has already grasped hold of us.

Here I believe we should re-express the relationship Tillich draws between revelation and culture; his own account should lead us further, to find revelation *within* culture as well as in the answers to its questions.[18] Revelation, as I have stressed, is not a message but God's coming to be present, as God's own self, with an unveiling of being and purpose. It is because God is always present in the world, in a self-opening to people, that they respond by opening themselves to what is of ultimate importance, even in the form of a quest. So there is revelation in the questions *and* in the answers; God opens God's own self to human hearts and they respond in questions, protests and prophetic voices. They reach towards the place where God is revealed in focus and fullness, in the story of Jesus. Saying this does not *confuse* revelation with culture. Culture is always a response to revelation, a reaction to the self-offering of God. And the response may need to be judged as well as encouraged.

Tillich urges that Christian believers should learn to 'read the style of a culture'. The style he read in the 1950s was marked by the protest of existentialism. It was the era of Sartre and Camus, of a novel such as *The*

Outsider in which the anti-hero expects to be led out to an execution in which the whole universe will greet him with cries of rejection.[19] The sense of not being at home in the world could be met with the Christian story of the healing of estrangement. If we read the style of our culture today, I think we may find the predominant spirit to be one of market forces, and the spirit of protest to be a relativizing of value systems.

This protest against modernism, usually called postmodernism, is worth considering in a little more detail. The *modernism* that Tillich reflects is in itself already a reaction against what we might call the *modernity* of the Enlightenment.[20] In the modern project from the mid-seventeenth century onwards, the human subject was exalted as the controller of the natural world, the supreme subject whose superior reason could bring order to everything else, which was therefore to be reduced to a mere set of objects. Because 'I think therefore I am', everything else is an object to be manipulated. Beginning early in this century, and certainly by the 1950s, writers and artists had seen the dangers of this project; they had reacted against the picture of the controlling ego, the masterful subject. This, they saw, had only estranged human beings from their world, and caused them to lose contact with it. So artists experimented with chaos, with the fragmenting of images, playing with multiple perspectives. But their protest assumed that the truth was still out there somewhere to be found; it just had to be reached through irony and discordance.

Postmodernism in our day has come to assert that the fragmentation is all there is. There are many separate language games, but no large story that unites them. There is, as we have seen, a crisis about how words can represent any reality beyond themselves. Truth is only the little truth, the relative truth, not a universal reality. Thus the term 'postmodernism', despite its descent into jargon, marks a reaction against both phases of the modern world – both modernity and modernism. With modernism, it rejects the attempt of the human mind to be master of all reality. Beyond modernism, it lives without the hope that a great truth might still be found among the broken pieces of the human endeavour. Driving this protest is the overwhelming suspicion that those who make great stories are seeking to oppress and dominate. Nietzsche is given credit for perceiving that the human story is one of will to power from the beginning. 'Violence is the master of us all',[21] and we must therefore avoid any pretension to large explanations and universal histories with which we might seek to get power over others.

Reading the culture means listening to the voice of the Holy Spirit, though not simply *as* the voice of culture. I have suggested that revelation is *in* culture, in the sense that God the revealer is present in the world, opening God's own self to human hearts and minds. The postmodern protest is surely a proper response to the self-offering of God, in so far as it awakens us to the danger of power games, to oppressive ideologies that hide under a mask of attractive stories about the world. It also challenges the kind of knowledge that subordinates an 'It-world' of objects to the human subject. God is not an object to be investigated, and the postmodern mood can move us towards a different kind of knowing, a knowing through participation rather than observation. I want to return to this suggestion shortly.

However, we must also judge the postmodern protest from the standpoint of the revelation in Christ. We notice that it is in fact involved in a contradiction; while it apparently shuns any meta-narratives, any large stories, it adopts at least two for itself. First, the claim that there are no such thing as universal truths is itself a universal theory. Second, it implicitly accepts Nietzsche's grand story that the will to power lies beneath the surface of *all* large-scale stories, that the cycle of violence is inevitable.

Indeed, it seems that one all-consuming story is emerging from globalization and multi-national commerce; it is the tale that all events are part of one imperious necessity, the will to exert power. In particular, the refusal of postmodern critics and artists to tell a universal story turns out to be capitulation to the predominant trend in our culture, the power of market forces. These continue unabated, above the intellectual clamour. The term 'postmodern' might then be claiming too much for itself; it might be more accurate to assess this mood of present culture as no more than 'very late modernism'.

5. The Story as judge of the stories

These observations bring us to tackle the first of our questions about relating the Christian story to other stories in culture, whether high or low. The question was how one story can be a critique of others, given that all stories are forms of culture. The Christian strategy is not to imagine that we have a point of vantage above or beyond culture, from which to survey other stories. It is rather, as Nicholas Lash puts it, that we are called to tell 'a more persuasive tale';[22] it is the power of the story to convince that will judge other stories; we are to 'out-perform' them by living by a better story.

The Christian story of peace, of reconciliation and *shalom*, counters the dominant narrative. It affirms that peace was the ethos of creation in the beginning, and peace is the goal of creation at the end. It denies that violence is the master of us all. As Paul Ricoeur points out, the dominant Babylonian creation myth in the ancient world was one of redemptive violence.[23] Tiamat, the chaos monster and 'mother of all' is murdered and dismembered; from her body the world is formed. Marduk, the young champion of the gods shoots an arrow into Tiamat that bursts her distended belly; he then pierces her heart and splits her skull. Dividing the corpse in two, he makes the sky and the earth. So chaos is to be brought to order through violence; the will to power is enshrined in creation itself.

This is a story repeated in the popular myths of our day. The heroine of the film *Dirty Weekend*, for instance, has had enough of being victimized by men; Bella has been treated badly by her boyfriend, spied on by a peeping Tom and threatened by phone calls. So she takes a gun and goes on a killing spree, taking a murderous revenge on those who have abused her. (The justification of this violence by the director, Michael Winner, was that it was a blow for women's liberation, breaking free from male oppression, but a number of women's groups immediately took issue with him.) This is the story not only of *Dirty Weekend*, but *Dirty Harry*, where the citizen tries to make justice from the barrel of a gun. In the world of fantasy, it is the story of a whole range of cartoon heroes - Popeye, Superman, Ninja Turtles, Spiderman. The Nietzschean *Übermensch* takes strange forms in our culture, from Wagner's Siegfried to Mighty Mouse.

All these perpetuate the myth that violence can be redemptive, a sub-myth of the larger story of the will to power at the well-springs of life.

But the Christian story claims that creation is not an act of violence; order is brought from chaos by the simple word of God, letting life be, and by the Spirit's brooding in a maternal way upon the waters. Redemption is brought into disordered human history by the resistance of Jesus to evil, a challenge to the powers which is not violent, but the way of suffering love. As John Milbank points out, those who exercise a will to power are imitating a certain cultural paradigm of strength;[24] they dedicate themselves to a particular story which fosters their oppressive acts. The weak then can also dedicate themselves to a story in which the true and surprising power of God to overcome evil is revealed.

Dedication to a story means 'indwelling the story', as Michael Polanyi puts it.[25] It means not only inhabiting it but enacting it, performing the story as others in our culture act out their own stories. But Lesslie Newbigin is surely right to insist that if we are to indwell the biblical story in a way that *relates* to other stories, we must also learn to dwell in imagination in the many stories too. In his book *The Gospel in a Pluralist Society* he testifies that as a Christian living in the biblical story he nevertheless shares his life with other members of society who inhabit a different world-view; he says that 'I do not live in that plausibility [structure], but I know what it feels like to live in it.' The debate between the two plausibilities is internalized, and as it goes on in our mind, so (says Newbigin), we are 'equipped for the external dialogue'.[26]

I suggest that this internalizing is especially important where other people's stories take the form of protest against the dominant story of our culture, as Tillich has pointed out. Nor is this just a technique for communication, as Newbigin tends to imply. If God is indeed present in the world, opening and offering God's own self, then in culture there will be many and diverse human responses to this self-gift. These responses may be inadequate, unworthy, or even mistaken, but as we enter into them we can listen for the divine Word to which they are reacting. We can catch the echoes of the Word in the silence, and so we can learn how to tell our *own* story, and to grasp more deeply what the story really means.

The Christian story of peace must then make its way among the other stories, and we can be confident that it will.[27] This is what it means to judge culture, not standing over it but in the midst of it.

6. What the story represents

But our second question therefore presses the more urgently: what is this story all about? Does it really refer to anything beyond itself?

One of the marks of our present culture has been an emphasis on the importance of language in its own right. Following the Enlightenment, for a long time language was seen simply as a means of exchange, as mere tokens to render our private thoughts public, a bridge between the thinking subject and the world of objects outside the mind. Language was just a coinage. But now (as Nicholas Lash discerns it)[28] there is a stress on the event of the word, word as happening, word as a phenomenon to be reckoned with. Culture, as I have suggested, is understood as a web of language and perhaps the world-wide computer web helps to foster this image. It may well be a result of the pressure of the Spirit of God within culture, a sign of the self-revealing presence of God, that there is this attention to the historicity, the sheer 'there-ness' of the word. God's Word, after all, has been made flesh.

However, there is a downside to this. Words, as we have seen, can become self-enclosed, an autonomous web. The net can close in upon itself. The human word can become God, or at least Narcissus. The reader can find the world of the text to be open to nothing outside itself, as a crisis of confidence befalls our culture about whether words can represent anything – God, the self, the world around. The 'coinage' of words can be thoroughly debased. Language can be regarded as an autistic network of signs and markers, showing mere 'traces' of the self and others. As I have already suggested, in our age the covenant between the word and the world seems to have broken down.

Again, there is an aspect of this we need to listen to as Christian believers, especially when we use words in talking about God and God's engagement with the world. This is our great story, but words are bound to fail us as we tell it. After all, if we believe that we cannot know about God without God's own self-revelation to us, then there is bound to be some crisis of representation. God is not an object to be put under the microscope and investigated; God is other than us, as holy mystery. As Karl Barth puts it, 'when God reveals himself he also hides himself'.[29] On the one hand this is because God always retains freedom as the Lord, giving the divine self to us but not in such a way as to become our prisoner. So when Moses encounters God at the burning bush and wants to get a hold over God by possessing the divine name, God eludes his grasp by telling him 'I am.... what I am' (Exodus 3:14). On the other hand, God will also be hidden in revelation because the medium of the world is unsuitable for God's transcendent glory: it is finite and sinful, so that we can always only see 'through a glass darkly' or 'puzzling reflections in a mirror' (1 Corinthians 13:12).

We need then to be uneasy with the claim that words can simply represent God in any unequivocal way. We need to be alert to the part that images, metaphors, ambiguities, echoes and multiple meanings play in any telling of the story. Words will always break apart in our hands. But for all this, we believe that the story does truly point to God, does represent God in a way that corresponds to the truth of God's being, and that this derives from the historic event of the word being made flesh. God has spoken the truth about God's self, so that we can speak the truth back to God.

The way that the story leads us to God is, however, not going to be the way of *observation*. This is made very clear by the supreme form of the Christian story I have already mentioned, the doctrine of the Trinity. This doctrine does not lead us to say, 'So now I know what God looks like!' One God who lives in a communion of interweaving relationships cannot be portrayed in oil paint, or etched in glass, or carved in stone. The doctrine of the Trinity makes little sense as an observation of God, as the report of an observer. But it makes a great deal of sense as the report of a *participant* in God's life. It is the story of being involved in relationships which are like those between a Father and a Son, and which are always being opened up in surprising ways by a Spirit of the unexpected.[30] It is a story of being involved in the sending of the Son by the Father, in the Son's obedient 'yes' to the Father, and the Spirit's openness to the future. That is, it is a story of being involved in God's own story of mission and glory.

The story then is truly about God, but in a mode of *participation* and not observation. It draws us into God, as any story draws us into its world. Revelation brings a crisis of representation; we are baffled as to how words can contain the coming of God. But this very crisis should lead us into a new covenant between the word, the world and God. There is a strong sense in our present culture that there is an *absence* at the heart of any story, or other work of art. There is a void, a vacuity. Nothing is present – neither the author nor the world, and especially not God. The Christian story tells us that there is not an absence, but a *hiddenness* of God, which entices us further into relationship.

To illustrate this kind of representation, let us consider *the name of the rose*. In his play *Romeo and Juliet*, Shakespeare's heroine laments her lover's name, for it marks him out as a member of the Montague family, and the Montagues are in a state of feud with her own family, the Capulets. She reflects:

> O Romeo, Romeo! wherefore art thou Romeo?…
> What's in a name? That which we call a rose
> By any other name would smell as sweet.

In distinguishing the flower from its name she is not rejecting the covenant between words and the world; she is not denying that the word 'rose' can represent the thing which is the flower. But she is pleading that this representation should be able to take new and flexible forms. She loves the real thing, the real person (Romeo), and wishes this could be re-named. She urges that the name, the word, should not obstruct the relationship it is meant to assist. In the nineteenth century, however, the poet Stéphane Mallarmé takes the same example, but now *exalts* the word over the thing. Here George Steiner draws attention to what he calls 'Mallarmé's repudiation of the covenant of reference'.[31] In affirming art for art's sake, Mallarmé believes that what gives the word 'rose' its attractiveness is 'the absence of every rose'; released from the dirty job of representing an actual object, the word is set free to weave its own magic. It has a 'purity', 'unsoiled by the tribe'.[32]

We are well on the way to my final example, where words cannot signify objects. In his book *The Name of the Rose*, Umberto Eco relates a series of murders committed in a Benedictine monastery in the Middle Ages, and a visiting monk becomes the detective who aims to solve the crimes. The central point is that he finds the villain (the librarian, by the way) totally by accident. The crimes have certainly left clues, but none of them turn out to have been pointing to the culprit. Unlike other detective novels, the signs are misleading. No theory can be constructed from them. There seems then to be no link between sign and event, between (as it were) the name of a rose and the rose itself. The person telling the story, who has shared as a young monk in these events, concludes, 'I leave this manuscript, I do not know for whom; I no longer know what it is about.'[33]

Eco might be called a postmodern novelist. He is making the point that there is always a gap between a sign and the object it points to – 'the thing signified'. This is true not only of clues for a crime but of all marks on a written page, all writing. It is a long road from Juliet's lament to the postmodern breakdown of the contract of trust between the word and the world, though Juliet already notices the fact of the gap. We need to listen to the witness of the pre-Enlightenment world: 'a rose by any other name would smell as sweet', says Juliet. For Shakespeare, as for Juliet, there will always be some gap between the word and the thing. But this does not mean the absence of the reality signified by 'rose', whether it is the flower or the love (of Romeo) that the flower symbolizes. When words falter, when names fail, this should lead us precisely to enjoy the rose – or in this case, to be engaged in a relationship of love.

The Christian story cannot exactly tell us what God is like. But in this breakdown of representation it leads us to participate in God's life and love; and it can also lead us to take a responsible participation in the world that God has made.

7. A Story that does not dominate

I have been drawing attention to the rejection in our present culture of all universal stories, on the grounds that they are oppressive. The irony, we have seen, is that this view itself is a 'grand story'. The Christian story, I have suggested, challenges this meta-narrative that the will to power has the last word.

In doing so, it shows that it is not a dominating story in itself, and so we begin to find an answer to our third question: *how can we tell a universal story*? The theme of the Christian story is that God shows the nature of true power by giving it away, by being willing freely to submit to the conditions of God's own creation, to take rejection and suffering into the heart of the divine life. God aims to establish covenant with creation through persuasive love and not by force or manipulation. This is the surprising story of the cross of Jesus. This is a universal story that is not oppressive, because the content of the story corresponds to the nature of the revelation through which we have the story. Revelation is not a matter of a forcing of God upon creation, overwhelming it; in self-unveiling, God hides God's self at the same time, enticing us to find God in the silence of the Word. Revelation is not a transmitting of propositions that cannot be denied, but a drawing of us into participation in the dance of persons in the triune life of God.

The content of the story, and God's own transmission of it, should shape our own strategy in telling the story. To its shame, the church has sometimes used the weapons of aggression, threat, infusion of guilt and manipulation in its mission. (Women especially have felt this.) God, we might dare to say, has known the pain of having the church use methods which contradict the story itself, and it is the humility of God to endure the anguish this causes. Facing the challenge of our postmodern age, we should not be ashamed to tell a universal story; but we should be ashamed to tell it in a way which denies its content, and which gives credence to the postmodern suspicion that all universal stories aim to oppress.

We began with Eliot's *Sweeney Agonistes*, and to this I want finally to return. I suggest we can now see the true extent of Eliot's failure to bring the Christian story together with other human stories, as well as to unite high and low culture. His analogy between the remorse of the murderer and the dark night of purgation in the way of ascent to God strikes us oddly. Perhaps we can now see why: Eliot has chosen an image of violence to portray self-denial; the killing of a lover is an analogy for the putting away of worldly loves. Eliot is employing an image of violence for a spiritual quest which should precisely challenge the story of redemptive violence. A sign of this incongruity is that neither Sweeney nor Eliot seem concerned about the girl: Sweeney in fact is rather jocund about the whole thing –

I knew a man once did a girl in.
Any man might do a girl in
Any man has to, needs to, wants to
Once in a lifetime, do a girl in....

Yet he knows that words cannot capture the ultimate concerns he is trying to express, the experience of guilt, remorse, death in life and the hope of reaching out to life in death. Several times he explains 'I gotta use words when I talk to you', but that in fact 'it don't apply'. It is in his poem *Four Quartets* that words about God finally cease to be tools of investigation that can be 'applied', and become sign-posts to draw us into the life of God:[34]

You are not here to verify,
Instruct yourself, or inform curiosity
Or carry report. You are here to kneel
Where prayer has been valid. And prayer is more
Than an order of words....

Notes to Chapter 4

[1] T. S. Eliot, 'Sweeney Agonistes', in *The Complete Poems and Plays of T.S. Eliot* (London: Faber and Faber, 1969), p. 125.

[2] T.S. Eliot, *The Use of Poetry and the Use of Criticism* (London: Faber and Faber, 1933), p. 153. Eliot writes: 'There was to be an understanding between this protagonist and a small number of the audience, while the rest of the audience would share the response of the other characters in the play.'

[3] See e.g. Grover Smyth, *T.S. Eliot's Poetry and Plays. A Study in Sources and Meaning* (Chicago: University of Chicago Press, 1956), pp. 112-13.

[4] T.S. Eliot, *Notes towards the Definition of Culture* (London: Faber and Faber, 1948), p. 31. Eliot also includes a third sense, the culture of a particular group, smaller than a nation.

[5] We must add that for Eliot, this means an unashamed perpetuation of the class structure; to keep culture worth living, there has to be a leisured upper class participating fully in the highest culture. Eliot, op. cit., p. 35.

[6] This is in line with the thesis of Clifford Geertz, *The Interpretation of Cultures* (New York: Basic Books, 1973), pp. 5ff, and the definitions of culture already offered by Alan Kreider and Jane Shaw in this volume.

[7] Eliot, *The Complete Poems and Plays*, p. 121.

[8] This is similar to the distinction that Karl Rahner makes between 'transcendental' and 'categorical' revelation: see his *Foundations of Christian Faith*, transl. W. Dych (London: Darton, Longman and Todd, 1978), pp. 42-61.

[9] Karl Barth, *Church Dogmatics*, transl. and ed. G.W. Bromiley and T.F. Torrance, Volume I, Part One (Edinburgh: T. & T. Clark, 1975), p. 304.

[10] Lesslie Newbigin, *The Gospel in a Pluralist Society* (London: SPCK, 1989), pp. 63-4.

[11] H. Richard Niebuhr, *Christ and Culture* (London: Faber and Faber, 1952), pp. 192-6, 235-9.

[12] *The Search for Faith and the Witness of the Church.* An exploration by the Missionary Theological Advisory Group of the Church of England (London: Church House Publishing, 1996).

[13] George Steiner, *Real Presences. Is there anything* in *what we say?* (London: Faber and Faber, 1991), pp. 90ff.

[14] This critique has been voiced most notably by Jean-François Lyotard, *The Postmodern Condition: a Report on Knowledge*, in *Theory and History of Literature*, Vol. 10, tr. G. Bennington (Manchester: Manchester University Press, 1984), pp. 72ff.

[15] See, for example, Jacques Derrida, *Speech and Phenomena*, transl. D. Allison (Evanston: Northwestern University Press, 1973), pp. 102f.; Mark Taylor, *Altarity* (Chicago: University of Chicago Press, 1987), pp. 64ff.

[16] Paul Tillich, 'Aspects of a Religious Analysis of Culture' (1956), in Tillich, *Theology of Culture*, ed. R. C. Kimball (New York: Oxford University Press, 1959), pp. 40-51.

[17] Paul Tillich, *Systematic Theology*, Combined Volume (Welwyn: Nisbet, 1968), Vol. I., pp. 88-93, 181-4; Vol. II, pp. 203-4; Vol. III, pp. 235-7.

[18] cf. Paul S. Fiddes, *Freedom and Limit. A Dialogue between Literature and Christian Doctrine* (Basingstoke: Macmillan, 1991), pp. 29-32.

[19] Albert Camus, *The Outsider*, transl. S. Gilbert (Harmondsworth: Penguin Books, 1964), p. 120.

[20] This distinction between 'modernity' and 'modernism' is made by David Harvey, *The Condition of Postmodernity* (Oxford: Blackwell, 1990), pp. 30ff.

[21] This is John Milbank's summary of Nietzsche's perception, in *Theology and Social Theory* (Oxford: Blackwell, 1990), p. 276, cf. p. 5.

[22] Nicholas Lash, *The Beginning and the End of Religion* (Cambridge: Cambridge University Press, 1996), p. 227.

[23] Paul Ricoeur, *The Symbolism of Evil* (New York: Harper and Row, 1967), pp. 175-210. On 'the myth of redemptive violence', see also Walter Wink,

Engaging the Powers. Discernment and Resistance in a World of Domination (Minneapolis: Fortress Press, 1992), pp. 13-32.

[24] Milbank, *Theology and Social Theory*, p. 283

[25] Michael Polanyi, *Personal Knowledge. Towards a Post-Critical Philosophy* (London: Routledge & Kegan Paul, 1958), pp. 270ff.

[26] Newbigin, *The Gospel in a Pluralist Society*, p. 65.

[27] It will also be more persuasive since it crosses the boundaries of many cultures. It is a form of culture, but it is itself multi-cultural.

[28] Lash, *The Beginning and the End of Religion*, p.83.

[29] Barth, *Church Dogmatics* I/1, pp. 165-78.

[30] I work out this 'participatory' knowledge of God in my book, *Participating in God. A Pastoral Doctrine of the Trinity* (London: Darton, Longman and Todd, 2000).

[31] Steiner, *Real Presences*, pp. 96.

[32] Stéphane Mallarmé, final paragraphs of 'La Crise de Vers', in H. Mondor and G. Jean-Aubry, Stéphane Mallarmé, *Oevres Complètes* (Paris: Gallimard, 1970), pp. 370ff.

[33] Umberto Eco, *The Name of the Rose* transl. W. Weaver (London: Pan Books, 1984), p.502.

[34] Eliot, 'Little Gidding', in *Complete Poems and Plays*, p. 192.

5
The Power of Story:
The Incarnation of Truth in Culture

MARJORIE REEVES

Great stories have been handed down from the past and have become archetypes in the heritage of the imagination. Sometimes these are called 'myths', though the word can be misleading if it is taken to mean an 'untruth'. Obviously, every culture inherits its own particular stories, but there is a treasure house of great stories for which it is claimed that they transcend cultural barriers, having in some sense 'universal meaning'. But what is the basis of this universal meaning? What constitutes its reality? Does a great story still speak across centuries and cultures to our human condition today, in a new millennium? In this essay I want to argue that 'myth' or 'story' still constitutes a vital element in the nourishment of the human spirit but that, in the light of modern critical theory, we have to re-state the nature of its reality.

1. Story and its relation to history

How far ancient peoples in general really believed their stories of gods and heroes to be true is an academic question we can perhaps leave aside here. But for a 'People of the Book',[1] in particular Hebrews and their heirs, Christians, it is a crucial question for today. The Bible has been the main source of spiritual story throughout the Christian centuries. Its historicity was for many generations a matter of fundamental importance to the development of Christian belief. God had revealed himself through the long succession of his 'engagements' in time and space with his people recorded in the Old Testament and their truth had been confirmed by the historical reality of the incarnation. History was the field of his activity and the inherited story of his actions was God's sign-writing. This shows us something of crucial importance about God's method of teaching his children; it was story rather than doctrine that nourished the spirituality of many generations because it fed the imagination. Story came first; doctrine afterwards.

This is demonstrated clearly in medieval religious life. Of course scholastic minds, wrestling with the intellectual problems of relating classical philosophy to theology, were of great importance in the education of Christian minds and we see the peak of their achievement in the majestic *summa* of the thirteenth century.[2] But 'story' influenced a much wider range of the devout. From the *lectio divina* of monastic community to the visual representations of sculpture and painting in churches, sacred story was 'read' by the many. Biblical exegetes, who so lovingly expounded the multiple meanings of each narrative or person, peopled the medieval imagination with actors in a world of many dimensions. The educational role of Old Testament story was essential. It was, to take but one example, in answer to questions by the monastic brethren that Hugh of St Victor expounded in two treatises both the historical reality and the spiritual symbolism of Noah's ark, carefully drawing and colouring the diagrammatic *figura* which illustrated his teaching:

> As an illustration of this spiritual building I shall give you Noah's ark, which your eye shall see outwardly that your soul may be fashioned to its likeness inwardly. You shall see colours, shapes and figures which please the eye; but know that they are set there to teach you wisdom, understanding and virtue, to adorn your soul. The ark signifies the Church, and the Church is Christ's body; so I have drawn the whole person of Christ, head and members in visible shape to picture it for you clearly.

And so he proceeds with his symbolic picture.[3]

It was of fundamental importance to these medieval interpreters of the Old Testament that the multiple senses they extracted from the text were founded on historical reality. Each event or person signified more than itself but the literal happening was the root of all prophetical significances. St. Augustine warned against the gnostic tendency to over-spiritualize the text:

> When you hear an exposition of the mystery of the Scriptures telling of things that took place... believe what is read to have actually taken place... lest, undermining the foundation of actuality, you seek as it were to build on air.[4]

In the West, to a large extent, St. Augustine's view was followed and thus the medieval concept of *figura* was developed. Erich Auerbach has defined it thus:

> *Figura*... is something real and historical which announces something else that is real and historical... Real historical figures are to be interpreted spiritually... but the interpretation points to a carnal, hence historical, fulfilment.[5]

That is to say, because history is God's sign-writing it can figurally illuminate historical experience yet to come. This is allegory in a special sense which is born directly out of the Judeo-Christian understanding of history as the work of God. Inspired by this concept of *figura*, medieval students of the Bible found an inexhaustible well of meaning. They drew up bucketfuls of it.

In his early work, *Convivio*, Dante made a distinction between poet's allegory and what he called theologian's allegory. The former was fiction, although it veiled a spiritual meaning, 'a truth hidden under a beautiful lie'. His example is the story of Orpheus taming the beasts, and moving trees and stones by his music, something which did not actually happen but which signified the power of wise men to tame and civilize. In theologian's allegory God reveals the truth about human choice and judgement through real human story. In the *Divine Comedy* Dante saw the truth about good and evil embodied in particular human stories but this particularity always carried multi-dimensional meaning. His people are true *figurae*. The *Comedy* swarms with real people but behind many of his 'stories' are biblical archetypes. His characters, especially his own contemporaries, are idiosyncratically portrayed to emphasize their particular reality but they embody universal human choices of acceptance or refusal of God's will. Behind each stand others. In 'limbo' or ante-hell, for instance, are the Trimmers, those 'neither hot nor cold', who 'never were alive', because they evaded the great choices of life. Among them is 'he who made the great refusal'. Many commentators think this was Dante's contemporary, Pope Celestine V, the hermit pope whose abdication let in the notorious Boniface VIII. But, if so, behind him stand biblical figures, such as Esau, the rich young ruler and Pontius Pilate, and perhaps too, the

Florentine Cerchi. And how many other cases of failure through cowardice could we not call up? Among the suicides in *Inferno* is Pier dell Vigne, the confidant of the Emperor Frederick II who came to disaster through passionate loyalty to a lesser god. He is the anti-type and behind him we see the great archetype of true loyalty clearly alluded to when Pier tells Dante, 'I am he who held both the keys to Frederick's heart'.[6]

As Dante and Virgil stand at dawn on the shore below Mount Purgatory, they see the Angel of God approaching across the ocean using his wings as the white sails of a ship which carries more than a thousand souls of the lately dead. They are chanting Psalm 114: 'When Israel came out of Egypt'. Released from the bondage of this world they are about to begin their pilgrimage towards the perfect liberty of the Son of God by the ascent of the Mount. The exodus from Egypt is the great archetype for all human souls who seek release from chains and journey towards freedom. Shepherding the souls on the shore, rather surprisingly, is Cato. He is described by Dante in terms that recall the representations of Moses in medieval art. But why Cato? Virgil explains to Dante that he is there because he valued freedom more than life, and here Virgil specifically links Dante himself with Cato. Dante's personal pilgrimage is from the bondage of a chaotic Florence to 'a people just and sane', from Egypt to Jerusalem, with the Israelites of every generation. Once again Dante's imagination, using the figural exodus, evokes a multi-dimensional human experience.

Dante's political philosophy was focused on the crying need for a universal ruler to bridle Italy, the riderless horse, that is, to quell the civil discord which was tearing society apart. Believing that the signs of God's providential purposes are implanted in history, he seeks clues in biblical and Roman story. One crucial sign is that, according to his chronology, King David was contemporary with the coming of Aeneas to Rome. Both are archetypes of divinely appointed authority. So in the heaven of Jupiter, where just rulers are assembled, the eye of the eagle, which is the symbol of all just rulers, is King David.

Finally, Dante's sense of the fundamental relationship of the individual soul to the whole of scriptural story is vividly embodied in the pageant which unrolls before his eyes in the Earthly Paradise. First come twenty-four elders, the books of the Old Testament, then the mystical chariot of the church, drawn by the Griffon which represents Christ himself. Next are the four *animalia* for the Gospels, then two figures for Luke (as author of Acts) and Paul, then four 'lowly ones' for authors of the lesser epistles, and finally a solitary old man walking in a trance, the author of the Book of Revelation. The procession halts with the chariot immediately opposite Dante. This is the moment of truth for the individual soul; Beatrice is revealed in the chariot and for Dante she is the representative of Christ. She confronts Dante with the whole of his past life, reproaching him bitterly for straying so far from the true path. He is utterly abased. But this is also the moment of individual resurrection. Under Beatrice's tuition Dante perceives that the whole dimension of time is contained in the Word of God that is the scriptures. Past, present and future are unfolded to his imagination and Dante is commissioned as one particular human soul to play his own proper part in history. It is historical memory that has liberated him and made him whole.

Medieval typology only gradually succumbed to the new humanist scholarship of the sixteenth and seventeenth centuries. The gulf between medieval and modern was only really established by the higher biblical criticism. This was signalled in England by the Hebraist Robert Lowth (1710-1787), one-time Professor of Poetry in Oxford, but the full onslaught on the text came mainly from German scholars. Their demythologizing critique found popular expression in Lessing's famous *The Education of the Human Race* (1780). English conservatism may have held back the tide for a time (Mrs. Trimmer's standard *Help to the Unlearned in the Study of Holy Scripture* [1806] was 'as firmly typological as any medieval monk's'[7]) but by the 1820s critical scholarship had become a major force to be reckoned with. By the time Mrs. Humphrey Ward (Matthew Arnold's niece) published her best-selling novel, *Robert Elsmere* (1888), she was highlighting the anguish, not only of one intellectual young cleric in wrestling with the conflict between scholarship and 'revealed truth', but that of a host of other thoughtful Christians.

2. Story and the dangers of relativism

Today many of the descendants of those thoughtful Christians of the nineteenth century have accommodated themselves to the findings of a historical critique, though there are still some tensions between history and faith. But in the meantime, the reading of biblical texts (as of other great texts) has faced a new type of attack, more subtle, more pervasive and more dangerous. This comes from literary criticism in its most negative, deconstructing form. We still sing in our worship:

> How purely hath thy speech come down
> From man's primeval youth.

But the critics reply: there is no descent of pure speech to succeeding generations; all is contaminated at source. No authentic message can echo down the ages. The Bible is no longer the Word of the Lord with universal relevance, but a multiplicity of transient voices, each trapped within its own cultural frontiers.

Whereas the debates on historicity had been largely between scholars, this later debate has entered the public arena of lay concern, even reaching the newspapers. The question is: can these texts speak? Or – to borrow Ezekiel's words – can these bones live? Peter Jenkins wrote in the *Independent* newspaper:

> In accordance with deconstructionist theories, the texts of the Western canon are seen as coded embodiments of the power structure of the society in which they were produced... Everything is relative, subjective, a matter of opinion.[8]

Again, Danah Zohar declared:

> In the place of truth or reality, we have only limited human discourse, the system of belief and acts of interpretation which each of us makes from within the prison of his own culture or language... Every value is equal to every other value, nothing is real or natural or authoritative, everything is up for interpretation.[9]

The balance of importance has shifted from author to reader, speaker to listener. Author's meaning vanishes behind reader's interpretation. This kind of theory undercuts any notion of learning through the reception of new ideas or beliefs which may be surprising, uncomfortable, even belief-shattering. Anything unpalatable is to be discarded. 'The truth, whatever is meant by that, if anything, is not the author's truth but the reader's, that is *whatever it is comfortable and convenient for him* to take from the text, if indeed he finds anything acceptable.'[10] Here we meet a type of ideological imprisonment which takes two closely connected forms. One is the widely prevalent mind-set, dubbed 'political correctness'; the other may be termed 'cultural correctness'. That this kind of pose is acting as a concealed censorship in the mind needs no proof. We may take an example from a recent book, *The War of the Words*, edited by Sarah Dunant, in which the writer of an essay on teaching English literature explains the method: you do not 'ban' books, but in the case of a text which upsets the reader (like the 'little Englishness' of Philip Larkin) you 'contextualize' it in the setting of the values most acceptable in Britain today. This puts the author in his rightful marginal place. A reviewer of this book commented that this is what happens to any author who 'reveals himself to be out of tune with the attitudes, beliefs and value systems of those who study him... What, are we to reshuffle Austen to the bottom of the pack for her snobbery?'[11]

3. Story as a challenge to an 'instant' world

Historical criticism and deconstructionist literary theory each in turn created obstacles to 'reading the Word'. Now a third has become the subject of debate. Is the rising generation boxed with an instant environment? Is it the case that few have any real interest in anything further back than the last ten years? Or do the myths of the past still speak? Day by day the media pour out a stream of instant news focused on the latest heroes, the current icons which rise and pass in a day. Are we all in danger of becoming trapped in this absorbing instant world?

For all of us the choice to live 'cardboard lives' of two dimensions only is all too easy to make. Yet voices of 'the other' insistently disturb our fragile peace. Their 'real presences', as George Steiner calls them, inhabit our imaginations but, he says, ' we crave remission from direct encounter with the "real presence"... The secondary is our narcotic.'[12] But, he maintains, such narcotics are deadly. He acknowledges some validity in the deconstructionist position but argues for a break out of complete relativism by what he calls a 'quantum leap', or 'a wager on transcendence' that there can be both meaning and a 'presumption of presence' in the voices from the past. He acknowledges that such a belief 'cannot be logically, formally or evidentially proved... but let there be no mistake, such "verification transcendence" marks every essential aspect of human existence'.[13]

Of course we can only view the past through our specific cultural spectacles but do these really distort the image and blinker the outlook to such a degree that we only see what conforms with and confirms our own cultural stance? The function of a great image or story is to challenge our presuppositions and upset our complacencies. Great texts are given to us to illuminate our imaginations with a new truth which lights up our own stories. The words 'story', 'narrative' and 'history', applied to personal lives, have lately been adopted into contemporary 'speak'. They are increasingly used in place of the conventional phrase 'personal experience' as the key to the human condition. Whereas 'my experience' spells out the ego-centred feelings of an *individual*, 'my story' assumes the involvement of the *person* in relationships over time. It is remarkable that, in the midst of today's culture of individualism and instant living, so many thinkers should be saying, in one way or another, that we all have a story which is an essential part of our self-identity.

> Nations and peoples are largely the stories they feed themselves [on]...
> All our actions are mediated through and defined within stories, stories
> of who we are, how we came to be here, of ourselves and the world
> around us. All of our knowledge is little else but stories which shape and
> define us. We live in a world of stories.[14]

Steiner's wager on the power of meaning or message to transcend cultural relativity, even under the pressures of today's cultural correctness, is confirmed by a wide range of contemporary story. It is only possible here to assemble a few types of example. Take an anecdote which could be matched many times by teachers. A student who – rather accidentally – opted for a Dante class was outraged by his imperialist theory in the *Monarchia*, refusing to touch it because it offended her politically correct mind-set. But, as the class progressed, she surrendered on the strange, alien but powerful vision of the *Comedy*. Urging the need for an extra class at the end, she said: 'I've got to get to Paradise!'

The constant appearance of foreign literature in new translations marks the attempt to overleap cultural and language barriers. A truly remarkable example is recounted by Eric Anderson:

> A delightful Chinese lady told me recently that two new translations of *The Heart of Midlothian* had appeared in the same year and that other novels of Scott's were in hand. She herself had first read the Waverley novels in secret during her years as a peasant during the Cultural Revolution, when possession of a foreign book meant death. 'You see, we find in *Old Mortality* and *Woodstock* exactly what we went through in China' she said, 'and... we recognize in Scott's peasants the Chinese peasants of today.'[15]

Gabriel Josipovici tackles the question of whether, in translation, we can really receive an authentic message: 'Are we locked for ever in our own cultural horizons?', he asks. He replies with a general principle: 'the greater our imaginative response to others, the more we shall be able to understand them'.[16] Imaginative empathy, rather than analytical scholarship, best opens the barriers of time and language, enlarging our own world by contact with those others. He also makes the point that great writers 'transcend the horizons of their culture... in the sense of recognizing the complexity and ambiguity inherent in all human motivation of all ages. Homer, Dante and Shakespeare are each rooted in a particular culture, but each transcends it in his portrayal of a grand but flawed human nature.'[17]

The power of great drama was exemplified in a production of the complete trilogy of the *Oresteia* at the National Theatre some years ago. It was long, it was archaic in its conventions and staging, but night after night the theatre was packed. On the night I was there, the atmosphere was almost palpable in its concentration. Those ancient and tremendous themes of violence, blood-feud and – finally – reconciliation could not have spoken more loudly to our human condition today. Turning to the visual arts, in a study entitled *Fra Angelico at San Marco*, William Hood remarks that 'works of art helped fifteenth-century Florentines to know who they were'. A large proportion of those paintings and sculptures embodied great religious and classical stories from the past. The artist's 'method', says Hood, was 'a way of representing the present as though it were an extension of the past, or, conversely, of representing the past as though it were synchronous with the present.' In this way of thinking, 'transient events derived their meaning from their accommodation to the eternal realities of revealed truth'.[18] Can we still say this? In some earlier twentieth-century works of art – for example, in Stanley Spencer's and Henry Moore's work – this was abundantly true of their 'speech'. The question today is how far young artists are absorbed in the reality of immediate things – beer cans, bottles, dead carcasses *et al.* – or whether they too are responding to the resonances of the past. Certainly the fifteenth-century work of Piero della Francesco can still inspire a present-day poet to meditate on the spiritual meaning of the material world. In a deeply anti-dualist response to specific paintings of Piero's, Anne Ridler reflects:

> The body is not fallen like the soul:
> For these are godlike, beings
> wholly of flesh, and in that being whole.
> Founded on earth, they seem to be built not painted -
> Nothing is tortured, nothing ethereal here,
> Nor would transcend the limits of material
> Being, for in the flesh is nothing to fear,
> And nothing to despise...[19]

This historical approach is backed up by Clive Wilmer writing on the art of memory:

> Poetry has always been richer and more resonant when it has drawn on its past. Without the historical echo chamber, you might argue, there can be no poetry at all.[20]

On a different plane, there has been an explosion of family and local history societies in the last twenty or thirty years. Significantly, these eager beavers researching into their past are predominantly adults in the third period of their lives, often retired. They have worked through the instant pressures and satisfactions of our consumer society and are now looking for the missing dimension of their lives. Organizations exchange information in a proliferating new literature, the Open University has instituted courses on methodology and officers in local record departments say they are inundated by amateur historians whose need for guidance strains their resources. This is a conscious movement acknowledging that to confirm our personal identity we need to relate ourselves to our roots as well as to our contemporary world.

4. Story, memory and liberation

In a world of political upheaval, of peoples on the move, of exiles condemned to eat a bitter bread, the song of the ancient Hebrew exiles touches a powerful nerve – 'By the waters of Babylon there we sat down, yea we wept when we remembered Zion...' (Psalm 137) – as it comes mediated to us in a contemporary pop song. On the other side of the coin a plaque with the date 1989 in St Vitus's cathedral at Prague celebrates the return of freedom to a people in the words of Psalm 126: 'When the Lord turned again the captivity of Zion, we were like them that dream. Then was our mouth filled with laughter, and our tongue with singing.'

The connection between memory and liberation is mysterious. T.S. Eliot wrote: 'This is the use of memory: For liberation'.[21] Could we say that linking ourselves with great past experiences liberates us from triviality and meaninglessness to give greater depth to our attempts at living? Sometimes the ringing voice of grand language can liberate us from a prison of debased or feeble words and in following the foot prints of our heroes we find a commitment whose service is perfect freedom. This source of strength from the past embraces both our own forebears and the long procession of shared heroes both in the secular and religious traditions: saints and martyrs, both Catholic and Protestant, political and social reformers, public-spirited worthies of all kinds, an innumerable multitude who fuel the enthusiasm of succeeding generations to attempt great things. When Mr. Valiant-for-Truth makes his testament before crossing the River, his words resonate far beyond the limits of any particular faith:

'...though with great difficulty I have got hither, yet now I do not repent me of all the trouble I have been at to arrive where I am. My sword, I give to him that shall succeed me in my pilgrimage, and my courage and skill, to him that can get it. My marks and scars I carry with me...'[22]

This could be the manifesto of many a modern champion.

But there is a dark reverse side to memory. It can be a terrible '*damnosa hereditas*'. Ironically, the very force that Eliot saw providing the key to liberation is also the key which can lock people into a dungeon of despair. Eliot acknowledges this in the lines: 'History may be servitude, History may be freedom'. Both at the personal level and at the level of groups, tribes and nations we see all around us the saddest tragedies of human beings imprisoned in a historical mind-set which impels them to a life of hatred and violence or breaks them psychologically. Human experience is always paradoxical in its juxtaposition of good and evil. Memory is two-edged, but its power is unquestionable.

5. The truth of story

Thus, for good or evil, common experience shows that powerful images from the past can still work in the present to influence belief and action. But if we take seriously the findings of historical and literary scholarship, we must face the fact that any inheritance received from the past is culturally conditioned. What, therefore, is the 'authority' of great stories and texts? Can they be a form of truth, or is their power to inspire and change only a subtle kind of deception? In claiming the reality of his 'presences', Steiner makes the bold proposal that their validity rests on a different platform from that of academic proof ; a 'leap of faith' is required.[23] There are two ways of justifying this leap, a general, secular way and a specifically religious way.

a. A secular argument

First, as we have seen from a range of examples, there are certain universal emotions – of love and hate, hope and fear, aspiration and despair, adoration and terror – which experientially transcend cultural boundaries.

Great myths encapsulate these and therefore have power to 'speak' to all generations. Writing about ancient classical myth, Roberto Calasso says, in *The Marriage of Cadmus and Harmony*, 'we do not have to believe in gods... But we do have to believe in the reality of the human conditions and aspirations that are stored in myth'.[24] Myths are about human reality, not in Ranke's sense of 'what actually happened', but as embodying universal human experience. Jung reflected profoundly on 'the need for mythic statement' which, he believed, was satisfied.

> When we frame a view of the world which adequately explains the meaning of human existence in the cosmos... [m]eaninglessness inhibits fullness of life. Meaning makes a great many things endurable – perhaps everything. No science can ever replace myth and a myth cannot be made out of any science. For it is not that 'God' is a myth, but that myth is the revelation of a divine life in man. It is not we who invent myth, rather it speaks to us as a Word of God. There is nothing about this Word that cannot be considered known and human, except for the manner in which it confronts and spontaneously places obligation on us...[25]

Thus myth nourishes a sense of meaning and is also a mysterious call to commitment. Jung's exploration of the great archetypal images reveals their continuing power to people our imaginations.

b. A biblical view

Secondly, with regard to biblical stories, the 'People of the Book' affirm that the one universal Creator God has chosen to reveal himself continuously to his people through *particularity*. He engages with them in encounters that take place in time and space. Handed down in memory these become universalized in particular stories. Archetypal experiences are clothed in flesh. For Jews and Christians in particular, the long story of these engagements which they share in the Old Testament – mixed though they are with nationalist propaganda – narrated experiences which carry their own mark of self-authentication.

For Christians this authority of the particular is sealed by the life, words and death of that most particular of human beings, Jesus of Nazareth. The affirmation that in this one man the God of Universes speaks in fullness is the most extreme case of particularity. The belief in the incarnation was a scandal to intellectuals in St Paul's day and still is. At the risk of repetition, once more we affirm our belief that the 'truth' – about ourselves, and our destiny, about community and nationhood, about divine love holding all things together – is revealed to us primarily through 'incarnate' human choices and actions in specific situations. The church did not find the need for credal formulations until the fourth century of its existence. Theology is the intellectual abstraction summing up what is first grasped as divine-human drama in the imagination. St Paul devoted much thought to the doctrinal implications of Christian experience, but when he wanted to emphasize the precious core of that which he had 'received', it was the words and actions of Jesus 'on the night in which he was betrayed' that the Apostle 'delivered' to the early Christians (1 Cor. 11:23-25).

Christian memory is here, of course, treasuring a range of stories which shade from the purely legendary to events which actually happened (though still liable to distortion in the telling). At the legendary end, take, for instance, the details in the myths of creation or beginnings. Norman Cohn's book *Cosmos, Chaos and the World to come*[26] argues that a constant theme in all cultures was the yearning to see order rise out of chaos. Faith 'leapt' to the answer in the concept of a Creator. Here we meet a striking example of the way a cultural shift does not destroy the main message. For early peoples, struggling with the harsh realities of survival, the Creator's promise 'Be fruitful and multiply, and replenish the earth and subdue it: and have dominion over... every living thing that moveth upon the earth' (Genesis 1:28) was reassuring, while today, in the affluent nations, we shrink from what Francis Bacon famously called the 'Adamright' to domination and try to identify ourselves with the welfare of all creatures. Yet faith in a Creator remains the same.

Historically, Abraham is a shadowy figure of moving tribes but he has become the archetype of all pilgrims who accept the call to go out into the unknown, seeking 'a city which hath foundations'. In wrestling Jacob we find the type of all those who strive on the frontiers of understanding to know more. But the strange story teaches that such a quest, though it earns a blessing is costly, and in the Unknown's refusal to divulge His Name we learn that human knowledge always reaches limits and cannot attain power over all mysteries. What happened at the Red Sea is still disputed but the famous crossing of the Israelites has become the classic *figura* of all liberated peoples. It encapsulated for Negro slaves their drama of freedom and was apparently saved for its archetypal power in the baptismal service of the Anglican Alternative Service Book by the vote of lay Sunday School teachers against historically minded clergy. Scholars may warn us that David and Solomon were not quite as they are portrayed in the Book of Kings, but the images of the poet-king and the paragon of wisdom form the counter-image to power-hungry tyrants. Questioning Job sets the stage for our continuing dialogue over conflicting experiences of evil and good, of devastating disaster, on the one hand, and the providential care and majestic beauty manifested by the Creator on the other. Jonah gives us a dramatic parable of stubborn narrow-mindedness transformed into a vision of God's universal care: 'Should I not spare Nineveh, that great city, wherein are more than six score thousand persons that cannot discern between their right hand and their left hand, and also much cattle?' (Book of Jonah 4:11).

The historic prophets come across to us as actual voices of people deeply involved in the social and political problems of their societies. They obey a divine compulsion, whether called to denounce the evils of their day or to point to the unattainable, yet always relevant, vision of a Mount Zion to which all nations come, the ideal of a community at peace with itself and with God. They are the prototype of all brave protesters and dissidents who suffer for speaking the truth against greed and brutality. A modern book of prophets could be compiled from the cases publicized by Amnesty International. Thus, when Amos cries out for the Lord, 'they sell the righteous for silver, and the poor for a pair of shoes' (Amos 2:6), we hear the echo of modern voices in an Amnesty report: 'they silenced those who called for justice, and let the poor rot in boxes'. When Jeremiah desperately tries to evade his bitter commission – 'Ah, Lord God! Behold I cannot speak: for I am but a child,' (Jeremiah 1:6) – we think of all those today who have taken up the cause of justice with deep reluctance and foreboding.

The New Testament brings us fully into the realm of history, yet we are still confronted by the problems of contaminated texts and cultural barriers. Faith affirms in the heart that here, supremely, divine revelation is speaking to us but the critical mind finds it hard to read these records simplistically. Within the scope of this essay it is only possible to consider briefly how we try to meet this tension in reading the Gospels. Anthony Harvey has wrestled with it at a learned level in *Jesus and the Constraints of History.*[27] A layman's attempt to resolve it might go something like this. If Jesus was truly Man, destined, like all human beings, to occupy a uniquely-shaped 'hole' in time and space, he could only grow up and work within the constraints imposed by being a first-century Jew. But the astonishing narrative of his encounters and dialogues with his fellow men and women reveals him bursting through those limits to grasp and declare truths for all time. His compassion transcends tribal taboos and frontiers. With a mounting realization that, in his deep obedience to the Father, his sonship was indeed unique, we reach the narratives of the passion, to acknowledge that – beyond any textual problems which they pose – they manifest the very God in all the mystery of divine love. Thus the Gospels give us the final affirmation that changeless and abiding truths are mediated to us through concrete story, reinterpreted by every changing culture.

This truth has recently been strikingly confirmed by the unexpected success of the exhibition at the National Gallery in London: 'Seeing Salvation. Images of Christ'. Ian MacGregor, the Director of the Gallery, commenting on its impact, writes: 'These are [images] that speak to us from whatever distance in time about life and death and suffering, pain, fear, compassion and, most of all, about love and hope.' Reflecting in particular on a Netherlandish sculpture of 'Christ on the cold stone', he says: 'This is Christ as Everyman – an archetype of suffering that speaks as clearly to our secular age as it did 500 years ago... To look at this sculpture is to be reminded – whatever one's view of the nature and teachings of Jesus – that we are all in some measure complicit in the sufferings of each other'.[28] The image is of Christ, abandoned, naked, seated on a stone, awaiting the crucifixion. It does not represent a moment recorded in any of the passion narratives. Thus the working of this tremendous drama within the imagination is so strong that it creates new images, but always of the same timeless face and figure which gave an extraordinary new meaning to the word 'Saviour'.

6. Getting inside the story

One thing is clear: the more precious the 'incarnated' truth, the more important it is to understand it, to 'get inside' the primary embodiment in which it is given to us. All great texts demand dedicated attention to unlock their full meaning and religious texts supremely so. We have now reached the point in this discussion where we can say that while cultural correctness can be an obstruction to faith, critical scholarship can be its great enabler.

John Barton brings this home when he adapts four stages in understanding a text, as proposed by George Steiner, to reading the Bible.[29] The first is the act of trust that there is a worthwhile truth to be discovered. The second is the stage of placing ourselves inside the text, of seeking in the imagination to comprehend, as far as possible, its particular cultural context. The third is the imaginative act of bringing it home and naturalizing it within our own frame of reference. This is the crucial stage when we open the door and welcome it in. It may involve an upheaval of 'furniture moving' – or even throwing some out – as we accommodate the new message or, in Steiner's metaphor, play its ideas back to ourselves. But Steiner has a fourth stage. If we appropriate it to our own use, we must also make an act of restitution, giving the text back to its own independent existence, for these great stories belong to themselves and therefore to all ages. In domesticating them to our own culture, we colour them by our own experience. Recognizing the inevitable relativity of our own interpretation, we must respect the integrity of an abiding truth. Steiner concludes that 'What the author wrote' and 'what I have made of him' thereby achieve an equipoise. A real meeting of minds has occurred across what may be a great cultural divide, and *there is something new in the world.*[30]

Steiner's conclusion on reading the text drops a hint of great importance. The transmission of stories across ages and cultures, like the reading of texts, is not simply preservative but also essentially creative. New perceptions and meanings are born, like new stars in the human firmament. Jung caught this same thought too: a myth must live and grow, he said, otherwise it is dead. The creative force of myth in human experience is an electric charge running between generations and cultures.[31]

Newspapers today feed us largely on stories of despair and bitterness turning into hatred. But among these one can find the occasional shining gem of a story telling of resurrected hope and inspiration ignited by a role model, either contemporary or re-embodied from the past. Our conclusion, therefore, must be that there is an urgent need today to nourish imaginations on great myth and story of heroes from the rich inheritance of the past, as well as from the role-models of the present. These gems of inspiration can be mined from many sources. For Christians the Bible remains the primary source. Even while we draw on the analytical skills of critical scholarship to prise out the jewels more carefully, we treasure them the more as divine speech to this, as to all generations.

Notes to Chapter 5

This chapter is the only one which did not begin as a lecture in the Centre for the Study of Christianity and Culture, but as a talk given to a theological society elsewhere in Oxford. Dr Reeves, however, has kindly re-written this piece specially for this volume.

[1] *People of the Book?* is the main title of John Barton's Bampton Lectures for 1988, subtitled *The Authority of the Bible in Christianity* (New edition: London: SPCK, 1993).

[2] *Editor*: the medieval *summa* ('the whole') was a comprehensive work on philosophy, theology or canon law, used as a textbook in the schools of theology; see especially the massive *Summa Theologiae* of Thomas Aquinas (begun in about 1260), dealing with every conceivable topic of Christian theology in the form of a dialogue.

[3] Hugh of St. Victor, *De Arca Noe Morali*, *PL 1*, ii, p. 622, quoted in Beryl Smalley, *The Study of the Bible in the Middle Ages* (Oxford: Oxford University Press, 1952), p.96.

[4] Quoted in Erich Auerbach, *Scenes from the drama of European Literature*, trans. R. Mannheim (New York: Meridian Books, 1959), p. 39.

[5] Ibid, p.17.

[6] *Editor*: cf. Christ's announcement in Revelation 1:18; the lesser archetype is Peter, as in Matt. 16:19.

[7] Stephen Prickett, 'Romantics and Victorians: from Typology to Symbolism' in Stephen Prickett (ed.), *Reading the Text. Biblical Criticism and Literary Theory* (Oxford: Blackwell, 1991), p.186.

[8] Peter Jenkins, 'The follies of the political correct', The *Independent*, 8 May 1991.

[9] Danah Zohar, 'A Wonderland without Wonder', The *Independent*, 19 December 1989.

[10] Jonathan D. Culler, *On Deconstruction. Theory and Criticism after Structuralism* (London: Routledge & Kegan Paul, 1983), p. 64.

[11] Z. Heller, review of Sarah Dunant, *The War of the Words. The Political Correctness Debate* (London: Virago, 1994), in The *Independent*, 29 October 1994.

[12] George Steiner, *Real Presences. Is there anything* in *what we say?* (London: Faber and Faber, 1991), pp. 39, 49.

[13] Ibid., p. 214.

[14] I. Merchant, 'The Sea of Stories', *Movement*, No. 96, Summer, 1997, p. 8

[15] Eric Anderson, The *Independent*, Magazine section, 17 August 1991, p. 46.

[16] Gabriel Josipovici, 'Breaking the Language Barriers', The *Independent*, 30 June, 1990.

[17] Ibid.

[18] William Hood, *Fra Angelico at San Marco* (New Haven & London: Yale University Press, 1993), pp. x, 17.

[19] Anne Ridler, *Collected Poems* (Manchester: Carcanet, 1994), p.88.

[20] Clive Wilmer, 'The art of Memory', The *Independent*, 20 October 1994.

[21] T. S. Eliot, *Four Quartets*, 'Little Gidding', III, lines 7-8, in *The Complete Poems and Plays of T. S. Eliot* (London: Faber and Faber, 1969), p. 195.

[22] John Bunyan, *The Pilgrim's Progress*, ed. Roger Sharrock (Harmondsworth: Penguin Books, 1965), p. 370.

[23] Steiner, *Real Presences*, pp. 212-15, cf. 167-70.

[24] Roberto Calasso, *The Marriage of Cadmus and Harmony*, transl. T. Parks (London: Cape, 1993).

[25] Carl Jung, *Memories, Dreams, Reflections* (London: Fontana, 1974), p. 372.

[26] Norman Cohn, *Cosmos, Chaos, and the World to come. The Ancient Roots of Apocalyptic Faith* (New Haven: Yale University Press, 1993).

[27] Anthony Harvey, *Jesus and the Constraints of History*, (London: Duckworth, 1982).

[28] Ian MacGregor, The *Independent*, in Holy Week 2000.

[29] John Barton, *People of the Book?* pp. 62-4; he is referring to George Steiner, *After Babel, Aspects of Language and Tradition* (London and New York: Oxford University Press, 1975), pp. 296-415.

[30] Steiner, *After Babel*, pp. 300-2.

[31] Jung, *op.cit.*, p. 364.

6
Theology and Poetry: The Word and the World in Human Culture

And chiefly thou, O Spirit, that dost prefer
Before all temples th'upright heart and pure,
Instruct me, for thou know'st; thou from the first
Wast present, and with mighty wings outspread
Dove-like sat'st brooding on the vast abyss
And mad'st it pregnant: what in me is dark
Illumine, what is low raise and support;
That to the highth of this great argument
I may assert Eternal Providence,
And justify the ways of God to men.

John Milton, *Paradise Lost*[1]

1. Poetry and explaining the faith

The primary movement of Christian revelation is one of disclosure. As a consequence of this there arises what we might call a secondary level of reflexion, which is the communication of what Karl Rahner termed 'the idea of Christianity'.[2] This is to *give an account* of theology not just to Christians themselves, as an act of higher reflection, but crucially to all people, of alternative faith or none, who, according to Christian belief, have nevertheless been addressed in some mysterious sense by God's speaking with us in his Word.

But as a kind of theology which gives an account of what faith is, both to those outside the Christian tradition and to those who are within, fundamental theology has need of material extraneous to itself. The temptation simply to perform theology, and to ask dogmatics to do the work of fundamental theology in a triumph of the analytical approach, has however proved strong over recent decades, as can be seen from the theological narratives of Karl Barth and Hans Urs von Balthasar.[3] Here fundamental theology becomes 'coextensive with the whole of theology'.[4]

But this seems in a sense to be the refusal of explanation and of the dialogue which is enjoined in 1 Pet. 3: 15: 'Always be ready to make your defence to anyone who demands from you an accounting for the hope that is in you'. The disclosive movement of revelation surely demands expression specifically at the level of *explanation*, however provisional and contingent this may be. Whether as 'foundational theology' for the Christian communities, or as 'apologetics' for non-Christians, self-description, as distinct from self-performance, is vital if theology is to avoid the suspicion of incomprehensibility and incoherence and is to claim its own proper place in the order of things.[5]

The task of explanation, of telling people what faith 'is like', has had to be thought anew in different ages, reflecting the changing paradigms of truth and explanation.[6] The model I am presenting here, that of poetics, ties in with a contemporary movement which is seeking to use aesthetics more generally as part of the project of fundamental theology. This looks back both to the 'theological poetics' of Hans Urs von Balthasar, which was markedly more open to the life of culture than most contemporary theologies have been, and to the privileged place of art in postmodern society, in which – by Michel Foucault's account – art has substantially taken the place of religion.

Drawing upon Blondel and Ricoeur, as well as von Balthasar, Gerhard Larcher has recently stressed the extent to which the revelation itself is communicated *aesthetically*, through the senses (*pulchrum*) and in a way that offers mediation of the theological (*verum*) and the ethical (*bonum*).[7] As a sensible modality of communication and attestation, art is thus protected from the fragmentation of reason which is a condition of the postmodern, and can continue creatively to mediate the primary elements of Christian consciousness and tradition within an environment that is generally hostile to their classical expressions. Where Larcher deviates from von Balthasar however is in his view that works of modern art, for all their 'techniques of negation' and counter-aestheticism, remain 'sense-events', intimately linked with Ricoeur's 'originary expressions' (*affirmations originaires*), which open out into mystery, and ultimately into the mystery of God made flesh. In Larcher's view, the visual dominates contemporary culture, and modern art – precisely in its confrontation with the 'unrepresentable' and sense of 'the end of art' –

offers a place of deep dialogue between church and culture, faith and 'reason', modernity and tradition. The outline of a fundamental theology based upon contemporary art and aesthetics is a development that is at ease both with postmodernity and tradition, and it promises much for the future.

I have preferred to treat poetry and poetics rather than the visual arts, however, in recognition of the role played by the 'linguistic turn' in Christian theology and literary hermeneutics.[8] There is a risk here, as with modern art in general, that poetry might be thought of only as an élitest pursuit for the most educated in society. But the democratization of art is one of the characteristics of the modern, and the enchantment of the poetic text wholly transcends the academic context of its systematic study, since in nursery rhymes, songs and hymns it has widespread popular appeal. I shall argue that one of the key factors which poetry and Christian speech have in common, and which grounds their natural affinity, is the fact that neither the speech of poets nor that of apostles can be said to be ordinary speech, but both are forms of human talking which are powerfully under the sway of some other power, or licence. To that extent therefore, both can be said to have distanced themselves from the conventional speech of human beings, to have undergone some degree of *deviation* from the norm, to be – in Shklovsky's phrase – speech 'made strange'.[9] The analogy of poetics then, and the generative field of the poetic text, is one way in which the Christian community can communicate through reflective understanding something of what it is like to discover in Christ the form of the living Word, and to live by its meanings.

2. The form of poetic speech

Although poetry, in the form of nursery rhymes and popular songs, belongs to the common inheritance of humanity, the science of 'poetics', which seeks to understand the structure of poeticity, does not. We can make use of a paradigm originally developed by Roman Jakobson in order to draw distinctions between ordinary and poetic speech. According to this model, the shape of the normal speech-act is a triadic combination of addresser, addressee and the message, in which it is the communicative intentionality of the addresser with respect to the addressee that governs the whole.[10] If the communication is to be successful, then the words used must efficiently serve as signs to those things to which they refer. The functionality of language here is fundamentally one of service, requiring the transparency of the signifier with respect to the signified. In the case of poetic language, however, the focus shifts from the intentionality of the addresser within the communicative act to *the message itself.* Now language no longer serves to point beyond itself, or at least no longer does this alone, but rather turns in upon itself and engenders a world not beyond language but contained within it.

a. Words set apart from ordinary speaking

The first aspect of poeticity then, to align poetic language with theological speech, is the determination on the part of the one who delivers the text that the words are not to be taken straightforwardly in their denotative function, as ordinary reference. In the case of poetry, this is reflected in the use of specific markers such as introductions, titles, the publication of volumes of poetry, the organization of poetry readings, to ensure that such literary or oral texts will be set apart from ordinary speaking. The privacy of the poem, or its non-referential function, is signalled not only by context but also by its recognisable 'poetic form', which is based in one way or another upon simple repetition. Prosodic elements such as stanzas, rhyme, metre, a fixed number of syllables and/or lines, assonance, are all different expressions of the principle of repetition, which immediately marks out poetic discourse to the listener or reader as being in some way speech made strange (after all, too much repetition or non-referential use of speech in other contexts can easily be taken as the sign of madness).

In the case of religion, of course, theological speaking is set apart from ordinary speech by its associations with the cult, that is with liturgy, worship and church gatherings, and with a reverential frame of mind. The mixing of Christian speech with ordinary speech is perilous, since the mysterious and invisible realities of which the Christian community speaks cannot be pointed to like objects in the world which are equally perceived by all. Indeed, a blurring of the boundaries between ordinary language and Christian speech which is 'set apart' in this special sense leads either to blasphemy or religious mania. As ways of speaking which are 'set apart' from ordinary usage, both poetry and theology must be protective of their distinctiveness.

b. Words with multiple meanings

But the setting aside of reference to the external world in the poem has the further consequence that poetic language tends inherently towards ambiguity. This is a second point of affinity with theology. In the case of the poem, this ambiguity flows from the prioritization of language itself within the speech-act, in which the communicative function of language is no longer controlled by the addresser's intention to speak to the addressee about the world. Rather, the boundaries of the poem serve to create an inner-linguistic space: a world within the poem. Jakobson has described this as the projection of 'the principle of equivalence from the axis of selection to the axis of combination'.[11] What this means is that when we construct a non-poetic sentence, we *select* a word from a number of broadly equivalent words which we exclude as not suiting our meaning, and then follow it with another word which we have similarly selected out from a range of alternative possibilities. In the poetic function of language however the choice of a word is determined in no small degree by the other words which surround it and which together construct the body of the poem.[12] The choice of the poetic word then is determined not by its opposition to alternative words from among which it has been selected but rather by its *combination* with the other words of the poem.[13] Thus 'the succession of similarities and differences are the forces which keep together and enhance poetic constructions'.[14] As Edward Stankiewicz has said, Jakobson's 'message' now becomes 'autotelic', possessing its own goals, and 'the Kantian formula of art as "purposiveness without purpose" epitomizes also the essence of verbal art: poetic language is purposive in terms of the internal organization of the message, and purposeless in terms of the external reference'.[15] This same point was made more succinctly by the critic Northrop Frye when he wrote: 'the word does not echo the thing but other words'.[16]

Within the extraordinarily rich context of a fine poem, the individual word becomes ambiguous, or polyvalent, as it takes on a superabundance of meanings. The properties of the poem may involve rhyme and partial rhyme, metrical sequence based on the quantity or quality of vowels, syllabic sequence or accentual sequence. Within the overall texture of the poem, such structures will interact both with the natural expressive tone of the language the poem is written in and with the meanings of the words themselves. Thus the significance of particular words may be heightened through their position in the metrical flow, or alternatively they may be veiled. But in any case, a strong metrical, or prosodic, environment will greatly enhance the interaction of the different elements and make available a whole range of unforeseen and multiple combinations and meanings which are the product both of the normal ostensible functions of the words (made strange of course in the context of the poem), the suggestive associations of the words, and their interaction through the phonological, metrical or accentual systems which together construct the poetic text.

Ambiguity then stands at the heart of poetic meaning, and is essential to it. But for the Christian too, language is rich in its different contextual associations. Christian speaking is deeply indebted to the language of the bible, with its metaphors, tropes and types. The unseen God is spoken of precisely in terms of the language of the world, which then becomes charged with new and extraordinary significance. Furthermore, the language of Christianity is recontextualized in every age and new cultural world, so that the content of terms sanctioned by Scripture are constantly taking on new meanings. The ambiguity of Christian language then is both a matter of the density and richness of new contextualizations and is the consequence of a divine excess of meaning which revelation commissions language to bear.

c. Words that are 'inspired'

A third affinity between poetics and theology lies in the area of origination. The loosening of the referential function of language in the poem leads to the displacement of the self as speaker and, finally, to the problematicization of the authorship of a poem. Of course, in any conventional or legal sense, a poem can rightfully be claimed by the individual who composed it; but there is a deeper issue here to do with the question of the poem's origin. The creative process is notoriously outside the control of the conscious self, relying upon inspiration, creativity and vision, as well as craft, stamina and skill.

In earlier traditions, the unfathomability of poetic genesis was expressed as a belief in supernatural agency, in divine or semi-divine beings, who could under certain conditions take over the speech functions of the individual, 'enthusing' them in Plato's sense with or as inspiration. Nor is there any reason to think that the survival of the Muse into the Baroque period was always a purely cosmetic device of strategic anachronism. Modern poets too frankly acknowledge their debt and obligations to some 'energy' which is the incalculable source of their creativity. A twentieth century poet such as Stefan George can still write of his muse in strongly personalist, pseudo-religious terms, exactly conveying the sense of being at the service, or ambiguously in the power, of another:

Lobgesang

Du bist mein herr! Wenn du auf meinem weg•
Viel-wechselnder gestalt doch gleich erkennbar
Und schön • erscheinst beug ich vor dir den nacken
[...]
Du reinigst die befleckung • heilst die risse
Und wischst die tränen durch dein süsses when.
In fahr und fron • wenn wir nur überdauern •
Hat jeder tag mit einem sieg sein ende –
So auch dein dienst: erneute huldigung
Vergessnes lächeln ins gestirnte blau.

Hymn of Praise

You are my Lord! When you appear on my path –
In ever changing form but always recognisable
And beautiful – I bow my head before you.
[...]
You cleanse impurity; the wounds you heal

And dry my tears with your sweet sighing.
In following and vassalage – if only we survive –
Each day ends with a victory –
So too your service: renewed homage
Forgotten smile into the blue of stars.[17]

A certain ambiguity concerning authorship of the poem, in whatever way it may be constructed in different historical periods, is an abiding feature of poetic discourse, and it is one which invites some comparison with the experience of the theologian, whose divinely sanctioned speech we have likewise interpreted as a form of dispossession.

d. Words that liberate

But if the poet is in a sense 'inspired', then why should his or her work not be in a sense 'revealed'? Indeed, there is a pronounced strain in modern poetry, from Charles Baudelaire to Gottfried Benn, that seems to claim just such a vatic or visionary function. In the work of Heidegger, looking back to J. G. Hamann, that disclosure is itself one that is ontological, and poetry itself becomes 'the establishing of Being by means of the word'.[18] But the 'revelatory' is a function also of the world-creating dimension of the poem, or what Paul Ricoeur calls the 'world of the text'.[19] This is specifically that domain of reference which the poem sets up in a liberating opposition to description or teleological reference. Accordingly, for Ricoeur, 'this suspension or abolition of a referential function of the first degree' releases 'a more primitive, more originary referential function, which may be called a second order reference only because discourse whose function is descriptive has usurped the first rank in daily life and has been supported in this regard by modern science'.[20] This disclosure is not something that becomes for the reader the object of cognition in her own world, as part of what Paul Ricoeur identifies as the 'subject-object relation', but rather itself manifests as a world in its own indeterminacy and 'pure sensibility' (in Hart Crane's phrase)[21], so that the manner of its reception is encounter with and entry into *a second world*. Thus the poem does not offer itself as experience to us, or at least not that alone, but rather offers itself to us as *the very possibility of experience*, discretely constituted and newly configured. And the reader finds herself restored to 'that participation-in or belonging-to an order of things which precedes our capacity to oppose ourselves to things taken as objects opposed to a subject'.[22]

The central role of the imagination in this revelatory and liberating function of poetry is captured by Wallace Stevens when he describes the poem as a place of imaginings or 'supreme fictions', constituting a counter-realm to the real, freed of the constraints of teleology and functionalism.[23] From this, poetry emerges as the possibility of a human liberation, a place of purification and renewal of the imagining mind, and a place also where, without condition, the mind can touch the tap-root of all experience. For Stevens, poetry represents a bulwark against 'the pressure of reality' which he understands to be not only materialism and commercialism of the modern era, but also an increasing tendency towards violence.[24] It places imagination on equal terms with reality, but 'the imagination gives to everything that it touches a peculiarity, and it seems to me that the peculiarity of the imagination is nobility'.[25] This nobility of the imagination is 'a violence from within that protects us from a violence from without. It is the imagination pressing back against the pressure of reality. It seems, in the last analysis, to have something to do with our self-preservation; and that, no doubt, is why the expression of it, the sounds of its words, helps us to live our lives'.[26]

e. Words that offer another kind of experience

As reflection upon experience, the poem also offers the reader the experience of itself: its own world as distinct from the 'other' world of which it is an accidental reflex. It is this which leads Robert Frost to speak of 'a better wildness of logic than inconsequence'. For the logic of the poem 'is backward, in retrospect, after the act. It must be felt more than seen ahead in prophecy. It must be a revelation, or a series of revelations, as much for the poet as for the reader'.[27] The special experience of the poem is one akin to love, for it 'begins in delight and ends in wisdom'.[28]

Abstracted experience can itself be experience, one akin to our experience of the ordinary world, though freed from it. We grow from it and are increased by it, gaining in wisdom. We can say then that the paths of a poem are for the reader a journeying into his or her own memories and associations, while being confronted with the thoughts, emotions and inner personal reality of another. In reading it, we encounter the interpretative parameters of our own self, structured on the experience of another. And so, like ordinary experience, it takes us in directions we cannot predict, marked with contingency and mortality; as Lorca put it in his *Theory and Function of the Duende,* 'the magical quality of a poem consists in its being always possessed by the *duende* [sense of the presence of death], so that whoever beholds it is baptized with dark water'.[29] But as abstracted experience, removed from the world and set up over against the world, the poet's imagination 'becomes the light in the minds of others' (Wallace Stevens).[30] It changes our experience of the world and thus the nature of the world itself. Indeed, in Bakhtin's phrase, art and life are held together in a relation of mutual *answerability* so that 'inspiration that ignores life and is itself ignored by life is not inspiration but a state of possession'.[31] The imaginative experience which poetry offers is a form of purification, in which the generative powers of the mind are returned to their own source and made available in a new way for the formation of our worlds. This is a process akin to the purification of the blood in the aorta, whereby the old blood is purged of its toxins and, as Paul Celan has it, made 'bright' for the furtherance of life.[32]

f. Words that are their own truth

The release of the imagination, and resistance to 'the pressure of reality', leads also to a sense of the 'truth' of poetry. But A. E. Housman's remark that 'poetry is not the thing said, but a way of saying it' should serve to remind us that the concept of poetic truth is necessarily a complex one.[33] Something of the same is conveyed by McLeish's adage that a poem should not mean but be.[34] W. H. Auden has criticized this latter phrase, saying: 'This is not quite accurate. In a poem, as distinct from many other kinds of verbal societies, meaning and being are identical. A poem might be called a pseudo-person. Like a person it is unique and addresses the reader personally [...] like a natural being, and unlike a historical person, it cannot lie'.[35] The claim that the poem has its own being is simultaneously the claim that somehow it stands above or beyond the world, and represents a second world, whose truth is both address and *aletheia*, or unrevealedness: the absence of falsehood.

The truth of poetry is its own being, as a sovereign hermeneutical space. The attempt to dragoon poets and their work into the functionalities of crudely political, socio-economic (or religious!) ideologies, cuts at the heart of the spontaneity and freedom of the poetic word, and European cultural history is littered with feeble paeons to establishment or ideology, explicitly coerced (as in the case of Mandelstam) or implicitly so (as in the work of some English Poet Laureates). The right precisely to resist accommodation to other kinds of discourse is part of the very essence of poetry as motion, and free generative play. Nor can the poet use the poem to articulate his or her feelings too directly. The creation of a successful poem requires a certain displacement, or even personal self-discipline (*ascesis*) on the part of the poet, as he or she seeks for what T. S. Eliot called 'objective correlatives' or 'significant emotion', that is, 'emotion which has its life in the poem and not in the history of the poet.'[36] Precisely because the poem exists as its own world, rather than serving merely as an interpretation of the empirical world, there can be no hegemony in the way that it is read. The poem offers the possibility of a multiplicity of interpretations and appropriations, and its very fecundity, 'the wonder of its unexpected supply' (Robert Frost) subverts any easy closure of interpretation.[37]

g. Words that create

In light of modern poetry's claim to be both 'revelation' and 'truth', it is no wonder that poetry has increasingly seemed to take on aspects of self-understanding previously reserved for the distinctively 'religious'. This is already apparent in the work of Mallarmé, who turns from his Christian faith to the new faith of poetry. Hugo Friedrich has remarked on the increasing trend towards a form of religious inwardness and 'transcendentality' in modern poetry, and notes the occurrence of the motif of angels which are however 'angels without God and without a message'.[38] For Michael Hamburger, 'a whole genealogy of such angels could be traced from Rimbaud to Stefan George, Rilke, Wallace Stevens and Rafael Alberti'.[39]

Among the religious, pseudo-religious or para-religious elements within modern poetry we could cite the notion of poet as creator and of his work as a *creatio ex nihilo*. This is originally a Romantic idea, and on this theme Gary Giddes quotes Byron's remark, ' 'Tis to create, and in creating live, a being more intense, that we endow with form our fancy, gaining as we give the life we image'.[40] The creative bringing of order within the poem to what is inchoate, fragmented and conflictual is the very essence of the function of the poem as what Bakhtin calls the *consummation* of our life and experience, or what for Rilke is *Auftrag*, that is our calling or task.[41] This reconciliation or integration of diverse energies within the body of the poem represents in itself a kind of release so that, as Wallace Stevens has it: 'after one has abandoned belief in God, poetry is the essence which takes its place as life's redemption'.[42]

It is finally the centrality of language and the supreme excess of language which poetry represents that lends it such a quality of the numinous. The ability to use language is in some sense a defining human quality, and so poetry is 'not an art or branch of art, it's something more. If what distinguishes us from other species is speech, then poetry, which is the supreme linguistic operation, is our anthropological, indeed genetic goal' (Joseph Brodsky).[43] Only in poetry is language used in the fullness of all its possibilities: referential, creative, phonemic. In Bakhtin's words: '(L)anguage reveals all of its possibilities only in poetry, since here maximal demands are placed upon it: all its aspects are strained to the extreme, and reach their ultimate limits. Poetry squeezes, as it were, all the juices from language, and language exceeds itself here'.[44] In poetry we encounter in an unparalleled way something essential to our own nature: the ability to govern language – as form – and to master reality – as content given or made available in form. And it also adds something essential to our experience of being alive, namely the sense of being answerable to and involved in fluid processes of creation and meaning which transcend the parameters of the self and locate us, 'carnivalistically' in Bakhtin's pregnant phrase, in the broader contexts of world and existence.

3. Towards the relation of theology and poetry

As language that is 'set apart', mysterious in its genesis, enchanting in its effects and burdened with an excess of meaning, as language which appears to speak in a revelatory fashion to the heart of things, as a second world, as a way of speaking which defies any appropriation by imperatives other than its own, poetry appears to offer a real analogy to the language of Christians and, above all, to the wisdom-speech that is theology. But for all these striking affinities, which are so valuable for a fundamental theology that seeks to give an account of faith for those outside it, the distinctions between poetry and theology need also to be pointed out. Otherwise there is a risk that theology itself will simply become a matter of language alone: a kind of poetry.

a. Differences with inspiration

We can see real differences with respect to inspiration, for instance, since although the poet may be said to experience a degree of dispossession through inspiration, the dispossession of the theologian is emphatically a coming into possession by another, by God as Spirit or illumining grace. And although the reader of the poem is called to give herself over to the aesthetic encounter with a world that is fundamentally shaped by the experience and feelings of another, the theologian is an individual who is summoned in the whole of her personal existence to participate fully in the trinitarian ground from which that sacred speech emerges. The theologian is herself to become part of the 'poem' she delivers. For the poet, on the other hand, there is no new dispensation, nor can there be, for the deity served by the poet is no more than a cypher – however graphic – for the mystery of the provenance of poetry.

b. Differences about revelation

We must also be careful in applying the term 'revelation' for the linguistic disclosure which is at the heart of the poetic text. Although both poetic and religious disclosure can be said to be not so much phenomenal as grounding the possibility of appearance (*phainesthai*) as such, as constituting a second world and thus allowing the emergence of a realm of new possibilities of experience and existence, revelation as a religious term in its highest manifestations implies some kind of transcendent communicative act, founded upon a divine communicative intentionality. Such a communicative agency is alien to poetry except in its most abruptly oracular forms. And if the reception of a poem by a sensitive reader can indeed have something of the force of a revelation, if we are opened up by poetry, confronted with new imaginings, associations and semantic possibilities, then we should remember that poetry in the final analysis is 'a revelation in words by means of the words' (Wallace Stevens).[45] What is 'revealed' as such then in good poetry is the generative function of language itself: the infinite play of its own free possibilities.

c. Different kinds of 'strangeness'

If both poetry and theology is language 'made strange', then the measure of the deviation is, arguably, the extent to which the language of poets is answerable to the mystery of its own genesis (as muse) and to the very particular discipline of the poetic art (as *technê*), while the deviation of theology is the extent to which theological language is answerable to God and to understandings that are illumined by processes of grace. This same distinction manifests also with regard to the respective types of metaphoricity which they embody. In the case of theology, metaphoricity disrupts normal referencing with respect to the world in order to speak of what is given to us *from beyond* the world. Theological language is human speech that is configured and refigured in response to a divine advent; and its expressivity is one which is ordered to that advent. Poetic metaphoricity on the other hand functions entirely *within* the world, since language referring to language, revelation 'in words by means of the words', never leaves the realm of the created, for all its generative fecundity and gifting of new possibilities of perceiving. Indeed, given the different relation between language and world that operates in theology and poetry, we can say that poetic metaphoricity determines the relation between poetry and world as one which is *aesthetic*, predicated upon irony and a horizontal perspective. Theological metaphoricity on the other hand determines the relation between theology and world as one which is *critical*, predicated upon judgement and a vertical perspective. If then with respect to inspiration we can say that poetry suffers a dispossession without coming into the possession of another, so too we can say that poetry delivers a revelation, but it is revelation without content.

d. Differences about creation and salvation

In the light of these distinctions, we should examine also the poet's claim to create. For W. H. Auden, poetic creativity is only 'analogous' to divine creation and 'is not an imitation, for were it so, the poet would be able to create like God *ex nihilo*; instead, he requires pre-existing occasions of feeling and a pre-existing language out of which to create'.[46] A necessary part of creation is the establishing of order, and it is of creative ordering that W. H. Auden prefers to speak in an extended metaphor of the poem as a 'verbal society' (perhaps making skilful use of motifs from Augustine's *City of God*). The poem itself stands for the 'form' of the Church constructed via a process of election by the ecclesial-poetic integration of the raw elements of life or humanity:

> The nature of the final poetic order is the outcome of a dialectical struggle between the recollected occasions of feeling and the verbal system. As a society the verbal system is actively coercive upon the occasions it is attempting to embody; what it cannot embody truthfully it excludes... In a successful poem, society and community are in one order and the system may love itself because the feelings which it embodies are all members of the same community, loving each other and it. A poem may fail in two ways; it may exclude too much (banality), or attempt to embody more than one community at once (disorder)'.[47]

Indeed, Auden warns against the explicit appropriation of Christian language at this point: 'Every beautiful poem presents an analogy to the forgiveness of sins; an analogy, not an imitation, because it is not evil intentions which are repented of and pardoned but contradictory feelings which the poet surrenders to the poem in which they are reconciled'.[48]

And he points too to the danger that poetic beauty will be confused for goodness:

> The effect of [poetic] beauty, therefore, is good to the degree that through its analogies, the goodness of created existence, the historical fall into unfreedom and disorder, and the possibility of regaining paradise through repentance and forgiveness are recognised. Its effect is evil to the degree that beauty is taken, not as analogous to, but identical with goodness, so that the artist regards himself or is regarded by others as God, the pleasure of beauty taken for the joy of Paradise, and the conclusion drawn that, since all is well in the work of art, all is well in history. But all is not well there'.[49]

This abrupt conclusion to the Augustinian metaphor of the poem as Augustine's transhistorical 'other city', is not a contesting of the poetic as idolatry (as we do find at times in the Christian tradition), but is rather a warning against a Nietzschean appropriation of poems as 'saving fictions', which sing the conscience to sleep and persuade us against an active and ethical involvement with the world. What we can discern here, then, once again is the difference between poetry and religion worked out in terms of a distance that is, for the former, aesthetic and for the latter, critique.

e. Differences about the loss of self

It is in terms of the ethical and the personal then that we must seek the locus of the radical distinction between poetry and theology, for all their symmetries. Christianity has a fundamental concern with the ethical, understood as a self-dispossessing ethics. Kenosis (self-emptying) needs a language of existential self-knowledge and self-possession if the kenotic self is to know itself to be put at risk for the sake of the other. Although the openness of reading, which Cixous refers to as 'a relentless process of de-selfing, de-egoization', has a kenotic structure in some degree, it is finally not that of a Christian ethics of enacted dispossession for the sake of a concrete other.[50]

While I recognize that language is central to the way in which we construct and experience the world as individuals, language also remains fundamentally a form of social and *interpersonal* communication and exchange. It is a sign system that is used by speech-agents, who thereby relate with other speech-agents in the construction (or destruction) of a common social reality. While language can in itself be generative, in accordance for instance with Ricoeur's view of the text as a form of 'generative poetics', and thus serve to refigure our world, it remains a phenomenon – albeit displaced through text – which presupposes a human speaker. We cannot unthink the one who speaks, the one who is performed in speech relations, whose self-possessing existence is the precondition for any self-dispossessing ethical act. For theology to retreat into language *per se* is to risk that ethical subject, and to risk also the divine self-communication to us through the self-dispossession of God for our sake in Jesus Christ. To take Jesus as 'essentially a linguistic and poetic reality' (John Milbank) then is to risk trading Jesus as the divine-human person in whom God speaks, for Jesus as a figure of speech.[51]

f. Differences with the diversity of meaning

This focus upon the singularity of *personal* as distinct from *textual* or *linguistic* revelation is apparent also in the significant difference between the seemingly unending play of interpretation of literary texts and the canonization of texts and closure of interpretation which we find in Christian tradition. Although the cultural expressions of Christianity show precisely this unending character, the credal texts of Christianity command a consensus of response and understanding. The *credimus* contrasts fundamentally with the free flowing diversity of meanings and form which characterize the reception of most if not all cultural artefacts. Within the Christian economy resistance to closure manifests not as a multiplication of meanings at the level of the horizontal, but rather as a vanishing into depth at the level of the vertical. The divine-human object of our understanding escapes what Levinas calls 'the hegemony of comprehension' not by a rapid Ovidian series of metamorphoses, but because the surface of that revelation – what David Ford, adapting Levinas, calls 'the face of God' – constantly dissolves into ever greater depth.[52] In Christian hermeneutics, we remain grasped by the personal mystery that underlies the text, of whom the text speaks, who speaks with us from

within the text, and we do so within a relatively stable unity of interpretation which is enriched but not fragmented by its diversity.

g. Differences in relation to history

This brings us finally to an assessment of how poetics leads us to the
threshold of theology but not beyond; and the issue is that of history. The
poem does at some subtle level remain tied to the empirical realm; that is
the foundation of its metaphoricity.[53] But in general, the poem is a semi-
otic system, or 'world', which is set up against the realm of ordinary
perception and existence. Abstracted from the 'real' world, it is in an
important sense other than it. Theology, on the other hand, if it is not to
become a purely rhetorical, de-mythologized space, has deep obligations
to history and to historical belief. This again is to reinstitute agency, without which we shall lose sight of that divine-human agency which was
exercised by Jesus in his self-giving for us and the commensurate divine-
human agency which is the condition of faith.

The otherness of theology as metaphor is not given by a stratum of
residual reference to ordinary objects in our world, therefore, as with
poetry, but rather by a point at which metaphor and empirical experience
converge. This occurs in our recognition of who Christ is which, for all
the complexities of the resurrection narratives and the nature of faith,
entails belief which is historical at its core. For as Kierkegaard noted, it is
only historical belief that can become truly dialectical, allowing us to
glimpse the coming into existence of the Infinite Paradox in history. And
only by undergoing what Kierkegaard called the 'passion of thought' can
our own existence become truly 'historical' in turn, as we are conformed
to God's revelation to us in Christ.

It is not, therefore, that a theological poetics lacks historicity, but
rather that historicity in the sense developed above is *the very condition of
the poeticity of a theological poetics*. The radical and dialectical antithe-
ses of Christian faith – of incarnation and Trinity, personally made
manifest to us in the hypostatic union – are the consummation, overflow

and 'passion' of human existence itself. Such an existence is accomplished in every form of human feeling, thinking and speaking.

Notes to Chapter 6

[1] John Milton, *Paradise Lost*, Book I, lines 17-26.

[2] Karl Rahner, *Foundations of the Christian Faith: an Introduction to the Idea of Christianity*, transl. William V. Dych (London: Darton, Longman and Todd, 1978).

[3] In the spirit of von Balthasar, Rino Fisichella (*La rivilazione: evento e credibilitá* [Bologna: Edizioni Dehoniane Bologna, 1985]) sees fundamental theology as based on the trinitarian mystery as revealed in Christ and the church.

[4] 'Coextensive de la théologie tout entière': Henri Bouillard, 'La tâche actuelle de la théologie fondamentale', repr. in idem, *Vérité du Christianisme* (Paris: Desclée, 1989), pp. 149-179 (here 178).

[5] On the different presuppositions of apologetics and fundamental theology, see Gerald O'Collins, *Fundamental Theology* (London: Darton, Longman and Todd, 1981), p. 23. But although these two differ by virtue of their respective contexts, they both draw upon a process of reflexion.

[6] René Latourelle, 'A New Image of Fundamental Theology', in René Latourelle and Gerald O'Collins (eds), *Problems and Perspectives of Fundamental Theology* (New York/Ramsey: Paulist Press, 1982), pp. 37-58 (here p. 37).

[7] Gerhard Larcher, 'Subjekt – Kunst – Geschichte. Chancen einer Annäherung von Fundamentaltheologie und Ästhetik', in Klaus Müller (ed.), *Fundamentaltheologie – Fluchtlinien und gegenwärtige Herausforderungen* (Regensburg: Verlag Friedrich Pustet, 1998), pp. 299-321.

[8] In his *Gott als Autor: zu einer poietologischen Theologie* (Tübingen: Mohr Siebeck, 1999), Oswald Bayer develops a theology of God's creative language as a 'Poesie des Versprechens', combining speech act theory with Hamann's identification of poetry with prophecy. See also Alex Stock, *Poetische Dogmatik* (Paderborn: Schöningh, vol. 1, 1995; vol. 2, 1996; vol. 3, 1998).

[9] Viktor Shklovsky first discusses his concept of the *priem ostranenia*, or 'strategy of alienation', as poetological principle in his articles *Potebnia* (1916) and *Iskusstvo kak priem* (1917), published in *Poetika*, Petrograd, 1919, pp. 3-6 and pp. 101-114 (discussed in Victor Ehrlich, *Russian Formalism*, 3rd ed. [New Haven: Yale University Press, 1981], pp. 76-78). John Milbank similarly takes poeticity as a creatively alienating force as a key notion for theology today in his

work *The Word Made Strange. Theology, Language Culture* (Oxford: Blackwell, 1997); see in particular pp. 24-32.

[10] Roman Jakobson, 'Linguistics and Poetics', idem, *Selected Writings*, III (The Hague, Paris, New York: Mouton Publishers, 1981), pp. 18-51 (here pp. 21-2).

[11] Ibid., p. 27.

[12] What this means concretely is that where the poetic function does not apply, we might say of a sleeping child: 'the child/ infant/ boy/ girl/ son/ daughter snoozes/ sleeps/ dozes/ slumbers'. Whichever one of these options we choose will depend on what seems most appropriate at the time (do we know the sex of the child?), and the chief criterion will be efficiency of communication within a specific speech context. Where the poetic function does apply however, then we shall have to take into account the semantics and phonology of what precedes and follows this statement within the overall unit of utterance. If it is followed by the words 'and the father snores', for instance, then we may opt for 'son' and 'snoozes' ('the son snoozes and the father snores'). 'Son' picks up 'father' in a way that 'boy' does not, and 'snoozes' seems to be appropriate for an infant in the way that 'snores' is for a full grown man. Thus perhaps we see the future man in the sleeping child (and the child in the man?).

[13] Poetic effects are not confined to such texts however and can be found in ordinary language; see Deborah Tannen, *Talking Voices. Repetition, dialogue, and imagery in conversational discourse* (Cambridge: Cambridge University Press, 1989), especially pp. 36-97. An argument for the interdependence of poetics and semiotics can be found in L. Dolezel and K. Hausenblas, *Poetika i Stilistika*, in D. Davie, (ed.), *Poetics, polish, russian* (Gravenhage: Mouton & Co, 1961), pp. 39-52.

[14] Edward Stankiewicz, 'Poetic and non-Poetic Language in their Interrelation', in Davie, *Poetics*, pp. 11-23 (here p. 15).

[15] Ibid.

[16] Northrop Frye, *Anatomy of Criticism* (Princeton: Princeton University Press, 1957), p. 81.

[17] Stefan George, *Gedichte* (Stuttgart: Ernst Klett, 1983), p. 64 (my translation).

[18] 'Dichtung ist worthafte Stiftung des Seins': Martin Heidegger, 'Hölderlin und das Wesen der Dichtung', *Erläuterungen zu Hölderlins Dichtung*, Gesamtausgabe, IV (Frankfurt: Klostermann, 1981), pp. 33-48; here p. 41.

[19] Paul Ricoeur, 'Toward a Hermeneutic of the Idea of Revelation', in Lewis S. Mudge (ed.), Paul Ricoeur, *Essays on Biblical Interpretation* (London: SPCK, 1981), pp. 73-118 (here p. 100).

[20] Ibid., p. 101.

[21] '[I]n poetry the rationale of metaphor belongs to another order of experience than science... the logic of metaphor is so organically entrenched in pure sensibility...' Quoted in James Scully, *Modern Poetics* (New York: McGraw-Hill, 1965), pp.161-2.

[22] Ricoeur, 'Towards a Hermeneutic', p. 101.

[23] Wallace Stevens, 'The Noble Rider and the Sound of Words', in idem, *The Necessary Angel* (New York: Alfred A. Knopf, 1951), pp. 3-36 (here p. 31).

[24] Ibid., pp. 19-20.

[25] Ibid., p. 33.

[26] Ibid., p. 36.

[27] Robert Frost, 'The Figure a Poem makes', in idem, *Complete Poems* (London: Jonathan Cape, 1967), pp. 17-20 (here p. 19).

[28] Ibid., p. 18.

[29] Federico Garcia Lorca, *Obras Completas*, I (Madrid: Aguilar, 1980), p. 1106: 'La virtud mágica del poema consiste en estar siempre enduandado para bautizar con agua oscura a todos los que lo miran'.

[30] Stevens, 'The Noble Rider', p. 29.

[31] M. M. Bakhtin, 'Art and Answerability', in M. Holquist and V. Liapunov (eds), *Art and Answerability: Early Philosophical Essays by M. M. Bakhtin* (Austin: University of Texas Press, 1990), pp. 1-3 (here p. 2).

[32] See the poem *Nah, im Aortenbogen,* in Paul Celan, *Gedichte,* II (Frankfurt am Main: Suhrkamp Verlag, 1975), p. 202: 'Nah, im Aortenbogen,/ im Hellblut:/ das Hellwort.' ('Near, in the bend of the aorta, in the bright blood: the bright word.').

[33] A. E. Housman, *The Name and Nature of Poetry* (Cambridge: Cambridge University Press, 1933), p. 37.

[34] Quoted in Michael Hamburger, *The Truth of Poetry* (London: Anvil Press, 1982), p. 34.

[35] W. H. Auden, 'The Virgin and the Dynamo', in *The Dyer's Hand* (New York: Random House, 1948), pp. 61-71 (here p. 68)

[36] T. S. Eliot, 'Tradition and the Individual Talent', in idem, *Selected Essays* (London: Faber and Faber, 1932), pp. 13-22.

[37] Frost, 'The Figure a Poem makes', p. 18.

[38] Quoted in Hamburger, *The Truth of Poetry*, p. 28.

[39] Ibid.

[40] Gary Giddes (ed.), *Twentieth Century Poetry and Poetics*, 4th. edn (Toronto: Oxford University Press, 1996), p. xvi.

[41] Rainer Maria Rilke, *Werke in drei Bänden*, I (Frankfurt am Main: Insel Verlag, 1966), p. 442.

[42] Wallace Stevens, 'Adagia', in idem, *Opus Posthumous* (London: Faber and Faber, 1957), pp. 157-180 (here p. 158).

[43] Joseph Brodsky, quoted in Geddes (ed.), *Twentieth Century Poetry*, pp. xv-xvi.

[44] M. M. Bakhtin, 'Content, Material and Form in Verbal Art', in Holquist and Liapunov (eds), *Art and Answerability*, p. 294.

[45] Stevens, 'The Noble Rider', p. 33.

[46] Auden, 'The Virgin and the Dynamo', p. 70.

[47] Ibid., pp. 68-69.

[48] Ibid., p. 71.

[49] Ibid.

[50] Deborah Jenson (ed.), and Sarach Cornell (transl.), *Hélène Cixous, Coming to Writing and other Essays* (Cambridge, Mass.: Harvard University Press, 1991), p. 156; quoted in Graham Ward, 'Kenosis and naming: beyond analogy and towards *allegoria amoris*', in Paul Heelas, (ed.), *Religion, Modernity and Postmodernity* (Oxford: Blackwell, 1998), p. 235.

[51] John Milbank, *The Word Made Strange* (Oxford: Blackwell, 1997), p. 3.

[52] David F. Ford, *Self and Salvation* (Cambridge: Cambridge University Press, 1999), pp. 193-202.

[53] In 'The Poet as Fool and Priest', *Journal of English Literary History*, vol. 25, no. 4, (1956), pp. 279-298, Sigurd Burckhardt argues that since words can never be totally severed from their meanings '[t]here can be no non-representational poetry; the very medium forbids it' (p. 280).

Part II
Contexts

7

'The Sacred Sound through Which All Creation Resounds': The Appeal of Hildegard of Bingen

MARK ATHERTON

1. Introduction: Hildegard in her time and ours

In a book entitled *The Dynamic of Tradition*, the Anglican writer A. M. Allchin asks his readers to consider the continuities which link apparently divided centuries. He urges the need for 'an ecumenism in time',[1] in other words 'a serious exchange, an active encounter between the Church of today and the Church of former ages'. He then proposes the following scenario: 'To a well-educated Englishman of the seventeenth, eighteenth or nineteenth century, it would have seemed mere folly to suppose that an uneducated woman of the middle ages, living the restricted and unnatural life of a hermit, would have been able to give us any serious illumination on the predicament of man or the nature of God.'[2] The woman whom A. M. Allchin has in mind is the English writer Julian of Norwich, but his words are equally applicable to the subject of this chapter, Hildegard of Bingen in the Rhineland, who in her music and her writings offers an ideal opportunity for the kind of 'active encounter' that he finds so useful and necessary.

In today's world Hildegard of Bingen has appeal, an appeal which rests principally on her songs and music, but also on her theological writings. Her music, unheard and unsung for centuries, was published in the twentieth century and is now frequently performed and widely available.[3] As for her visionary theological writings, these have tended to be neglected until recently but are now admired for their wisdom and learning,[4] for their inclusivity and emphasis on wholeness – their 'Creation spirituality'.[5] Her medical writings and herbal remedies have also attracted enthusiasts in some circles.[6] Of great interest too is her life story – this biography of a woman asserting herself in a male world is often heard in radio talks, plays, novels, and lectures.[7]

My question in this chapter, however, is this: was Hildegard famous in her own time for the same reasons? What aspects of her work appealed to her contemporaries?[8]

For the first half of her life, her work received no responses and no recognition from her contemporaries. Hildegard herself seems to have suppressed her visionary experiences, her theological knowledge and possibly her music as well. It was only on the death of the strict ascetic abbess Jutta, at the convent on Mount Disibod (Disibodenberg) that Hildegard felt a pressure from within to take up her new vocation. She became abbess, and made her own appeal, an appeal for support, at first locally, then more widely afield. Even as abbess, she still needed permission to put her visions into writing.

2. The letter to Bernard: a new vision of unity

In 1146 she wrote to Bernard of Clairvaux. At the time, Bernard was a celebrated spiritual writer and head of the important Cistercian Order; arguably he was the most influential person in western Christendom; even the Pope, Eugenius III, was a former pupil and protegé. I would like to look in detail at this important letter, as a way of gaining access to the twelfth-century world in which Hildegard lived and worked.[9]

We recall that the letter is in Latin, which was not only the language of the Church but also the international language of the day, studied thoroughly for its grammar and rhetoric,[10] and used mostly by men in the male-dominated worlds of law and administration.[11] We note also the structure of the letter, with its salutation, exordium, narration, petition and conclusion: the classic arrangement as taught in the schools. Hildegard has had help. Although most of the words are undoubtedly Hildegard's, the format should probably be ascribed to Volmar – her scribe and secretary, a monk from the local monastery at Disibodenberg. The date of the letter is clear from the reference to the Second Crusade, for which Eugenius had enlisted Bernard's support: Bernard had gone on preaching tours urging men to take up the cross for the defence of the Holy Land.

In a typical epistolary salutation Hildegard emphasizes Bernard's fame and her own unworthiness, before moving to her main point.

Despite her minimal education, she claims sophisticated theological visions which come to her in Latin and not German; she also claims to have direct access to interpretations of the Bible and other books. But she is worried and 'speaks as one in doubt'. As a mere uneducated woman, she is uncertain whether to 'say these things openly' or whether to keep quiet.

So far the letter is standard, and it has been shown from parallel cases that men too wrote similarly humble letters to their superiors asking for permission to undertake a work of writing.[12] But consider the conclusion. Hildegard closes her letter with a petition the like of which Bernard had almost certainly never seen or heard before, appealing to him in a series of injunctions, some conventional, others new and strange. She entreats him not only 'by the brightness of the Father and by his miraculous Word', a familiar idea, but also 'by the sacred sound through which all creation resounds', a more unusual concept; and perhaps even more startling she makes her entreaty 'by the Word from which all the world was created, by the height of the Father who through the sweet power of green vigour sent the Word to the Virgin's womb where it took on flesh like the honey in the honeycomb'.

What does she mean by all this? The 'sacred sound' implies an idea of music as an essential part of the basic fabric of the cosmos. A whole world of ideas lies behind this short phrase.[13] The expression 'green vigour' (*viriditas* or 'greenness' in the original Latin) is similarly rich in connotations. In Hildegard's ecological way of thinking, 'greenness' means the force which gives life to the body and renewal in nature. It also has a theological significance: firstly as the power of the Spirit at work in the world and secondly as the moral force that gives life and fruitfulness to human actions.

With Hildegard's later work in mind, we can see the significance of such metaphors and concepts; they are the first expressions in writing of a new Christian thinker who already by 1146 had her own theological system. The final phrases of the letter to Bernard are well-formed thoughts, the product of her visionary experiences and meditative devotion over a period of many years. They point to a musician with her own philosophy of music; they reveal a writer endowed with the gift of creating fresh and startling images and ideas. Moreover, they are expressed in a rough and ready Latin which she had learned apparently without formal study – while singing the psalms and prayers of the Latin monastic services in the daily life of her convent.

Bernard was impressed, and his short reply was positive. This is surprising. Bernard was convinced of the need for absolute doctrinal unity in the Church, and by the liberal standards of today his level of tolerance was poor: a few years before, at the Council of Sens, he had secured the prohibition of the teachings of the great Paris philosopher Peter Abelard and his supporter Arnold of Brescia, and at the time of Hildegard's letter he was also agitating for the condemnation of the doctrines of Gilbert of Poitiers, a theologian who had made some unorthodox statements on the unity of the Godhead.[14]

Eventually, a commission was sent to investigate Hildegard's work at Disibodenberg and report their findings. At the Synod of Trier in the winter of 1147-8, some passages from Hildegard's writings (possibly some sections of the book of visions known by its Latin title *Scivias*) were heard and considered by Pope Eugenius III and others. Bernard of Clairvaux spoke in her favour, and papal approval was given for the work to continue. It is interesting to note that Eugenius in the same period also approved another difficult literary work, the *Cosmographia* of the Paris-trained scholar Bernard Silvester. Both the *Cosmographia* and the *Scivias* are large-scale allegories concerned, among many other themes, with the relationship of the human being to the divine order of creation. We will consider the early parts of *Scivias* in the final part of this chapter. First the music.

3. Hildegard's music: a new song

Hildegard's music must have been discussed at the Synod of Trier, at least briefly. As early as 1148, in a letter to Hildegard from Odo of Soisson, a master at the schools of Paris, we learn of her activities as a composer. As we shall see, Odo is mainly concerned in his letter with Hildegard's opinion on Gilbert of Poitiers, but his preliminary remarks touch on various matters of relevance to Hildegard's music:[15] 'They say that you are taken up in the heavenly places and see many things which you bring out in your writing; also, that you bring forth the melodies of a new song although you have not studied any of these things.'

It is stated quite clearly here by an acquaintance of Hildegard that she was accomplished as a musician, although she had not studied music. The same claim is made in the autobiographical section of the *Life of Hildegard*: 'But I also composed and sang songs with melodies in praise of God and the saints, again without any human instruction, although I had never learnt neums or singing.'[16] Hildegard had not studied musical notation – the 'neums' which indicate changes of pitch in medieval manuscripts – but it seems unlikely that a nun who took part every day in the offices of the liturgy had never learnt 'any singing'; presumably she means that she lacked formal knowledge of choral music, in the same way that she had not officially studied any formal grammar.

In this respect, the actual content of her music is informative. Hildegard's musical technique is so different from the norms of Gregorian plainchant that her claim must be taken seriously. It seems she really had not undertaken any study of the traditional forms. Instead, guided by her inspiration, she was following her own path. These 'melodies of a new song' (to use Odo's phrase) often range over two octaves, frequently leaping suddenly from a low note to a high and varying their phrases and motifs. Although they are based on the accepted patterns of the liturgy, particularly the antiphon, they have a surprising spontaneity and exuberance.[17] Furthermore, the harmony and melody are shaped carefully to the form and content of the text. Hildegard chooses an appropriate scale or mode to the theme of the song, as heard for instance in the following two antiphons composed for the dedication of a church:[18]

O virgo ecclesia[19]

O virgin church, you must lament
that the most savage wolf
has seized your children from your side.
Woe to the cunning serpent!
But how precious is the blood of the Saviour!
In the banner of the king[20]

he has pledged the church to himself
so that she now seeks her children.

Nunc gaudeant [21]

May the maternal heart of the Church now rejoice
that her sons have been gathered to her lap
in heavenly harmony.
Therefore, shameful serpent, you are confounded,
because those you thought were in your heart
now shine in the blood of God's son.
Praise to you, King on high, alleluia.

The first antiphon is a lament that fierce enemies (the wolf and the serpent) have assailed the church and seized her children, while the second
rejoices that the church has finally triumphed and gathered together her
sons in heavenly harmony – in itself a fitting musical metaphor for the
message to be proclaimed. In each case the mood of the song is captured
fittingly by the melody.

Another technique Hildegard consciously employs to match together
text and music is that of 'word-painting'; a good example is the melisma
(i.e. the lingering of the melody) on the word *sonante* ('sounding forth')
at the end of the song *Cum processit*:[22]

O laudabilis Maria,
celo rutilante
et in laudibus sonante.

The way the final word *sonante* ('sounding forth') relates to the theme of
the song is best understood in the context of the whole piece, which
translates as follows:[23]

When creation came forth from the finger of God
fashioned in God's image
created of mixed blood
along the exile-path of Adam's fall:
then the elements received

the joys of life.
O Mary, worthy of praise.
As heavens shine red
they sound forth your praise.

In the very compressed patterns of thought in this song Hildegard combines ideas of creation, fall and exile with the notion that the four elements (out of which all matter is made) also participate in the joys of life and the praise of Mary the mother of Christ. The final word of the Latin text *sonante*, drawn out in the melody for a relatively long period of time and rhyming as it does with *rutilante* ('reddening'), effectively summarizes the pattern of thought. In this way, the idea of 'the sacred sound through which all creation resounds', of which Hildegard wrote to Bernard of Clairvaux, is embodied in the external form of both the text and the music itself.

It will be clear from the above that Hildegard's 'new song' is not simply a new style of music set to traditional words. Hildegard's texts are also new and innovatory, and they reflect her distinctive ideas on the purposes of music in the spiritual life of the Church. On this point, there is an interesting passage in the final vision of her book, *Scivias*. Hildegard writes here a kind of musical morality play, later to be developed into the famous *Ordo virtutum* or 'Play of the Virtues'.[24] Her own summary of the events of this play is as follows (*Scivias* III, 13):

> Then I saw a bright layer of air in which I heard wonderfully diverse types of music within the aforementioned symbols: songs of praise for the joys of the citizens of heaven who persevere steadfastly on the way of truth, songs of lament for those who had to be called back to the praise of such joys, and songs of exhortation for the Virtues who urge each other to secure the salvation of the people struggling against the wiles of the devil. But the Virtues compel the faithful people finally to pass from their sins through penance to the heavenly heights.[25]

The notion of 'wonderfully diverse types of music' in the quotation above illustrates very well Hildegard's moral and spiritual purposes in making music to supplement the liturgy.

For Hildegard, therefore, the daily practice of music was essential, and any disruption to that process could hardly even be contemplated. This did in fact happen towards the end of her life, during the row over an interdict (a ban on singing the liturgy) imposed on the Rupertsberg abbey in 1179.[26] It is Hildegard's correspondence with the Mainz prelates who had imposed the interdict that provides further insights into her ideas on music.[27] In Hildegard's theology, the human soul is 'symphonic'; music is part of the profound nature of the spirit, by which a human being can recall the heavenly harmony and 'divine sweetness and praise by which with the angels, Adam was made jubilant in God before he fell'. And just as David called for every man and woman to praise the Lord in the Psalms (the basis of the liturgy, it should be remembered), so also the prophets of the Old Testament composed different types of songs and used different kinds of musical instruments. The forms and qualities of the instruments themselves, Hildegard asserts, can nurture the listeners as much as the meanings of the words. One remarkable passage in this letter reads like a meditation on the opening ideas of the song *Cum processit* (with which it should be compared above):

> Eager and wise men imitated the holy prophets, inventing human kinds of harmonized melody by their art, so that they could sing in the delight of their soul; and they adapted their singing to [the notation indicated by] the bending of the finger-joints, as it were recalling that Adam was formed by the finger of God, which is the Holy Spirit, and that in Adam's voice before he fell there was the sound of every harmony and the sweetness of the whole art of music. And if Adam had remained in that condition in which he was formed, human frailty could never endure the power and resonance of that voice.[28]

Music was thus a powerful force in the life of Hildegard's monastery, and, as her writings show, it is an essential force in her theology. Hildegard sent copies of her songs to nearby monasteries, and they were preserved in the memory of later generations of nuns at the Rupertsberg; perhaps surprisingly, however, there is no evidence that the songs had a wide circulation in the later middle ages. Music was important to Hildegard, extremely important, but its importance at the time remained local.[29] For the twelfth century, Hildegard's fame lay elsewhere, and to explore the wider influence Hildegard had on her contemporaries, we must turn now to another major area of her career, her theology, and consider her visionary work, *Scivias*.

4. Hildegard's writings: a new way of seeing

Hildegard's *Scivias* (a title meaning 'Know the Ways'), written in the period 1141-51, is a book of visions with commentary, together forming an encyclopedic survey of salvation history and church doctrine. It would be intriguing to know which part of it was read by Eugenius III at the Synod of Trier in 1147-8. Presumably it was work still in progress, and some clues are given in Hildegard's letter to Odo of Soissons, part of the correspondence mentioned above, which shares a number of themes with the first vision of part two of *Scivias*.[30] In fact very similar themes were being discussed at the Synod of Paris in 1148, when Gilbert of Poitiers was attacked by Bernard of Clairvaux and others for his views on the nature of God. Various passages in *Scivias* II, 2, a vision of the Trinity, emphasize the unity of the Godhead, and can be seen as a response to this debate. The following is typical:

> And just as there are three powers in the glowing heat of a flame, so the one God is in three persons. How is this? The flame consists of splendid brightness, purple vigour and fiery glow. It has a splendid brightness so that it can shine its light, a purple vigour so that it can maintain its existence, and a fiery glow so that it can burn. Consider the Father in the splendid brightness, for he sends out his brightness to the faithful through the goodness of his fatherhood; and in the purple vigour held within the flame and containing its strength, consider the Son, who assumed a body from the Virgin in which the godhead declared its marvels; and in the fiery glow perceive the Holy Spirit, who pours his fire over the minds of believers. But the flame will not be seen if there is no splendid brightness, or purple vigour, or fiery glow; in the same way, God is not worthily honoured in any place where neither the Father, Son, or Holy Spirit are venerated. Therefore just as three powers are discerned in the one flame, so three persons are to be understood in the unity of the Godhead.[31]

Scivias II, 1, a vision of the Fall, also deals with the nature of God, creation and redemption.[32] The theme of the vision is best understood by looking first at the illustration which accompanies this text in the Rupertsberg manuscript of *Scivias*.[33] The top of this attractive and colourful illustration is dominated by a bright sphere, a vibrant series of red, golden and blue concentric circles, so vibrant, in fact, that they appear to break out from the confines of the frame of the picture. This is the Godhead, described in the text as 'a shining fire, unfathomable, inextinguishable, fully alive and existing full of life; with a flame the colour of the air, brightly burning in the gentle breeze'. As Hildegard recounts her vision, the flame begins to glow white, as though a moment of great import has arrived. Glancing from text back to picture, we see, in the middle of the picture below the concentric circles – and taking up about a third of the space – a broad band of night sky filled with white and golden stars and luminaries. This provides the backdrop against which the next part of the cosmic drama is set.

In this night sky, just below the bright sphere and in contact with it, there is a dark sphere containing six images: sun and sky, planets, angels, trees and water, birds, and animals – almost certainly representing the six days of creation.[34] In the corresponding text the speaker declares: 'And suddenly a dark circle of air appeared, huge in size, which struck many blows against the shining flame, and at each blow a spark flew up so that soon the circle of air was brought to completion, and heaven and earth shone forth in the fullness of perfection.' The most dynamic effect in the whole scene is the figure of Christ emerging from the Godhead in a blaze of light to the succour of the man Adam, who has fallen into the darkness after smelling a flower in the top right of the picture. The text tells this story at length, and the ensuing commentary clarifies its meaning and significance. The familiar story of the creation of the heavens and the earth, the story of the fall, and the act of redemption here take on new and striking forms in this combination of vision, text and image, the style of which has been compared to the poetry and painting of William Blake, for like Blake Hildegard gives the impression that *she really saw* what she describes in her vision. This way of writing is also a way of seeing.

Such is the explicit claim she makes. As her opening words say, she is a human being with the 'fragility' of a woman, and 'neither ablaze with

the zeal of strong lions nor learned in their exhalations'. Hildegard professes neither the energy nor the learning of the male scholar, and in this
respect she is very different to Bernard Silvester whose allegorical works
were also approved at the Synod of Trier. She writes *as she sees*, and as
her inspiration, 'the voice from the living flame' directs her:

> Nevertheless you are touched by my light, which touches your inner
> being with fire like the burning sun. Shout and tell! And write down
> these my mysteries which you see and hear in the mystical vision! Do
> not be afraid, but tell the mysteries as you understand them in the spirit,
> as I speak them through you. May they be ashamed who should be
> showing my people the path of justice!

Hildegard is a prophet in the Old Testament tradition, touched by 'fire
like the burning sun', rather like Ezekiel, or like Job and Hosea whom she
cites later in the text of *Scivias* II, 1. As a prophet, she has a social message for her contemporaries; this she expounds in later parts of the
Scivias, in her letters and sermons, and in her later writings. The message
is urgent and demands to be told – it is the 'way of justice'.

Hildegard's teachings and prophetic advice were most sought after,
either in her letters or in the larger visionary writings; from dissemination
of manuscripts and other evidence, the most widely known and discussed
of her works in her own day was *Scivias*. A remark in a letter to a colleague by the contemporary English writer and churchman John of
Salisbury illustrates the point:

> If you do not come on anything else not available to our folk, at least the
> visions and prophecies of the blessed and most famous Hildegard are
> available to you. I hold her in commendation and reverence since Pope
> Eugenius cherished her with an intimate bond of affection. Look care-
> fully too and let me know whether anything was revealed to her at the
> end of this schism.[35]

Such requests are typical. It is the prophetic aspect of Hildegard's work
which held the attention of her readers in the twelfth century.

The rest of *Scivias* II, 1 goes on to explain the details of the initial vision in terms of the religious understanding of the day. Following in a teaching tradition that goes back to St Augustine's idea of the 'catechism of the unlearned', Hildegard in the one short piece covers creation, fall, the patriarchs and prophets, the defeat of the devil, redemption, Christ's resurrection and appearances to his followers, and finally the adornments of the Church as the bride of Christ; in brief, she gives a survey of salvation history, all based on a step-by-step explication of the details of her vision. If this was the material that the Synod of Trier heard at their deliberations on Hildegard, it is little wonder that Eugenius and Bernard responded favourably and gave their approval for her to continue with her work.

Such writings constitute the appeal of Hildegard in the twelfth century, not primarily as the musician, the spiritual writer or the woman writer (the aspects which interest today's audiences); instead, for the twelfth century she was a unique mixture of prophet, personal adviser, and popular teacher.

Notes to Chapter 7

[1] A. M. Allchin, *The Dynamic of Tradition* (London: Darton, Longman and Todd, 1981), cites this phrase from the Eastern Orthodox theologian George Florovsky (without reference), pp. 1, 95.

[2] Ibid., pp. 1, 4.

[3] One of the first recordings to gain recognition was by Gothic Voices, *A Feather on the Breath of God: Sequences and Hymns by Abbess Hildegard of Bingen* (the title refers to a phrase in Hildegard's writings). In addition the many recordings by the music ensemble Sequentia are also recommended. Other ensembles and choirs who have recorded Hildegard's music include the Augsburg Early Music Ensemble, Ensemble Mediatrix, Musica Sacra, Oxford Camerata, Voices of Ascension and Vox Animae. Most appropriately, the music has also been performed and recorded by the Choir of the Benedictine abbey of St Hildegard, Eibingen, the Rhineland abbey which Hildegard herself founded in 1165.

[4] The sapiential tradition in Hildegard's writings is explored by Barbara Newman, *Sister of Wisdom. St Hildegard's Theology of the Feminine* (Berkeley: University of California Press, 1987), while her breadth of learning is emphasized in Peter Dronke, *Women Writers of the Middle Ages* (Cambridge:

Cambridge University Press, 1984), and studied in detail in such publications as Peter Dronke, 'Platonic-Christian Allegories in the Homilies of Hildegard of Bingen', in Haijo Jan Westra (ed.), *From Athens to Chartres. Neoplatonism and Medieval Thought. Studies in Honour of Edouard Jeaunea* (Leiden: Brill, 1992), pp. 281-96.

[5] Matthew Fox (ed.), *Illuminations of Hildegard of Bingen* (Santa Fe: Bear & Co., 1985).

[6] Margret Berger (ed. and transl.), *Hildegard of Bingen. On Natural Philosophy and Medicine* (Cambridge: D.S. Brewer, 1999).

[7] June Boyce-Tillman, *The Creative Spirit. Harmonious Living with Hildegard of Bingen* (Norwich: Canterbury Press, 2000).

[8] Hildegard's increasing status is revealed in recent work by respected historians of the period. The thoroughly revised third edition of Christopher Brooke's *Europe in the Central Middle Ages 962-1154* (London: Longman, 2000) now sports an illustration from one of Hildegard's manuscripts on the front cover and contains 'one major new chapter' — on the role of women. Hildegard is discussed here (pp. 132-4) and compared for her intellectual achievements with (the perhaps better known) Abbess Heloise. Though brief on Hildegard, Brooke's book is an excellent survey of all aspects of the twelfth-century world in which Hildegard lived and worked.

[9] For the full text of the letter, and Bernard's reply, see chapters 1 and 32 in Mark Atherton (ed. and transl.), *Hildegard of Bingen. Selected Writings* (London: Penguin, 2001). For the original Latin, see letter 1 in the edition of the letters by Lieven Van Acker, *Hildegardis Bingensis Epistolarium* CCCM 91-91a (Brepols: Turnhout, 1991 and 1993). Other translations are found in Joseph L. Baird and Radd K. Ehrman, *The Letters of Hildegard of Bingen*, 2 vols. (Oxford: Oxford University Press, 1994 and 1998), and in Fiona Bowie and Oliver Davies (eds), *Hildegard of Bingen. An Anthology* (London: SPCK, 1990).

[10] R. N. Swanson, 'Educational Structures', chapter 2 of his *The Twelfth-Century Renaissance* (Manchester: Manchester University Press, 1999), pp. 12-39.

[11] A few women received a Latin education, sometimes by private tutor, as in the case of Heloise. See R. N. Swanson, 'A Renaissance in the Twelfth Century?' in his *The Twelfth-Century Renaissance*, pp. 188-213.

[12] For more discussion of this issue, see Sabina Flanagan, 'Opportunities and Constraints', chapter 3 of her *Hildegard of Bingen. A Visionary Life* (London and New York: Routledge, 1989), pp. 41-56.

[13] Hildegard's theology of music is most famously expressed in her letter to the prelates of Mainz; see the translation in Bowie and Davies (eds), *Hildegard*.

[14] G. R. Evans, *The Mind of St Bernard of Clairvaux* (Oxford: Oxford University Press, 1983) and Michael T. Clanchy, *Abelard: a Medieval Life* (Oxford: Blackwell, 1997).

[15] Atherton, *Hildegard of Bingen. Selected Writings*, chapters 4 and 32.

[16] Ibid., chapter 33.

[17] The antiphon, or song composed to be sung by two choirs during the alternate chanting of verses of the psalms in the liturgy, is a favourite form in Hildegard's music.

[18] Atherton, *Hildegard of Bingen. Selected Writings*, chapter 15. The two songs are recorded as tracks 13 and 14 on the CD by Sequentia, *Voice of the Blood*, Deutsche Harmonia Mundi 05472 77346 2.

[19] For the Latin text and further commentary see Pudentiana Barth and Immaculata Ritscher (eds) *Hildegard von Bingen. Lieder* (Salzburg: 1969), no. 56 and Barbara Newman (ed.), *Hildegard of Bingen. Symphonia* 2nd edition (Ithaca: Cornell University Press, 1998), no. 66. The song uses traditional imagery of the Church as mother and bride of the King.

[20] The 'banner of the king' signifies the cross.

[21] Barth and Ritscher, *Hildegard von Bingen. Lieder*, no. 57 and Newman, *Symphonia*, no. 67.

[22] *Cum processit* is track 4 on the CD by Sequentia, *Canticles of Ecstasy*, recorded in Cologne, June 1993, Deutsche Harmonia Mundi 05472 77320 2.

[23] Atherton, *Hildegard of Bingen. Selected Writings*, chapter 23, p. 118.

[24] The text is edited and translated by Peter Dronke, *Ordo virtutum*, in *Nine Medieval Latin Plays* (Cambridge: Cambridge University Press, 1994), and there is a recording by Sequentia, *Ordo virtutum*, Deutsche Harmonia Mundi 05472 77395-2.

[25] For more discussion see the Introduction in Atherton, *Hildegard of Bingen. Selected Writings*, p. xxxviii.

[26] This incident is discussed in detail in Flanagan, *Hildegard of Bingen. A Visionary Life*, pp. 184-92, and more briefly in Atherton, *Hildegard of Bingen. Selected Writings*, p. xiv.

[27] The discussion here follows closely my Introduction in Atherton, *Hildegard of Bingen. Selected Writings*, p. xxxix, with kind permission of my publishers, Penguin Books.

[28] Bowie and Davies, *Hildegard of Bingen. An Anthology*, p. 151.

[29] Probably the largest audience her music ever had was the performance of *Ordo virtutum* at a London 'Proms' concert in 1998, the 900th anniversary of her birth.

[30] For the correspondence between Hildegard and Odo, see Atherton, *Hildegard of Bingen. Selected Writings*, chapters 4 and 32.

[31] Atherton, *Hildegard of Bingen. Selected Writings*, chapter 5.

[32] Ibid., chapter 3.

[33] The most convenient reproduction of this picture is on the front cover of Christopher Brooke, *Europe in the Central Middle Ages 962-1154* (London: Longman, 2000). See also Matthew Fox, *Illuminations of St Hildegard*, p. 66 or the Latin edition of Adelgundis Führkötter and Angela Carlevaris (eds.), *Scivias*, CCCM 43-43a (Turnhout: Brepols, 1978), which also reproduces the manuscript illustrations.

[34] The detail of this picture is reproduced in Heinrich Schipperges, *The World of Hildegard of Bingen. Her Life, Times and Visions* (Tunbridge Wells: Burn and Oates, 1998), p. 87.

[35] W.J. Millor and C.N.L. Brooke (eds and transl.), *The Letters of John of Salisbury. Volume 2. The Later Letters (1163-1180)*, (Oxford: Clarendon Press, 1979), Letter 185, p. 224.

8
Sor Juana Inés de la Cruz: Poetry and Women's Experience in Latin American Spirituality

FRANCES KENNETT

The life and work of Sor Juana Inés de la Cruz epitomizes baroque Latin America: two centuries of a golden age of literature, music and art in the empire of New Spain.

Sor Juana has become a literary figurehead in modern Mexico, their Shakespeare. She was the only woman to be published in prose, poetry and plays, secular and religious, in both Spain and Latin America, and to be famous in her lifetime. Her works were read and performed all over the Spanish speaking world, in Madrid, in Peru – even as far away as Manila (through the work of the monastic orders in the Spanish Empire). In her day she was eulogized as the 'Phoenix of Mexico', or the 'Tenth Muse'.

Sor Juana was neither saintly, nor a mystic, (although her cast of mind may have led her fleetingly to direct knowledge of truth, as a form of the divine). Indeed, she was not a lot of things that have been attributed to her over the centuries of re-definitions that her achievement has prompted. The anomaly of her brilliance has led to theories that she was a narcissist, a spurned woman or a self-destructive neurotic. It is only fair and safe to assert that Sor Juana Inés de la Cruz had a brilliant intellect, a strong faith, and a resolute love of life.

Besides her poetic gift, she was an inventive theologian, and a proto-feminist. She might be thought of as Latin America's counterpart to Hildegard of Bingen in the range of her talents and her ability to speak to different centuries – none more so than now. Due to the studies of (latterly feminist) scholars this century, Sor Juana once more enjoys a growing international reputation. Not before time.

1. The making of a poet

Juana Inés was born in 1648 or 1651[1] at Nepantla, a little village on a plain lying between the volcanoes of Popocatapetl and Iztacihuatl. Her mother was Isabel Ramírez de Santillana, and Juana Inés was second of six children, three fathered by one partner, three born during a second relationship. Juana Inés' father was a Basque, Pedro Manuel de Asbaje, who travelled to Mexico to make his fortune. He left Doña Isabel after several years. She remained, raising her three offspring on the paternal family estate. (Her family rented and worked lands from a Dominican monastery near Panoayan.) Doña Isabel's second liaison was with a local landowner, Diego Ruíz Lozano, probably a business acquaintance of her father's. Juana Inés was second-generation *criollo*: of Spanish blood, but Mexican by birth. (The term does not mean half-caste, as 'creole' may in other contexts.)

In view of Sor Juana's later career, it is significant that her mother could not read or write, never married either of her lovers, but managed her father's landholdings quite successfully for thirty years. Such irregularities often occurred, although colonial and creole society papered over the cracks with great formality in the observance of a strict racial hierarchy. The absence of a father and the unorthodox competence of her mother influenced Juana Inés's reading of reality later; she knew of her illegitimacy and her peninsula ancestry: shame and pride were formative elements in her defiance.

There were six slaves working as domestics to the family, and numerous Indians and other African slaves labouring in their fields. Juana Inés learnt Nahuatl in childhood, and had an ear for dialectal speech. She also made up Spanish verses from infancy and won a prize for writing a religious poem at a local church in her early teens. This background led her to be eulogized later as a 'piece of nature', or as representing another form of Latin American gold: metaphors abound for her life.[2] It was as if the only explanation for Sor Juana's later achievement was to see her as some sort of indigenous, 'natural miracle', so remote was she from all that was conventionally deemed womanly.

The fictional or metaphorical *personae* of Sor Juana were in part created by the poet herself. In *The Response* (a defence of woman's rights to an education, of which more later) she recalls persuading an elder sister to take her to school long before she was old enough to attend formally, where she soon learnt to read and write. This ' Dame school' or *Amiga* school, proved insufficient. At six or seven years of age Juana Inés was what was called a *Marisabia* (or 'Wise Mary') – a female know-it-all – an interesting use of Mary's name. At home, her grandfather, Pedro Ramírez de Santillana, let her have the run of his extensive library and the child taught herself a little of everything. Doña Isabel ensured that all her daughters were educated, and no one seems to have stifled this particular and unusual talent. Juana Inés was still a girl when she heard about the university in Mexico City which was two days' ride away, and plagued her mother to send her there, ignorant of the fact that not just her youth but her sex prohibited her. She would not accept, even as a child, that things were beyond her reach or that she would have a life plotted out by others. At the age of 10/13, she was sent to Mexico City to live with an aunt, who was married to a wealthy nobleman, Juan de Mata. There she was to enjoy a wider social and intellectual world.

2. The city and the culture

There would have been good reason to have young girls secluded and well-supervised by relatives or other connections in Mexico City in the second half of the 17th century. It was a city of public luxury, mercantile energy and general licentiousness. Octavio Paz's monolithic but wayward account of her life describes the Spanish project thus: [3]

> ...whereas the English founded their communities [in North America] to escape an orthodoxy, the Spanish established theirs to expand one. For one group the founding principle was religious freedom; for the other, the conversion of the natives to an orthodoxy and a Church. The conquistadors undertook the Conquest at their own risk; in a way, it was a private undertaking. But it was also an imperial enterprise. Cross, sword and crown - a fusion of the military, the religious and the political. Two words define Spanish expansion: conquest and conversion. These are imperial words, and medieval words as well.

However, it is misleading to see Sor Juana's cultural and religious world as still locked in a medieval value system, as George Tavard makes clear:[4]

> New Spain was, by virtue of its dominant classes, an image of Spain itself. The viceroy in Mexico represented the king in Madrid and acted in his name. Juana Inés's religious universe was therefore that of the Spanish Counter-Reformation, not a belated form of the Middle Ages. In turn, the Spanish Counter-Reformation is part of a broader movement of the Counter-Reformation in general, whose effects in theology, piety and church architecture and decoration were felt first in central and northern Italy and in the southernmost German-speaking areas of Austria, Bavaria and Switzerland. This broader movement is commonly designated in art and literature as the baroque, a term that gains wider meaning when applied to the period: the baroque age. Militant against the inroads of the Reformation, the baroque's triumphalism is more moderate in France than in Italy, Spain, and the Germanic territories. It is the most exuberant kind that Juana Inés knew.

A history of the conquest of Mexico is beyond the scope of this essay, so to summarize rapidly: that enterprise was complete by about 1560, and led into a period of stabilization, whereby a minority, European population of 100,000 people in the mid-sixteenth century grew to about three million towards the end of the colonial period, and was capable of an organized, coercive political regime over a mass of 517 million multi-racial workers – at the same time as the indigenous Indian population was in catastrophic decline. It could fairly be said then, that triumphalism took a political as well as a religious character; that the two went hand in hand. Sor Juana lived in that hiatus of empire which had an appearance of stability, before the creoles perceived their own interests to be in conflict with the colonial power.

The urban setting into which she stepped with inquisitive expectations, Mexico City, demonstrated checks and balances between its administrative, educational, religious and military life. Imperial triumphalism was presented (and reinforced) in a succession of parades and fêtes through the streets of the capital, many to mark important Catholic festivals, but also celebrating the arrival of the Spanish Fleet with new dignitaries, merchandise, travellers, settlers, and news from the peninsula. The Catholic Church continued its expansion in the empire. The first wave in the sixteenth century was largely mission work undertaken by the monastic orders, (predominantly Franciscan) amongst a native population who had been deemed suitable for conversion, after much debate. Many aspects of Nahua and the later Aztec culture had surprised the Catholic missionaries of this first generation with their obvious parallels to Christian symbolism – for instance, the use of sacrifice, a cult of blood and flagellation, and the symbolism of bread in rites – facts that Sor Juana later exploited in her religious plays and poems. Her knowledge of the processes of evangelization was sophisticated – she used Juan de Torquemada (O.F.) and José de Acosta, (S.J.) for example – but manipulated for her own purposes.[5] Essentially she developed an early *criollo* perspective on the conversion process, expressing the fears and thoughts of the poorest elements of society as a sub-text in her conventional work for the court and church hierarchy.

The second wave of evangelists in the seventeenth century, rising to power in Sor Juana's era, were the Jesuits, who rapidly became the dominant ideological force, aiming to shape creole society as fervently Catholic, culturally Eurocentric. One can parallel the growing disenchantment with the Indian as a potential catechist with the rise in identity of the creole as truly 'Mexican'. All education of the white élite was in this order's hands, and they had great influence at the vice-regal court. In educating the creoles indistinguishably from peninsula-Spanish society, but without any hope of real power in the colony, the Jesuits never imagined that they were laying the ground for frustration and rebellion against the Crown, or distancing creole from Indian. Colombian writer Alvaro Uribe Rueda also points out:[6]

> Checks and balances of power-groupings extended beyond the court to forces within the church itself: between bishops and the various religious orders, between the bishopric of Mexico City and that of Puebla. In summary, there were endless tensions between a society full of hierarchies, rules and regulations, and a population shifting up and down the social range, due to fast money made, births or other errors concealed,

and power-broking patronage constantly plied. While this activity generated an atmosphere of excitement and originality, it also led to a
measure of display for the sake of it, concealing a ruthless world of allegiances and counter-allegiances.

The state was inherently unstable and, as more contemporary research is
finding, even the overlay of Catholicism on the numerous ethnic cultures
and beliefs in their domain was more chain mail than cast iron, at best a
syncretistic exercise. No wonder the baroque in all its manifestations
flourished in New Spain: nothing could be taken for what it seemed.

Sor Juana's relatives introduced her to life at court, and she became a
favourite of the viceroy's wife. For the next five years, Leonor Carreto,
Marquise de Mancera was a decisive figure in her career. Her first biogra-
pher, the Jesuit Father Diego Calleja, describes the legendary encounter at
court between the teenage Juana Inés and forty 'savants' whom she bested
on numerous topics, from astrology, through classics, philosophy and
mathematics. It is possibly mere hagiographic convention to say she had
won 'like a galleon sailing through a horde of small canoes' but even so,
the victory was cited in that Latin American image.[7] The Baroque Age
loved all kinds of marvels, including precocious, beautiful young girls
who could spout Latin, name the constellations, recite chemical formulations, and quote historical dates.

Her physical beauty might have placed her in jeopardy, were it not for
Juana Inés's distaste for (or given her discerning wit, boredom with) the
shallow and the corrupt, which she satirizes harshly in elegant courtly
sonnets. Her desire for intellectual freedom and disinclination to marriage
led her to take the veil in her late teenage years, although the Jesuit court
confessor, Antonio Nunez de Miranda, a brilliant but ambivalent influence on her life, claimed her 'vocation' as his greatest prize. After a brief
stay with the Carmelites (the severity of whose order caused her to suffer
a life-threatening illness) Juana Inés spent the rest of her days as a nun in
the Hieronymite order, a branch of the Augustines. She ran a virtual salon
from her cell and knew anybody and everybody of any importance in the
city. All visiting dignitaries came to see her in the *locutorio*. Sor Juana is
reputed to have collected the largest private library in Mexico City – as
many as 4,000 volumes are cited. She died young, in her mid-forties. The

events surrounding the end of her life have been much debated, and will be dealt with at the conclusion of this study. It is part of my 'hermeneutics of suspicion' in this introductory essay to dwell on her documented achievements, not on the myths of her eventual silence.

3. A poet of divine and human love

Sor Juana wrote in many styles and for many purposes, and there are few certain dates of composition. Some of the peaks of her range will indicate her diversity. These are coupled with some of my own translations in the appendix.

Some critics see her early love sonnets and lyrics as a reflection of her experiences at the court of Don Antonio Sebastián de Toledo, Marquis de Mancera (Viceroy 1664-1673), and his wife, Dona Leonor Carreto, Marquise de Mancera. Naturally there are those who surmise she became a nun after a failed romance. Other critics see her secular poetry more as a demonstration of her consummate skill with verse-forms, rather than auto-reflexive. The rapid succession of editions of Sor Juana's poetry (first published as *Inundación Castalida* in Madrid, 1689) evidences the popularity of her work in Spain and in Mexico during her lifetime. One poem in particular has never fallen from view: *'Hombres necios que acusáis'* (*'Silly, you men - so very adept/at wrongly faulting womankind'*). Schoolchildren in Latin America and Spain still learn it by heart. Nothing of the sexual *mores* of her time escaped her criticism.

Sor Juana's poetry addressed to women has also won her a sort of fame as a Sapphic. These, among other romantic sonnets and lyrics, made occasional appearances in anthologies or smaller editions throughout the next two centuries in Latin America and Europe. This partial reputation did not and still does not do her justice. There are current feminist critiques that question the oppressive features of gender norms, since they have been created under patriarchal power systems. Judith Butler for instance has argued that we need 'a variety of incoherent configurations that in their multiplicity exceed and defy the injunction by which they are generated.'[8] Sor Juana is an apt figure to consider from this viewpoint. She represented herself ambiguously at all times, as can be seen not only in the differing vocatives (female, male, neuter) used in her poetry, but also in her repeated descriptions of Self, as a person of 'no sex' or as a 'soul without gender', or as a 'mystery' beyond the understanding of the public:[9]

> ...I am not at all what you think.
> What you've done is attribute to me
> A different nature with your pens,
> A different talent with your lips.

Aside from her courtly verse, approximately one third of Sor Juana's literary output was written for the stage in the form of satirical verse comedies for the court, and in complete contrast, *autos sacramentales* – religious plays performed in Holy Week. One in particular, *El Divino Narciso (Divine Narcissus)*, published in Mexico in 1690, is a daring, syncretistic piece, drawing on Sor Juana's classical, theological, and mythological knowledge – from ancient Greece, hermetic Egypt, the Old and New Testaments, the Church Fathers, and the recent chronicles, written by Spanish priests, of Aztec Mexico.

Sor Juana Inés de la Cruz was also commissioned by the Catholic Church of New Spain for numerous cycles of Christmas carols, known as *villancicos*, which make up about one-quarter of her preserved output. They were performed in various cathedrals in New Spain and produced throughout Sor Juana's writing career. Sor Juana made a considerable fortune from her writing, besides acting as *contadora* or book-keeper to the convent with efficiency. Most of her creative work was undertaken at night when her duties were completed.

Her thought took flight in the silence. Sor Juana's most personal religious poem, the *Primero Sueño (First Dream)* appeared in the second volume of her work, *Poemas de la unica poetisa americana, musa decima*, published in Madrid in 1692. It stands in a category of its own in her work: many have ignored it in the belief that its ornate baroque imagery and hermetic atmosphere render it inaccessible. On the contrary, it is a vivid work that succeeds through its strong narrative drive, its daring or 'illicit' voice and revelatory content. Interpretations of the poem have tended towards detailed exploration of the poem's many esoteric sources, and in so doing the imaginative reach and spiritual strength of the poem has not been appreciated.

Sor Juana's conflict with the episcopate in New Spain was publicly revealed in a polemical epistle written in a baroque scholastic style, entitled, *Carta atenagórica de la madre Juana Inés de la Cruz, que imprime Filotea de la Cruz etc. (Puebla, 1690) (A Letter of Madre Juana Inés de la Cruz, worthy of the wisdom of the Goddess Athena, printed by Filothea of the Cross)*. The name of the printer was a female pseudonym taken by the Bishop of Puebla, Manuel Fernández de Santa Cruz, who added his own letter as a prologue. As a matter of etiquette, a Bishop could not address a nun in a public document but no one in Mexico City interested in this theological debate would have been in doubt about the identity of 'Sor Filothea'. In the prologue the Bishop of Puebla praises Sor Juana's work but admonishes the author for not putting her efforts into more 'holy matters' in private.

Sor Juana's reply is one of her most famous prose works: a defence of women's rights to an education and an autobiographical sketch, known as *La Respuesta a Sor Filotea de la Cruz (The Answer to Sister Filothea of the Cross)*: ironically Filothea means 'lover of God' in feminine gender. Sometimes entitled *The Response*, the content of which contains elements of riposte as well as a justification of the author's life, (a distortion of the conventional *apologia pro vita sua*), this text ranks as the most important piece of proto-feminist writing in the Spanish language. It has been extensively examined in both English and Spanish, and translated into English.[10]

Sor Juana also wrote *Ejercicios* (Devotional Exercises), for the nuns of her order and a lay readership, which have received much less attention than her poetic works, or her other prose texts, but attest to her liberal cast of mind and attention to the humbler spiritual needs of others.

4. The creation of an identity

a. The making of the self

One of the most interesting early voices with a positive assessment of Sor Juana's work was that other respected Spanish essayist and polemicist,

Miguel de Unamuno, who in '*Sor Juana Inés, hija de Eva*' [daughter of Eve] addressed the role of the intellect in Sor Juana's creative work and was precursor to modern opinions of this Mexican writer:[11]

> Sor Juana had an intensely intellectual love for the magical images she shaped, the creatures of her mind. It was an exquisite sort of love, akin to Spinoza's thoughts on the subject. She loved her very self amongst these beings, as something she had created by her own hand, for there is a refined self-love that consists in loving the epitome, the best that one can make of oneself, or the myth of oneself, if you like.

This is an ingenious, sensitive way of looking at that streak of narcissism in Sor Juana which male writers post-Freud, notably Ludwig Pfandl,[12] have found to be verging on the neurotic. The mortal, philosophical, or spiritual natures of love – all forms of love – are essential to any discussion of Sor Juana and her work. Unamuno was one of the first to address the idea of self-invention in Sor Juana's writings which in turn underpins a great part of her theology: the theme of how humankind can come to a realization of its full nature as formed in the image of God without falling into the sins of self-absorption or pride. For Sor Juana, the work of the imagination, the re-creation of self through intellect and feeling were appropriate, not sinful means of aspiration.

b. The making of a role

Sor Juana contributed to the challenge of change in her time, which we are still working on in her theories, and even further in her *praxis*. She resisted the identity or role allotted to her in a patriarchal society well before there was a public discourse or theory to go by. It is ironic today that at the same time as women begin to assert themselves, in postmodernist theory the very notion of a 'subject' begins to unravel. Yet it is precisely some destruction of notions of subject, object, gender and 'sites of discourse' that can provide the excitement and the impetus for new theologies, besides new theories of feminism, that must move beyond oppositional and dualistic thinking. What I am trying to do is to try to follow a guideline laid down in general by Rosemary Radford Ruether: 'the critical principle of feminist theology is the promotion of the full human-ity of women.'[13] I aim to make known Sor Juana as a *subject* of that authentic and full humanity. To 'recapitulate from a feminist, critical per-spective this journey of Western consciousness' includes to learn from the roles that Mexican nuns undertook (willingly *and* unwillingly) in the cre-ation of New World life and culture, and to recover the voices of those *Untold Sisters* (to use the title of a book that collects examples of colo-nial women's writing together for the first time).[14] From this flows the need to assess the role that Sor Juana played in her time, and could play now, by example and inspiration, in shaping an appropriate contemporary Christianity.

Sor Juana took risks to set down on paper the flights of her imagina-tion, secular poetic, philosophical and religious. These helped to shape new ways of worship for her sister nuns and were influential on a public audience composed of various social, cultural and racial groups. They can also help to shape our own ideas of woman, worship, and problematic notions in the doctrine of the Trinity. We can look for the autonomous impulses in her creativity and thinking, as a counter-balance to the aston-ishment sometimes expressed that centres on the supposed 'duality' of a great (i.e. 'masculine') intelligence in a female body.[15]

Sor Juana believed the soul to be without gender, yet consistently her writing lays bare the cultural marks of female experience. She seldom wishes to be thought of as a man writing: rather, she often wishes to be read as a woman *writing as a man*, purely to demonstrate her own (femi-nine) prowess. That is only an enigma to those who find clever women difficult. It was a feature of her age that writing was considered exclu-sively a male pursuit: writing was considered a diabolical activity for nuns. Even when barred from theological debate in public, it was through their work as nuns, believers, or servants of one sort or another that women demonstrated and exercised their peculiar spirituality, and in which we see positive elements for building feminist theology now.

c. The re-making of a history

Sor Juana always thought and wrote in terms of 'the highest that she knew',[16] and in this sense, adds another dimension to modern debate: she is a lively polemicist who stands against time. She focused on the best in the lives of the women she used as her exemplars and was not above certain distortions of her own to achieve her effects – as in her use of rhetorical devices in *The Response* – tricks that emulate those of Teresa of Avila, as examined by Alison Weber.[17] To give but one example from this same text: Sor Juana is responding to the criticism from a Bishop that she ought to focus on her religious duties and do no writing at all, as it is an unsuitable occupation for a woman. Part of her defence is to list all the intelligent and learned women in the Bible and in history. A second defence is write a brilliant and highly artificed account of her own upbringing, to emphasize the 'inevitability' of her intelligence, a God-given attribute. The third, and most damning, is to claim that her work was published without her knowledge (by the bishop himself, in an act of treachery) although the said prelate praises her skills as 'worthy of Athena':[18]

> ...could I have foreseen the happy destiny for which it [my letter] was born... I should have drowned it with these very hands to which it was born, for fear that the dull-witted scribbles of my ignorance should appear before the light of your knowledge. *Thus we know the extent of your noble beneficence; for your good will applauds precisely what your most brilliant discernment should repudiate.*

Hypocrisy offended Sor Juana, but she had ways to exact her revenge. How baroque yet subversive the image of a literary infanticide would have read from the pen of a nun. Although women's ways were shaped to satisfy man's needs of them as religious beings, some women also shaped the orthodoxy to their own needs. We can see signs of unorthodox constructions of belief or worship where they shine through in New Testament references and in the life of the early church. Sor Juana draws on such references frequently in her own work: she scanned history for the benefit of her female contemporaries, (and also the other oppressed elements in her society) and in so doing, modelled an early typology in use amongst feminist theologians today. It would appear that Sor Juana was well aware of the use of history by the centres of power in her time (the church and the court), and indeed, she participated in the process in her public, commissioned works. But she also subverted that duty, by creating her own personal history, and a specific female history, in an attempt to define another space of discourse in her own salon and a literary place for it in her writings.

There is only space to mention briefly how Sor Juana ignored the contemporary cult of the Virgin of Guadeloupe, and created in her public poetry, her *villancicos,* a vision of the Virgin much closer to the Wisdom figure of the Old Testament. Her miraculous image is not of a pregnant Indian maid, a submissive indigenous patroness for the masses, but an altogether more astounding and powerful femininity: [19]

> Alien being in Heaven and Earth,
> yet deemed in both of utmost worth,
> too female was she for Divinity,
> too Heavenly for Humanity.
>   Nature itself was cast in doubt
> If it could fashion her true throughout
> Too fecund was she for a Virgin's life,
> too pure was she for a married Wife.

This is a particularly important aspect of Sor Juana's achievement: her protagonistic stance in an age when such courage was rare. Other critics, including Octavio Paz, have seen this as self-obsession, but it was very far from that – it was the *praxis* of a devout woman who believed that her intelligence was part of her 'divinity' and that she shared her suffering with Christ, whose wise brows were spiked with thorns. Sor Juana moves away from the more conventional view of the female suffering of her sister nuns as respectfully embodying the silent, humiliated Christ. Her Christ, and her Mary, are active participants in a world of suffering, offering understanding and hope. Sor Juana did not dwell on the diabolic in human nature, but on the creative, redemptive possibilities in all classes of men and women.

5. The end of Sor Juana's life

From the appearance of her first biography by Father Calleja, tradition has held that Sor Juana eventually repented of her public literary fame, abandoning all writing in the last years of her life, giving away her valuable library and astronomical instruments, and dedicating herself to reconciliation with her Maker. The Catholic Church praised her 'conversion' and claimed her death, in 1695, while nursing her sister nuns during an outbreak of plague, as saintly in its sacrifice. Recent documentary evidence brought to light by Elías Trabulse[20] indicates that Sor Juana was subjected to an episcopal trial in 1693, and sentenced to forfeit her goods to the archbishop of Mexico City as well as abandon all work in the public eye. Sor Juana continued to write in private until her death, and was neither the tragic victim of self-pride nor a pious convert. The making and destruction of this myth is exactly in accord with Sor Juana's understanding of her 'identity', as something which was always to be newly constructed.

Appendix: Selected poems of Sor Juana Inés de la Cruz
Translated by Frances Kennett

Sonnets of love and discretion

Sonnet 164 (*Obras Completas* Vol 1 p. 287).

In which she puts paid to jealousy with the rhetoric/wordless proof of tears

> At dusk, my love, when I spoke to you,
> your face and gestures made me see
> that words would no longer work for you,
> and I wished that my heart could speak for me;
>   So Love, understanding, helped me out,
> and rescued me from hopeless fears,
> for he turned all my sorrow into tears,
> and distilled the pain of my broken heart .

Enough of suffering, my dear, enough,
let jealousy's vile torment be all forgot,
let evil doubts no longer plague your mind
 with telltale signs and gloomy doubt,
for in that flow of tears you saw and felt
my heart , in your hands, with sorrow melt.

Sonnet 165 (*Obras Completas* Vol. 1, p. 287)
Sonnet in which she explores the same theme but with a livelier wit.

Feliciano adores me and bores me rigid;
Lysardi loathes me but I adore him;
I wail over a wimp who doesn't fancy me,
and I don't fancy the drip who cares tenderly.

I offer my soul to the man who's all scorn
I snub the one who bares his heart and soul;
I sneer at the man who sings my praises,
and worship the fool who runs me down.

If I scorn this one with my nose in the air,
that one's rudeness gets to me more,
and I end up miserable whatever the score.

So both men end up driving me mad,
this one asking for what I can't give,
and that one for not taking what would be had...

Philosophical satire (Obras Completas No. 92 Vol 1. p. 228)

*In which she demonstrates the contradictions in men's taste for criticism,
blaming women for what they themselves have brought about.*

You men are so silly to find such fault
in women without the slightest cause,
failing to see that you yourselves
have brought about those very flaws.
 After laying chase and winning the prize

you make it plain whom you despise;
how can you hope that she'll behave well
when it's you who leads her on to hell?
  You spare no effort to wear her down,
Then you're first to claim that she's quite weak,
gravely judging her feebleness
more sinful than your own bald cheek.
  You like to play the real hero,
though truth to tell you look quite mad,
like a child who make-believes he's wild
and suddenly fears that he's really bad.
  With presumption that's the ultimate
you want the woman you're yearning for
to be wild as Thais when you're in pursuit,
and cold as Lucrecia when she's yours by law.
  What whim or wish could be more odd,
as this, beyond all rhyme or reason,
to smear the mirror with thick mud
and then regret it's lost reflection?
  Whether you're in or out of favour
neither way brings peace of mind,
you moan when she's a cruel monster
and scoff when she's been sweet and kind.
  No one wins a word of praise,
for if a woman holds a bit back,
denying you access, she's called a bitch,
while the one who yields is just a slag.
  Your attitude's completely stupid
to judge all women by this cruel code
accusing this first of being frigid
and shrugging the second one off as bold.
  So how can a woman be in between,
if once she's caught your roving eye,
she's either cold if she turns you down
or just a whore if she lets you try?
  So what with all your rage or pain,
both of which is entirely your own,
Good luck to the girl who keeps refusing,

no matter how much you fuss and moan!
  It's precisely protests that feed her whims,
so that she flies off in wilful schemes,
for if you've helped to make her bad,
there's no point wishing that she'd be good.
  For who do you think is more illicit
succumbing where such passions lead,
the man who sins in asking for it,
or the one who's begged to do the deed?

Endechas

> *Words to 'St Joan of Lima', another local dance, tune*
> *and accompaniment.*

Agrisima Gila...

Gila you're the tartest dish
who'd rather not be sweet,
but likes all lips to pucker up
and wince with saucy relish:
    I'd like to have you drawn
to Joan of Lima's tune,
to add the tang of lime
to all your acid lemon;
    With amber and with myrrh
your melting hair flows down;
to see that is to marvel
how bitterly it's grown;
    Your brow might be adorned
with jasmine's sweetest flower
but that is far outdone
by lemon blossom's power;
    A splash of inky dyeline
gives colour to your brows
spiced up with capers fine
and pinch of pickled gallnuts.
    Olive to perfection,

your eyes deepen in tone,
with salt and oregano
in well adjusted season.
        The press that yields the wine
might hope to tint your cheeks
but since you're still so young
the juice unripely reeks,
        Plump with vivid carmine
your lips are full of zest
a pleasurable sight,
but pepper to the taste.
        Your neck in fair perfection
is snowy white and shining,
a lemon rind in pithy white
a pinch of salt for frosting.
        Your hands will take their colour
from creamy curdled milk
that in the calm of dawn
turns goodly sour and thick.
        All eyes can't help but follow
when your trim gold boots flit by
but who would want to swallow
one dose of the girl they spy.
        And if this little draught
needs any sharper feature
just add a dash of bile
the essence of your nature.

From *Villancicos a la Asuncion, 1679*
Villancico VI

Jácara

She's that bravest of women of old
who appeared in a similar image
to John, secluded in Patmos
rewarding the good of his soul;
        She's that woman dressed up by the Sun

more brilliant than Sardanapolis
with sunbeams wound on her spindle
to weave up her golden gown;
    She's that woman, had Diana ventured
to challenge in beauty's lists,
would have seen her off with a slipper,
so peerless her beauty persists;
    For even the brilliant stars
just twinkle as dots of her grace
mere sparks of that greater splendour
burnished gold to rest on her brows.
    She's the woman that all of Heaven
in numberless shining spheres
consents to let wander at leisure
for her roamings exceeds all its realms;
    She's the woman whose lustrous hair
and finely woven gown
would take every starry gem
to fashion as fine as her own.
    She's the woman that all the world
has used for a measure of worth
but its beauties are merest scrawls
that fail to capture her truth;
    She's the pattern for every beauty
the clue to all that's rare
the ultimate word for fair,
the *sine qua non* of awe
    And that's not all, for in fear
of her cheeks in fairest bloom,
April shivers and grows quite pallid,
and May loses the charm of its hue
    Those eyes! How I'd love to see you,
Blushing Youth of the morning sun:
If she shot you the smallest of glances,
You'd abandon your chariot of dawn.
    For her lips, there is no equivalent
that comes within miles of their charm,
Her smile makes a waif of orient pearls

A beggar the western sun;
    Why ever would jasmine bud
leaf by leaf, with petals apace,
if it has to steal from her face
every luminous white and red?
    By the sum of all her perfections
This Mary, great *Mare Magnum,*
you could reckon up everything marvellous,
if any ruler could cope with the measure.
    For she is just terribly beautiful
So brave she inspires holy dread,
so brilliant she dazzles all eyes,
so bright she catches your breath.
    And whatever is lifted to Heaven,
by spirit is born from the earth,
for she spans with a single leap
too small a distance for one so fleet.
    Enter in, blessed Maid of God,
your celestial palace of gold
for going in or venturing out,
is something I shall never do,
    You might be pictured in majesty,
breaking through all heaven's bounds,
but I can only speak of you
as I am bound to, here below.

From *El Divino Narciso*

Scene XVI (Finale)

The allegorical figure of GRACE explains the Incarnation:

All Fishes in their wombs of dark
made offer of their deepest praise,
while all the loving Sea rose up
in glassy altars of adoring waves.
    All Nature made Him offerings

devoutly rendered by all things,
from the lowliest blade of grass
to the tallest forest pine.
   He manifested in his Grace
a plethora of perfect things
that infinite in beauty flowed
unceasing from his own fairness.
   Thus everything inanimate
the rational and the sensitive
came into being from His care
and would be lost without His thought.
   This is beauty's miracle,
amidst the meadow's blossomings,
to take delight in every rose
and feed upon the creamy lilies,
   Seeing all the splendour rare
of all His Beauty made a mirror,
seeing in His image, man,
Beloved of His own nature.
   His very own similitude
was all His love's attraction,
for only God of God himself
is worthy object of attention.

Oh let me lift my voice to sing His Glory,
The Mystery Supreme of His great ransom,
that to redeem us He gave up His Body,
generous Royal Fruit of the purest Womb!
   May we revere this finest Sacrament;
may ancient Mysteries yield duly to the New,
supplying through our Faith what is deficient
raising the senses to all feeling virtue.
   All glory, honour, blessing and acclaim,
nobility and power to the Father and the Son,
let them be rendered here, and Love that comes
from both, may we in equal praise to them return!

Notes to Chapter 8

[1] Documents support both birth dates: see Ramírez España, G. (ed.), *La Familia de SJIC; documentos ineditos* (México: Imprenta Universitaria, 1947).
[2] Luciani, F., 'Octavio Paz on Sor Juana Inés de la Cruz: The Metaphor Incarnate' *Latin American Literary Review* 1987, Jul-Dec., pp 6-25; p. 23. Fn 6. See also Glantz, M., *Sor Juana Inés de la Cruz: Hagiografía o Autobiografía?* (Mexico: Grijalbo, UNAM, 1995).
[3] Octavio Paz, *Sor Juana, or, The Traps of Faith* (Harvard: The Belknap Press, Harvard U.P. 1988), p.15.
[4] Tavard, George, *Sor Juana Inés de la Cruz and the Theology of Beauty: The First Mexican Theology* (Notre Dame, Indiana: University of Notre Dame Press, 1991), p. 34.
[5] Sor Juana may not have read widely in depth, but what she knew, she put to good use. Octavio Paz portrays her as a dilettante, but a study of her play, *El Divino Narciso* reveals a profound understanding of conversion issues. See Kennett, F., 'The Theology of The Divine Narcissus', *Feminist Theology* 25, September 2000, pp. 58-83.
[6] Uribe Rueda, Alvaro, 'Sor Juana Inés de la Cruz o la culminación del siglo Barroco en las Indias' *Thesaurus* Bogota, 1989, Jan-April, Vol 441, 112-148, p. 124.
[7] Calleja, D., S.J., *Vida de Sor Juana* in Castorena y Ursua, J.J. de., (ed.) *Fama y Obras póstumas del Fenix de México* (Madrid: 1700).
[8] Butler, Judith, *Gender Trouble: Feminism and the Subversion of Identity* (New York: Routledge Press, 1990), p. 142.
[9] From *'To the matchless pens of Europe, whose praise only enhanced her works. Lines found unfinished'* in Trueblood, A. A., tr. *A Sor Juana Anthology* (Cambridge and London: Harvard University Press 1988), No. 36, p. 103.
[10] See Arenal, E., and Powell, A., eds and transl., *Sor Juana Inés de la Cruz: The Answer/La Respuesta* (New York: The Feminist Press at The City University of New York, 1994), pp. 38-143.
[11] Unamuno, M. de., 'Sor Juana Inés, hija de Eva' in *Obras Completas* (Barcelona: Vergara, 1961), Vol VIII, p. 602.
[12] Pfandl, L., *Sor Juana Inés de la Cruz, la decima musa de México. Su vida. Su poesía. Su psique* (Mexico: Estudios fr Literatura, No 2., UNAM, 1963). The German original was published in 1946 but the impact of Pfandl's work really started when his work was made available in Spanish.
[13] Ruether, R. R., *Sexism and God-Talk* (Boston: Beacon Press, 1993), p. 18.

[14] Arenal, E. and Schlau, S. (eds), *Untold Sisters: Hispanic Nuns in Their Own Works,* with translations by Amanda Powell (Albuquerque: University of New Mexico Press, 1989).

[15] Cf. Judith Butler, *Feminism and the Subversion of Identity* (New York: Routledge, 1990), p. 142: 'Construction is not opposed to agency; it is the necessary scene of agency.'

[16] This is a phrase that Daphne Hampson uses of the Apostle Paul, with regard to his view of human (and gender) equality in his own cultural context, as expressed in Gal. 3:28; Hampson, *Theology and Feminism* (Oxford: Blackwell, 1990), p. 27.

[17] Weber, Alison, *Teresa of Avila and the Rhetoric of Femininity* (New Jersey: Princeton University Press, 1990).

[18] Arenal E., and Powell A., *The Answer/La Respuesta* (New York: The Feminist Press, 1994), p. 97. My italics.

[19] Villancicos a la Asunción, 1679, *Villancico* III, no 253; from Méndez Plancarte, A., ed., *Sor Juana Inés de la Cruz: Obras Completas* (Mexico: Fondo de Cultura Económica, 1955), Vol II, p. 64.

[20] Trabulse, E., *La Muerte de Sor Juana* (Mexico: Centro de Estudios de Historia de México, Condumex, 1999), p.63.

9
Unwilling Unbelief:
Kingsley Amis, the Novel and Faith

JULIAN THOMPSON

1. Half-belief and 'a hunger to be serious'

The father of the future novelist, Kingsley Amis, taught his boy that there was no obligation to believe in God. Having begun as a Denmark Hill Baptist, and having met his wife in the chapel where his prospective father-in-law played the organ, Amis Senior became in matters of religion what in his time would have been called a 'terrific liberal'.[1] It must have been with great difficulty that young Kingsley brought 'himself to see his father as any sort of rebel against anything',[2] but the upshot was that, as a matter of 'policy' (*AC*, p. 225) he never had 'God and the prophets and hell and damnation shoved down his throat when he was a youngster' (*YCDB*, p. 42). Like his 'best friend' (*AC*, p. 64) and 'inner audience',[3] the poet Philip Larkin, Kingsley became one of the generation glimpsed in retrospect in Larkin's poem 'High Windows', for whom there was no God any more, all going 'down the long slide/Like free bloody birds'.[4]

This enfranchisement, like most of the cultural relaxation Amis and Larkin contemplated in their work and correspondence, led to anything but bird-like freedom. In Larkin's poem, cutting oneself off from the past and its traditions, whether by disbelieving in God or immersing oneself in sex, culminates not in enlightenment, but in a difficult, if compelling, symbol. The 'deep blue air' beyond the 'thought' of high windows represents a kind of spiritual weightlessness, drifting between euphoria and stupor, the poem ramifying rather than stabilizing once the hawsers of conviction have been cut away. Though Amis claimed he couldn't understand the mysticism of 'High Windows', a warrant not to believe in God released in him comparable – though more vigorous and more bulky – ambiguities.

Parts of Amis's unbelief came easily: 'I have no belief in the existence of God, not the first beginning of one, not a shred, and never have had as far back as I can remember – not no belief in him as all-wise, all-loving, all-powerful, difficult as these might be to acquire, just no belief in him as an eternal supreme being' (*AC*, p. 226). And yet he confesses his unbelief is not 'uniform', he is an 'unwilling unbeliever', stirred and tantalised by the possibility of belonging to God, of reaching out to him in prayer, of accepting his human incarnation (*AC*, p. 226). Like the young Thomas Hardy reading the works of John Henry Newman, Amis believed his unbelief might harden into belief if he could accept 'other things, anterior things' (*AC*, p. 226); yet there seemed no 'first link' to the 'excellent chain' of Christian reasoning.

Belief drifting over unbelief like clouds over a still pool, Amis distinguishes himself sharply from the 'truly godless, those who care and know nothing about God at all' (*AC*, p. 226). Released from his ancestral Baptist tradition, Amis embraced the spiritual diversity and institutionalized tolerance of the City of London School, where he attended first as a day-boy, and later, after wartime evacuation to Marlborough, as a boarder.[5] That entailed Sunday chapel, and voluntary enlistment in the chapel choir, bringing with it a steady, seeping immersion in the cultural significance of English Christianity, so that, for Amis, as for Jake in *Jake's Thing*, the 'church he didn't go to had remained Anglican' (*JT*, p. 100). Although never an enlisted believer, Amis's allegiance to the church ran deeper than he had suspected or expected. It wasn't just his conviction that 'human beings without faith are the poorer for it in every part of their lives' (*AC*, p. 226); contemplating the ways in which traditional Christianity was busy modifying itself to accommodate the tastes of an increasingly secular society, Amis started to wonder if the Church of England, or, at least, the church in England, would see out his time, or, at the very furthest stretch, the time of his grandchildren. He explored the mournful truth that, once 'no longer current', a religious belief can never be revived by the pious efforts of cultural historians or, worse still, political executives (*AC*, p. 228), and this became one of the subjects of his 'alternate world' novel of 1980, *Russian Hide-and-Seek*. 'Godforsaken' (the title of a 1987 *Spectator* essay on his religious opinions, from which I have already quoted) and still residually iconoclastic on religious matters, Amis kept 'surprising' within himself something like the 'hunger to be more serious' of Larkin's poem on 'Church-going'.[6] Faith Amis thought of as a 'gift' he had never received (*AC*, p. 226); yet he found himself dragged, sometimes even dragged himself, to the level of the numinous, celebrating the traditions of the ancestral church, and mourning the likelihood of its passing.

The resilience of a half-belief very like Amis's own is explored in his major late novel, *You Can't Do Both* (1994). Written in the wake of the publication of Amis's *Memoirs*, and at the time Eric Jacobs was going through material for his biography of Amis, the novel is steeped in auto-biographical suggestions, not least the way in which Mr Davies, a kind of cipher for Amis's own father (Davies, for example, also exempts his son from any religious 'training and doctrine' [YCDB, p. 195]) tries to come to terms with having turned his back on the church. For the most part Mr Davies's struggles are inward and invisible, except in terms of the scars of anxiety and uncertainty he comes to wear increasingly with the years. Amis presents the old man's agonies with much sympathy, touching the heroic in the pages that describe his crimped, unbending end. He remains apostate on his deathbed, and beyond, insisting that the only ceremony at his funeral should be a bitter oration on the impracticality of a belief in God. The implication is that Mr Davies has himself written the words his son reads out, insisting that people who believe in God don't behave any better or more consistently than those who don't; nor does their 'apparent belief reduce the fear of death'. Yet the effect of this parting lecture (*YCDB*, pp. 204-05), delivered in a bleak crematorium, heard in silence by an uncomfortable grieving family, is to rekindle the possibility of faith in those left behind, rather than confirm them in godlessness. One of the characters who hears it, and who has 'been into' these matters 'a little' (*YCDB*, p. 209), promptly offers, as a kind of antidote, a characteristic Amis defence of the second person of the Trinity at the expense of the first ('Christ's much nicer than God, he hasn't got that capricious, arbitrary, prohibitive side, he's more human, what?' [*YCDB*, p. 209]). Mr Davies's son Robin, the novel's central character, also slides into familiar Amis spiritual territory, denying his father's aptitude for rebellion, stepping up his appetite for sexual encounters, reaffirming as his watchword 'the principle that you never know' (*YCDB*, p. 209). Thus what is perhaps the most unequivocal statement of godlessness in Amis's fiction (certainly, in terms of the canon, the latest) extracts the customary paradoxical surge of unwilling belief. It would be going too far to say that, for Amis, 'belief and unbelief are interchangeable expressions' (he considers *that* the sort of mental gymnastics best left to trendy bishops [*AC*, p. 229]), yet his novels are filled with unbelieving believers. They can, and must, do both.

The most obvious examples of this phenomenon are the trademark anti-heroes of Amis's best-known *bildungsroman* novels. Jim Dixon, John Lewis, Patrick Standish and Roger Micheldene of *One Fat Englishman* (especially he) are overlooked contemplating spiritual issues far more regularly than the young Amis's reputation for post-Christian downrightness – and his thoroughgoing repudiation of T. S. Eliot's tenet that 'beliefs were necessary if you want to do any serious writing' *(AC*, p. 21) – might lead us to expect. John Aneurin Lewis, hero of *That Uncertain Feeling*, considers why so many things should hurt human beings. Why, for instance, should mosquitoes replace your blood with tumour-inducing secretions of their own? 'Perhaps [the mosquitoes] wouldn't get so much fun out of it any other way, and that was quite enough reason, from the point of view of the Great Architect, for things remaining as they were' (*TUF*, p. 223).

Jim Dixon, in *Lucky Jim*, regularly foregrounds the Almighty's enjoyment of retributive slapstick. Bored with listening to a list of things that 'impressed' Professor Welch, Jim finds he is watching a fat man ogling a couple of pretty girls, so he turns his embarrassed attention away – just in time to take in a fat cricketer floored by a bouncer he aspires to hook. 'Uncertain whether this pair of vignettes was designed to illustrate the swiftness of divine retribution, or its tendency to mistake its target, Dixon was quite sure that he felt overwhelmed'(*LJ*, p. 177). At a higher, or lower, level than the rational, the protagonists of Amis's early novels posit a world sustained, even driven, by the malice of an ironically disposed creator. What Patrick Standish, in *Take a Girl Like You*, calls the 'Great Bastard' of 'Bastards' H.Q.' (*TGLY*, p. 41) sports with humanity like a Cold War spymaster, or (to borrow another concept from Hardy) like the President of the Immortals, more reprehensible as the object of human aspiration and intercession because this is a 'Bastard' who does not exist. For Roger Micheldene of *One Fat Englishman*, God does exist, of course, and even impels some cumbersome prayers.

In some ways this represents Amis's exploration of the pervasive claims upon the half-believer of Roman Catholicism, with its complacent assents and involuted denials, but the result fits in naturally with the spiritual trajectory of the earlier novels, the increasing spiritual awareness and vacillation of their central figures, and possibly owes something to an increasing 'hunger to be more serious' in Amis himself, at this time of personal realignment (1963). He had ended his academic career, contemplated ending his marriage, confronted the onset of middle age. He had also, in an essay in the *Sunday Telegraph*, 'On Christ's Nature' (1962), arranged his religious beliefs for public contemplation. The results might not have edified the Baptists of Denmark Hill; but they suggest the religious impulse in Amis and his fiction was moving from the margins to the centre, even if the moment when he might confess something like the gift of faith in anything like an accepted, traditional sense, seemed as far off as ever.

2. A protest against the culture of the time

One effect of Amis's increased absorption in spiritual matters (he was absorbed rather than questioning, for he knew that 'belief does not come by looking at the answers to questions' [*AC*, p. 226]) was to confirm his intolerance of the 'wholly godless', those 'pauperised' (*AC*, p. 226) intelligences for whom life is largely a matter of ignoring rather than confronting the inconvenient solidity of God's non-existence. Douglas Yandell, the narrator of one of the finest novels of Amis's middle period, *Girl, 20* (1971), is such a sturdy beggar. For all his superficial sophistication as a music critic, and despite the fact he contributes to Amis's personal crusade to rehabilitate the reputation of that neglected composer, Weber, Yandell is an unthinking materialist: complacent, sensual, and with an un-Amis like predisposition to detachment and timidity.

For much of the book Amis shields him with superficial sympathy, though holding his inner life at the arms-length that the device of 'the limited narrator' affords. At its crisis, however, Yandell's spiritual torpor is exploded. He is grilled, in a sort of Socratic catechism, by his prospective father-in-law, Mr Copes. Copes' method is as stealthy and feline as Father Brown's, though of the large cat variety. Copes begins – more like Swift than Father Brown, this – by lamenting all the ills of the permissive society, and offering his ironic 'Modest Proposal' for some remedies. He wonders, since we have such trouble preserving decency, if it might not be instituted 'by martial law' (*G20*, p. 186). The undesirable elements - the strikers, coloured people, football hooligans – might be respectively imprisoned, deported, or shot down in the street (*G20*, p. 186). That would help a bit. At least, it would save on taxpayers' money, which might then be spent much more usefully on the Space Race (*G20*, p. 188). Of course, Douglas – the catechized (since he's after Mr Copes's daughter) – is unlikely to take much verbal exception to this, though he privately questions Mr Copes's sanity. But it gets him off his guard. Sensible questions on the unduckable issues of life follow immediately: Do you sleep with your girlfriend? Do you believe in God? Mr Copes makes Douglas squirm:

> 'With respect, Doug, what an extraordinary number of things you don't think about and haven't got time for. Science Fiction. Religion. Whether the country's heading for moral anarchy. Marrying Vivvy or evidently anybody else either.... Very, very nearly everybody who's ever done anything has believed in something, and by anything I don't mean anything important, I mean anything whatever. Rather in the same way as very, very nearly everybody who's ever done anything whatever has had two arms and two legs. But I seem to have interrupted you again' (*G20*, pp. 193, 192).

The novel seems to approve pretty thoroughly of spiky Mr Copes, and to disapprove pretty forcefully of spineless Doug Yandell, who, when a middle-aged woman tells him on the last page about the freedom and serenity she has achieved on drugs, can only mumble about the 'lasting' qualities of Beethoven's music (*G20*, p. 233).

Amis thinks that a world without religion in it would be as 'sad and dreadful a place' (*AC*, p. 226) as a world without art (a world in which Beethoven would have found it impossible to write great music – not that Amis himself was ever quite sure he had – and in which the music he had written could not be fully understood); yet this does not mean that his novels are susceptible to the workings of cheap surrogate religions, sensational heresies, pagan superstitions and New Age placebos. On this subject Amis is a staunch disciple of Chesterton, arguing that religion should work as reason's ally against all such bogus mysticism and folly. In *Russian Hide-and-Seek* the twenty-first century *apparatchiks* who try to bring back Anglican services as spiritual medicine have to reckon with a culture that has long embraced the decadent and half-baked, given over, for instance, to a belief in 'Cartomancy' as 'a recognised form of proper divination' *(RHS*, p. 200).[7] Things had not gone quite so far in the England of 1979, when the novel was written, but the reception of one of Amis's earlier works suggested it was only a matter of time. In 1972 he broadcast a spoof ghost story[8] in the brashly unmistakable style of A.J. Alan in which he claims to have visited the very public house in his novel *The Green Man*, met most of its characters, and witnessed the materialization of a fertility God in its garden while his wife was busy copulating with the Deity. Having broadcast his story, Amis was at first amused but later amazed and even curiously appalled by the number of people from close friends to television producers to psychical researchers who contacted him to ask if the absurd events he recounted in the story could possibly be true. It seemed to him, like the widespread wishful delusions concerning the reality of the characters in television soap-operas, to demonstrate how blurred the line 'between belief and disbelief' had become.[9]

3. Problems with God's providence

If superstitious guesses are discounted, what does Amis consider to be the purpose of the universe that the God, in whom he half-believes, has allegedly created? Alec, the hero of one of Amis's most moving works, the short-story 'All the Blood Within Me', is an unpretentious soul, and his thoughts on the subject seem reasonably trustworthy. The woman he loves has died, and a preacher tries to comfort him at her funeral. This is his response:

> The next moment after Alec felt he was going to cry he started crying; he could no more have prevented it than he could have prevented himself from gasping if a bucket of icy water had been thrown over him. How did it help the dead to have made the living aware of certain things? What good to anyone were ideas about lovable qualities? What

use was it to learn about tenderness? What could you do when you were illuminated about human possibilities, except go round telling yourself how illuminated you were? What was knowing in aid of? And what was it to have loved someone? *(CSS,* p. 120).

Alec is honestly bemused, and Amis seems to share his perplexity. If there are answers to questions about the meaning and purpose of life, they emerge very slowly, and in the midst of what seems a huge mass of trivial, irrelevant and even competing data. In a review of Anthony Powell's *The Acceptance World,* the third instalment of his *Dance to the Music of Time,* which appeared in 1955, Amis views Powell's vision in terms that are something like the idea that Larkin claims inspired his poem 'Dockery and Son': an 'acceptance' of those peculiar innate assumptions that do so much to shape our lives, but which seem to have no basis whatever in upbringing or experience.[10] As Powell puts it in *The Acceptance World,* 'in a sense, nothing in life is planned - or everything is - because in the dance every step is ultimately the corollary of the step before; the consequence of being the kind of person one chances to be.'[11] Something hidden from us, to paraphrase 'Dockery and Son', chooses what we are: we get on with being that person, whether nice or nasty, and thus the world unwinds, much in the manner of a series of novels, full of complexity, vigour and dissonance, but not in the end demonstrating a clear design, and frequently (remember the mosquitoes and the cricket-ball in the gut) a malign one. The analogy with Powell's novel-sequence was probably still in Amis's mind when he wrote 'The Great Artifice', a poem in which the creation is criticized as an underwritten *'roman à fleuve',* where the good are frequently punished, and the undeserving go scot free:

> Enough of this great work has now appeared
> For sightings to be taken, the ground cleared,
> Though the main purpose - what it's all about
> In the thematic sense - remains in doubt.
> We can be certain, even at this stage,
> That seriousness adequate to engage
> Our deepest critical concern is not
> To be found here. First, what there is of plot
> Is thin, repetitive, leaning far too much

On casual meetings, parties, fights and such,
With that excessive use of coincidence
Which betrays authorial inexperience.
We note, besides these evident signs of haste,
A great deal more in questionable taste:
Too many sex-scenes, far too many coarse
Jokes, most of which have long lost all their force.
It might be felt that, after a slow start,
Abundant incident made amends for art,
But the work's 'greatness' is no more than size (*CP*, p. 88).

It is notoriously difficult to end a series of novels. But perhaps it hardly matters how the sequence ends. Or how the world does. Cataclysm will be as meaningfully meaningless as diminuendo, given that 'The seriousness adequate to engage / Our deepest critical attention is not / To be found here.' At best, it depends on how you look at it. A curious late short-story by Amis, 'A Twitch on the Thread', makes this point clearly, even a little diagrammatically. Separated at birth and ignorant of each other's existence, a pair of identical twins give up alcohol and enter the church at the same time, and for very similar reasons. Meeting in middle-life and comparing notes, they come to very different conclusions about their spiritual experience. For the American twin the 'twitch on the thread' comes, as in the Chesterton story that furnishes the title, as evidence that there is a fisher of men on the other end of the line. The English twin is less enchanted. For him 'God's thread has turned out to be the sort that controls the movements of a puppet' (*MBS*, p. 111).

On balance, then, in life and writing, Amis does assent to a notion of providence, even if its workings, as in the test case of 'A Twitch on the Thread', seem to him unacceptably vague and ambiguous. At one period in his writing career (the late 1950s and 60s), he goes further than this, seeing the puppeteer not just as exploitative, but disturbingly vindictive. Bernard Bergonzi is only one of a number of commentators who have found something 'profoundly animistic' about the universe of Amis's earlier novels. 'Its characters,' he writes, 'are constantly in the toils of a powerful and malign governing force.'[12] In the essay that most clearly signals his religious beliefs, 'On Christ's Nature' (1962), Amis admits his liking for William Empson's opinion in *Milton's God* that 'the traditional God of Christianity' is 'very wicked', resembling an avuncular bully at the head of a totalitarian state.[13] For Empson, God the Father 'is astonishingly like Uncle Joe Stalin [or Big Brother]; the same patience under an appearance of roughness, the same flashes of joviality, the same thorough unscrupulousness, the same real bad temper.'[14] A similar instability and irritability characterizes the deity of Amis's most ambitious novel, *The Anti-Death League* (1966), a book which the novelist admits he wrote under Empson's influence, where humanity's newly discovered Nuclear Capability gives it the chance to inflict just as much 'lovely death' as its creator. The novel has a Cold War setting, and features (rather appropriately) a military clergyman who is an undercover atheist – or, at least, an 'anti-theist' (Robert Conquest's intriguing label for Amis's own religious opinions).[15] As this character summarizes his views, 'To believe at all deeply in the Christian God,' or

'in any sort of benevolent deity, is a disgrace to human decency and intelligence. Of course it is. We can take that as read. I was so convinced of it when I was about your age that I saw the Church as the embodiment of the most effectively vicious lie ever told. I declared a personal war on it. That was why I joined – so as to be able to work against it more destructively from within. I used to have a lot of fun in those days with things like devising an order of service that would please God much more than merely grovelling and begging for mercy or praising him for his cruelty in the past and looking forward to seeing more of the same in the future. Selected members of the congregation getting their arms chopped off and/or their eyes put out as a warm-up. Then a canticle about his loving-kindness. Then some whips and scorpions treatment on children under sixteen, followed by a spot of disembowelling and perhaps a beheading or two at the discretion of the officiating priest, with the choir singing an anthem about the beauty of holiness. Then an address explaining about God's will and so on. Then a few crucifixions, bringing out the real meaning of the Christian symbol. Finally a blessing for the survivors, plus a friendly warning that it'll probably be their turn next. I used to think it was the Aztecs who came nearest to establishing the kingdom of God on earth. What was it they

were notching up, a thousand human sacrifices a week? But then the
Christians arrived and soon put them down. He's a jealous God (*ADL*,
pp. 266-67).

A jealous God. And death is his great weapon. Amis down-played
Larkin's notorious fear of death: he considered 'Aubade', Larkin's most
concentrated statement of his terrors, a morbid work, and recommended a
Dick Francis at the bedside as an antidote to small hours' angst (*Memoirs*,
p. 63). Nevertheless Martin Amis feels that, though less luridly and frequently expressed, his father's attitude to death had much in common
with Larkin's: 'I always knew how it went with him and death, how personally he took it, how viscerally he feared and hated it.'[16] For many of
Amis's characters – ordinary Alec, superheated chancers like Patrick
Standish, queasy librarians like Lewis, for whom it is the most 'Uncertain
Feeling' of all – death is the defining moment of life. Amis includes those
gloomy mortality-bill poems, Nashe's 'In Plague Time' and Shirley's
'The Great Leveller', in his anthology of favourite recitation pieces,[17] and
a number of poems he wrote in middle-age explore the way both 'lovely'
and 'shitty' things become distanced by the way you feel about your
impending end (*CP*, pp. 121-24).

For Amis the smell of Death was 'the worst odour in the world' (*GM*,
p. 139), and he should have known; as his friend Robert Conquest
reminds us, accompanying a party of Free French through the Falaise Gap
in 1944, Amis saw Death, 'and miles and miles of little else' (*Listener*
'Profile', p. 485), all of it the handiwork of a 'malicious, malevolent'
God.[18] Even as late as *You Can't Do Both* (1994) Mr Davies's funeral testimony (not necessarily Amis's own opinion, of course) declares that the
only God 'available' for belief is a 'wicked' one, or, failing that, 'impotent' (*YCDB*, p. 205). In his recent autobiography, *Experience*, Martin
Amis writes that 'perhaps the most revealing thing my father ever said
was in response to Yevgeny Yevtushenko's question (in King's College
Chapel, Cambridge, 1962), "You atheist?" He answered: "Well yes, but
it's more that I hate him"' (*Experience*, p. 189).[19]

4. The ancient witness of the church

The case Amis the 'anti-theist' makes against his putative Death-wielding half-God is strong, and seems at times to have engaged him, or part of him, very deeply. It does not, however, seem to me to sum up what is deepest or most constructive in Amis's view of religion: his preoccupation with a living faith that can inspire 'a living, believing, practising Church' (*AC*, p. 228), and which will enrich the thin soil of people like Douglas Yandell's bland hedonism and soul-less hankerings. In the last thirty years or so of his life, Amis came to regard the church, which he admitted he had never, or only partially embraced (*AC*, p.228), as one of the most effective bulwarks against what he believed to be the destabilizing forces of modern society. Called in as guest columnist for the *Daily Express* in 1969, he gave its readers very much what they wanted to hear - perhaps more than they wanted to hear. Though an agnostic 'totally unattracted' by the church, Amis could not help recognizing:

> that it was the Church that gave our grandfathers the moral authority and the confidence to hand on belief in those virtues which we now so much miss. And I cannot help wondering what would be the reaction of those who first began to topple Christianity, back in Victorian Times, if they could see the contemporary results of their handiwork. What to do about it? I really wish I knew. But I do know one thing not to do about it, and that is to get the Church to follow the trend, to point the way 'forward' to more permissiveness.[20]

In the late 60s and early 70s Amis thought the church was hurrying to follow that trend, with 'risky' consequences for its integrity and utility. In particular, stress on the corporate guilt of society was rapidly replacing the old view of personal sin and salvation. It was thinking about the consequences of this that led Amis to write *We Are All Guilty*, originally a television script in the mid-seventies 'Against the Crowd' series, but attractively reconditioned as a novel for adolescents in 1991.

In this novel Clive, a young offender, comes to the church hoping for absolution. Though he does not realize it, there is a sacramental element in his craving, and the novel comes close (though it wavers a bit at the crucial moment) to making Clive a kind of surrogate Christ, taking upon himself the burden of sin that seems to be the human portion. But the glottally-stopped clergyman who represents Anglicanism in the novel has disinfected his ministry of the slightest doctrinal content. The church of *We Are All Guilty* is very welcoming ('God bless you, mate!');[21] but it merely offers Clive more of the same kind of indulgence (everyone is guilty except Clive). Going in for self-fulfilment, self-forgiveness and self-expression, and peopled by 'the kind of bloke nobody would expect to find in a church from the top of his teased blue hair to his red running shoes' (*WAAG*, p. 47), the church is so anxious to change 'as the times change' (*WAAG*, p. 48), it forgets its ancient obligation as sin-eater. 'Forgive yourself, my son,' says the wacky Revd Foster, 'and be healed' (*WAAG*, p. 50).

This is the crux of Amis's case against theological modernism, against the churches which take it up, and the society that countenances their doing so. He demands that the church bear immemorial witness on the ancient ground of faith, rather than merely exchange its old 'canting pietistic nonsense' for new 'canting humanistic nonsense' (*WBJA?*, p. 222). The church has obligations to Amis's half-believing sort of person, as well as to its regular communicants, and so she must 'pursue or regain her role as a force for order and continuity, stay as she is or was until the times move back to her, still or once more preach, not indeed torments or sectarian hatred, but an all-powerful, all-loving God and his divine Son' (*WBJA?*, p. 223). When 'On Christ's Nature', which includes this pronouncement, was reprinted in *What Became of Jane Austen?*, reviewers accused Amis of intellectual laziness and duplicity. 'Surely a rationalist,' wrote an old sparring-partner, W.W. Robson, 'especially a rationalist like Amis, should not ask other people to propagate what he believes to be false.' The charge has some validity, which Amis partially recognizes himself (*AC*, p. 228); but it does little to deflect Amis's criticism of those reformers who, in seeking to accommodate the church to their own waning beliefs, demolish the traditional foundations which constitute for its lukewarm adherents the chief part of its imaginative appeal. Amis is not lamenting the decay of the church out of a whimsical hedonism, such as led Lytton Strachey to hope there would always be picturesque

Muggletonians.[22] He is repining at the loss of the rich mixture of custom, poetry and witness that, in part, had shaped his outlook and his being.

To this end, Amis asserts the energy of the Christianity he has gathered, via cultural exposure, disinterested enquiry, bursts of intellectual enthusiasm, such as the work he put in on the Greek Testament in the sixth form (*AC*, p. 225), and aesthetic sympathy (with the poetry of George Herbert, for instance, or of 'that great heroine of mine, Christina Rossetti).[23] He tells us that throughout his life he has avoided using 'obscenity and the name of Jesus Christ in the same phrase' (*WBJA?*, p. 212). He admits to some churchgoing at Easter, Christmas and (like Philip Larkin)[24] on Remembrance Sunday, and confesses he held it a 'point of honour' to be 'C. of E.' during his service in the armed forces (*WBJA?*, p. 212). He prides himself on his biblical knowledge, insisting that knowledge of the Bible must remain an essential part of our culture if we are to escape a 'barbarous incuriosity about fundamentals' (*WBJA?*, p. 212). *The Faber Popular Reciter*, which Amis compiled in 1978, bristles with hymns familiar to him from childhood, expressive of confidence in shared faith and community. Beginning with 'Jerusalem, My Happy Home', Amis includes Bunyan's 'To be a Pilgrim', Watts's 'O God, Our Help in Ages Past' and 'When I Survey the Wondrous Cross', Wesley's 'Jesu, Lover of my Soul', Toplady's 'Rock of Ages', Blake's 'Jerusalem', Heber's 'From Greenland's Icy mountains', Keble's 'New Every Morning', H.F. Lytes' 'Abide with Me', Newman's 'Lead, Kindly Light', Jane M. Campbell's 'We Plough the Fields', S. Johnson's 'City of God', C.F. Alexander's 'All Things Bright and Beautiful', William Whiting's 'Eternal Father, Strong to Save', John Ellerton's 'The Day Thou Gavest', Sabine Baring-Gould's 'Onward Christian Soldiers' and 'Through the Night of Doubt and Sorrow', W. Chatterton-Dix's 'As with Gladness Men of Old', and A. C. Ainger's 'God is Working his Purpose out'.[25] Amis approves of the 'clarity, heavy rhythms, strong rhymes and the rest' these hymns display (*FPR*, p. 18). Their persistence, at least into the second half of the twentieth century, reflects not only a kind of wholesome 'innocence', but also a society in which it is still possible to be a Christian, and to reach towards sacred truths through the suggestive dignity of appropriate religious language.

A society in which nobody could be a Christian, Amis reckons, would be as nasty as one in which nobody could be a poet *(AC,* p. 293); for poetry, as Arnold pointed out, asks many of the same questions as religion, and is a fundamental component of all spiritual communication. This is why Amis was so distressed by what he saw as the linguistic crassness of the New English Bible. 'One would have to try hard,' he wrote in 1973, 'suppressing all humour, all sense of style and reverence, to achieve some of the ineptitudes of the New English Bible. A single example must suffice: the King James Bible has "Save me, O God, for the waters have come in unto my soul"; in the *NEB,* "the waters have risen up to my neck!" (exclamation mark in text)' *(AC,* p. 292). Such a staggering contempt for the operation of metaphor turns 'the faith it professes to embody into something literally unbelievable' *(AC,* p. 292).

We may contrast the linguistic power rekindled, albeit fitfully and ultimately fruitlessly, in Amis's novel *Russian Hide-and-Seek* (England has been subject to a maundering state atheism by its Russian occupiers) when one old priest delivers with 'naturalness' and 'warmth' the cadences of the 1662 *Prayer Book* he has 'learned in childhood', sings a couple of hymns (significantly Amis's aforementioned favourites, Bunyan's 'To be a Pilgrim' and Charles Wesley's 'Jesu, Lover of my Soul'), and preaches a traditional Anglican sermon *(RHS,* pp. 169-76). But by the Revd Mr Glover's time the process of linguistic, and indeed mental deconsecration has gone much too far. Even if, with 'practised skill' *(RHS,* p.174) the preacher's address avoids the problem of the evil prevalent in God's world (which once so preoccupied and distracted Amis), neither his brave, if possibly over-courteous burst of Liberation Theology, nor his conviction that 'a world without purpose except that of survival is a miserable place' *(RHS,* p. 175) has much effect on his polite, bemused listeners. The best that can be said is that the 1662 *Prayer Book* proves less explosive than attempts to revive *Romeo and Juliet* under Russian occupation (ending in riot and conflagration), and less baffling than efforts to celebrate 'the composer of Ta-ra-ra-boom-de-ay' or Duke Ellington ('taken to be an English nobleman of some sort') *(RHS,* p. 183). Of the 'two hundred people who had been present at the start' of Glover's service, only eleven remain to hear him out to the end *(RHS,* p. 176). Those who hope that St Paul's words, or Cranmer's gloss on them, or

Glover's, or the 1662 gloss on those, might inspire a cultural revival are depressed to the point of despair. The old clergyman himself concludes he has gone 'above the heads of most of his audience', but propitiated the 'more discerning' (*RHS,* p. 176).

Amis's view in this novel seems to be that dead faiths cannot be revived merely by dusting off their cultural artefacts, even those as solemn and inspiring as the cadences of the Authorised Version and *Prayer Book.* A wholly demythologized Christianity would lead to apathy and eventually to the atrophy portrayed in *Russian Hide-and-Seek.* Amis's treatment of Anglicanism in novels with contemporary settings suggests he thought the church had gone a long way down this road.

Wales is hardly England, but the Church of England in Wales is represented in the late novel, *The Old Devils,* by little more than some brutally deconsecrated churches: St. Paul's in *The Old Devils,* now a cinema, 'Adult movies on screens 1 and 2' (*TOD,* p. 33), and St Dogmael's, converted 'not into a pornographic cinema but, less offensively, some might have thought, into an arts centre' (*TOD,* p.110). Elsewhere in Wales – and back in the forties, this time – there ministers the Revd Hopkins, he of the posturing sibilants, actorish gestures, studied rudeness and slippery failure to engage in any kind of theological debate, even when confronted with Robin Davies's delivery of the familiar Amis-Empson case against God (*You Can't Do Both,* pp. 167-73).

Back in England the beliefs of apparently unbelieving clergymen prove harder for Amis to get at, but their calculated assaults on what he considers proper hymns and liturgy give him the clue, as do the antics of the originals of the displaced rock musicians and television bishops in mufti who people his novels from the sixties onwards. To the Revd Foster of *We Are All Guilty* may be added the liberal bishop – "'Call me Barry' Kesteven" – of 'A Twitch on the Thread' and, trendiest and most crisply satirized of all, the Revd Tom Rodney Sonnenschein from *The Green Man.* For him spirituality is a dignified label for political activism of the sort that goes on where Bacardi and Pernod is drunk (*GM,* p. 126). As for the central doctrines of Christianity, the Revd Tom Rodney thinks the 'trend undoubtedly is for a committed God to go the same way as the immortality of the soul, with a twenty – or perhaps a twenty-five – year consciousness lag' (*GM,* p. 127). He likes parties, blatantly secular rock-music, keeping in with the upper-classes and (though not much is made of this, perhaps because of Amis's sympathy with homosexuals) is noticeably gay. Diana Maybury, mistress of Allingham, the novel's central character, challenges him in the familiar Amis style: 'What's the point of somebody like you being a parson when you say you don't care about things like duty and people's souls and sin? Isn't that just exactly what parsons are supposed to care about?' (*GM*, p. 128). Not exactly, according to the Revd Tom Rodney. The 'truth as he sees it' is to set about 'changing society so as to give everybody a meaningful and organic existence here on earth' (*GM*, pp. 129, 124). Christ is, inconveniently, part of the Christian baggage; but the Revd Tom Rodney does what he can to keep Christ in His place: 'Quite frankly,' he says, 'the Jesus of the Gospels can be a bit of a wet liberal at times, when he's not taking off into flights of rather schmaltzy Semitic metaphor' (*GM*, p. 125). Christ, for Sonnenschein, is too much of a 'suburban Mao Tse-Tung' (*GM*, p. 143). It is because he cares for the ancestral witness and cultural importance of the Anglican Church that Amis renders Sonnenschein's opinions and locutions so precisely.

5. An ambiguous attraction to Christ

It is because Amis cares for Christ, too, that he refuses to leave Him in the hands of a 'posturing idiot' like Sonnenschein (*GM*, p. 143). We have seen that Amis has a Blakean disrespect for the first person of the Trinity. Whether by accident or design, he says little about the third person, though a character in *Russian Hide-and-Seek*, possibly exploring a version of Amis's own views, does refer to 'the third Christian God, about whom even less seemed to be known than about God the Father; a sinister figure, even scaring if taken seriously' (*RHS*, pp. 172-73). On the subject of the 'second Christian God', whether Amis's feelings be hospitable or critical, they are profoundly engaged and appropriately complex. He expresses them in concentrated form in the 1962 article, 'On Christ's Nature'. Here he is clearly attracted to the healthy and energetic qualities of the embodied Christ. He likes his capacity for taking risks, his wit, his good-natured demolition of cant. Christ's comparison (Luke 7:34) of his own eating and drinking with the severity and abstemiousness of the

Baptist (neither Jesus nor John pleases his implacable auditors) strikes Amis as 'one of the most delightful jokes in the whole of ancient literature' (*WBJA?*, p. 219). Christ's interest in liquor particularly engages Amis – as befits the author of *Amis on Drink, Everyday Drinking, How's Your Glass?* and the alcohol correspondent of *Penthouse* magazine from 1972 to 1980. The Evangelist's description of the wedding at Cana engages him, less because it is one of the richest symbolic and proleptic passages in the Gospels, than because St. John is so explicit about the quantities of wine involved. Six waterpots at two or three firkins apiece constitutes for Amis twenty gallons of the best available, and prompts the question 'how many guests were there at that wedding?' (*WBJA?*, p. 219).

Amis's insistence on the physicality of Christ and his miracles is amusing. But it also has some rich pay-offs. Discussing Luke's resurrection narrative, he quotes 24:41 where the risen Christ asks for food. 'If I envied Christians anything,' writes Amis, 'I would envy them a God who could feel hungry' (*WBJA?*, p. 219). This tells us a lot about Amis's Christ. A man who experiences hunger and thirst, a healthy sensual charmer, by no means the pale Galilean, tender rather than paternalistic, protective rather than authoritarian: 'Have ye here any meat?' It is a novelist's Christ, an effort to reach into a human personality, for as Amis puts in the 1987 essay 'Godforsaken', if he could take the first step, and know that God was God, he could 'take the second step as soon as I had taken the first, and accept a God who became man' (*AC*, p. 226). At times in 'On Christ's Nature' Amis is touchingly generous to the Saviour: 'He loved children for themselves,' he writes, 'in a way that reinforces his theme that the good man must cultivate childlike qualities, and his use of traditional shepherd-and-flock imagery seems appropriate to one so instinctively protective and, like the lamb he made his emblem, so gentle. (I know he was tough as well.)' (*WBJA?*, p. 219).

But Amis's Christ 'made so little difference to anything' (*GM*, p. 144). After the oblation to Christ's goodwill, comes a criticism of his limitations. In the first place, Christ habitually speaks indirectly, often equivocally, with 'a sometimes overriding inclination to the striking phrase' (*WBJA?*, p. 217). He can be as 'oddly sidelong' (*WBJA?*, p. 221) as the Delphic Oracle, one moment liberal, another authoritarian, usually disturbingly ambiguous. Secondly the Sermon on the Mount does not seem conscious that 'overt justice involves covert injustice' (*WBJA?*, p. 217), that, as William Blake puts it:

> Pity would be no more,
> If we did not make somebody poor;
> And mercy no more could be,
> If all were as happy as we.[26]

Thirdly – and a little oddly, given his strictures on the literalism of the *New English Bible* – Amis is chary of the symbolic level at which Christ pitches his speech and sometimes his actions. 'Let the dead bury their dead' makes little sense to Amis (*WBJA?*, p. 217); and the episode of Jesus's walking on the water is merely 'an arbitrary display of power' (*WBJA?*, p. 218). But the most telling indictment of Christ's ministry in Amis's eyes, as we shall see, is that Christ's tremendous pontification is based upon such limited first-hand experience. Christ seems to have exposed himself slightly, or not at all, to 'war, disease, starvation, madness, also to those subtler engines from Jehovah's armoury of maleficence, the pain incidentally accruing from sexual love and the begetting of children' (*WBJA?*, p. 220).

'On Christ's Nature' appeared in *The Sunday Telegraph* in 1962, and may well have been the germ of the intervention which Christ – or, at least, a 'piece' of him (*GM*, p. 144) – makes from eternity in *The Green Man*. The visitor certainly resembles the 'bright young rabbinical intellectual' (*WBJA?*, p. 218) of 'On Christ's Nature', updated to 1969, with his 'humorous', interestingly 'not very trustworthy' face, spruce but not dapper appearance, and most particularly his 'fully modulated' speech, 'like that of a man interested in discourse, and his accent educated, without affectations'(*GM*, p. 138). He is elegant, generous, and accepts (recalling perhaps the Wedding at Cana) a couple of drinks; but there is also a gift-wrapped sternness about him, a tendency to remind Maurice Allingham, the object of his visit, that he 'can be very hard on those who don't behave as I feel they should' (*GM*, p.141). He also makes it clear, by a rather grisly display of skeletal fingers clicking on the whisky-glass, not only that he has died, but also that he is Master of Life and Death (*GM*, p. 139). Maurice puts the usual Amis-objections to the Christian dispensation: God's 'record' does not impress him; why should 'children and such' suffer; why isn't foreknowledge invoked to avert catastrophe? (*GM*, p. 141). The Presence, moving and drinking 'like a young man' (*GM*, p. 144), shuffles off the answers, not at all wearily or petulantly, but still perhaps with an atmosphere of that mystic arbitrariness and self-containment which, to Amis, always seems the most distasteful characteristic of the Deity. The young man says he has neither power to foresee the future, nor unmake the past – or rather, such potential power as he does possess must not be used, for fear of un-making the complex 'run of the play' that the operation of human free will over many centuries has set up (*GM*, p. 141). Incarnation was a rash experiment, which might have broken the bank were it not (Amis's Christ tells us what Amis himself frequently asserts) that Christ's appearance on earth 'made so little difference to anything' (*GM*, p. 144). As it stands the young man still hankers after being 'down on the board among the pieces, just for two or three moves, to get the feel of it, without at the same time stopping running the game' (*GM*, p. 142). And, lest we think a game is too undignified an image for the grand total of human dealings, the young man has another, more potent image, strongly reminiscent of the one we have already encountered in 'The Huge Artifice': 'it's not unlike an art, an art and a work of art all rolled into one. I know you think that's rather frivolous. It isn't really. It's entirely a matter of how it's all grown up' (*GM*, p. 142).

In *The Green Man* God is an urbane presence, simultaneously convivial and rather chilly, the master of a gigantic game which sometimes aspires to the dignity of a work of art. He makes occasional appearances to 'lean on' those who threaten the rules of his game, taking care to cover his tracks and discredit importunate witnesses – Maurice Allingham, an hallucinating alcoholic, is scarcely a 'security risk' at all (*GM*, p. 140).

It would be naive and irresponsible to pretend that every view expressed by Amis's Christ neatly encapsulates every view the mature Amis came to hold about Christ. This would be as foolish as pretending that Maurice Allingham was an unrefracted self-portrait of his creator, or that the pattern of the novel in which he appeared owes everything to Amis's meditation on first and last things, and nothing at all to his enjoyment of Science Fiction novels or his delight in pastiching the monsters and antiquarian enclaves of M.R. James. *The Green Man* is at bottom a comic novel and a genre piece, its serious effects depending much on the slickness with which they are carried off. And yet it does seem to me to include the most penetrating religious meditation in the Amis canon. The young man, like Shakespeare's Hal, will never be an 'entirely trustworthy' companion for ordinary humanity; instead he is something of (another fine, barbed Amis phrase) 'a royal tourist' (*CP*, p. 90). It seems pretty clear from *The Green Man*, and from almost everything else Amis ever says or writes about God, that the novelist sees in Christ no kind of embodied ideal. The notion of Christ the King sets up envious levelling tendencies in Amis. The divine love, either as a concept or a human aspiration, never figures in Amis's work. And yet, as the young man makes ready to depart, he reminds Allingham, and the novel reminds its creator and us, to 'use the Church where appropriate' (*GM*, p. 143). Not frequently, of course. But in the big things. Sacraments. Prayer. In the novel, the service of exorcism. Even the egregious Revd Sonnenschein 'is a priest of the Church, and as such he has certain techniques at his disposal' (*GM*, p. 143).

Bottom-line religion? Perhaps. But, though Amis may not like Christ, he cannot quite say he has no need of him; or if he does say he has no need of him, he wants at least to be sure Christ knows it. And if the world is a Grandiose Mistake, if 'The Huge Artifice' is turning out to be a self-replicating and lurid picaresque, more a creation of Smollett than of Amis's beloved Fielding, it is hard to see how it might be improved unless (on a larger scale than in *The Green Man*) there is a redemptive visit from beyond – probably from that eternal youth whose élan and lack of experience are such a trial to the middle-aged and elderly Amis ('does one ever feel quite the same about the incarnate Christ after one passes one's thirty-fourth year?', one hears him say).

6. The half-believer at prayer

I finish with a look at the poem 'New Approach Needed', which appeared in 1967 (*CP*, pp. 90-91). This strikes me as one of Amis's most cantankerous meditations on the nature of Christ. Its crisp trimeters bark like an instructing sergeant at some celestial debriefing, a flea in the ear for a delicate rookie who came late, swanned around a bit and went west in the first encounter:

Should you revisit us,
Stay a little longer,
And get to know the place.
Experience hunger,
Madness, disease and war.
You heard about them, true,
The last time you came here;
It's different having them.

Yet the asperity is studied. Amis may not like the manner of the
recruit from eternity, but he cannot deny his power, nor prevent tremendous suggestions from emerging in the poem's rich sub-text. 'New
Approach Needed' is not only a suggestion that God turn over a new leaf;
it is a sort of hard-bitten request for an imminent Second Coming. Like so
much Amis writes on this subject the poem trims suggestively. Its precise
tone is difficult to judge. Amis suggests rather loftily that there are worse
wrongs for humanity to suffer than death on a cross - then concedes that
you won't get him up on one of those things. The poem ends in a crossfire
of wordplay that is an honest and full statement of Amis's religious inde-
cisiveness. 'So, next time,' is the poet's last move, 'come off it'. Come off
what? The Christian high horse? Christ's high horse? The cross? What
kind of a high horse is the cross? 'Come off it, / And get some service in,
Jack.' Is that meant as an insult for the carpet-knight and shirker? Doesn't
'Jack', a common name for all men, the poet Gerard Manley Hopkins' pet
name for his lagging human soul, seem a bit too familiar, even (unexpect-
edly) too affectionate for that?[27] 'Get some service in, / Long before you
start / Laying down the old law.' By now the puns are triumphantly
explicit. 'Laying down the old law.' Christ as patriarch and pontificator,
the Sunday-school speechifier, the iron hand in the velvet glove. As likely
– perhaps more likely – Christ the bringer of the New Covenant, gently
supervening over the Law of the Prophets, the maker of all things new.

The poem ends with a fine, unexpected prayer: so cocksure, so downright, so like Amis; and yet so disturbingly genuine, both in its energy and
its direction: 'Tell your dad that from me.' This is the agnostic's prayer,
afraid to use the normal channels of Christian communication, yet aware
of where they run; surprised, but not unpleasantly surprised to find that,

as with most of the best, most spontaneous, and most heartfelt prayers, he was using them all the time.

Notes to Chapter 9

Where possible, references are to the Penguin reprint of Amis's works (Harmondsworth: Penguin Books), as this is most readily accessible; failing this, reference is to the first edition. The following abbreviations are used in the text:

> *Lucky Jim (1954), LJ.*
> *That Uncertain Feeling (1955), TUF.*
> *Take a Girl Like You (1960), TGLY.*
> *One Fat Englishman (1963), OFE.*
> *The Anti-Death League(1966), ADL.*
> *The Green Man (1969), GM.*
> *What Became of Jane Austen? and Other Questions (1970), WBJA?*
> *Girl, 20 (1971), G20.*
> *Jake's Thing (1978), JT.*
> *The Faber Popular Reciter (1978), FPR.*
> *Collected Poems 1944-79 (1979), CP.*
> *Collected Short Stories* (1980), *CSS.*
> *Russian Hide-and-Seek* (1980), *RHS.*
> *The Old Devils* (1986), *TOD.*
> *We Are All Guilty* (1991), *WAAG.*
> *Mr Barrett's Secret and Other Stories* (1993), *MBS.*
> *You Can't Do Both* (1994), *YCDB.*

[1] Kingsley Amis, 'Godforsaken', *The Amis Collection: Selected Non-Fiction 1954-90*, introduced by John McDermott (London: Hutchinson, 1990), pp. 225-29, p. 225; hereafter cited as *AC*.

[2] Eric Jacobs, *Kingsley Amis: A Biography* (London: Hodder and Stoughton, 1995), pp. 50-51; hereafter cited as Jacobs.

[3] *The Letters of Kingsley Amis*, ed. Zachary Leader (London: HarperCollins, 2000), p. 1126; hereafter cited as *Letters*.

[4] Philip Larkin, *High Windows* (London: Faber and Faber, 1974), p. 17.

[5] See Kingsley Amis, *Memoirs* (London: Hutchinson, 1991), pp. 10, 33-34; and Jacobs, pp. 50-52.

[6] Philip Larkin, *The Less Deceived* (Hull: The Marvell Press, 1955), pp. 28-29; in a letter of 11 August 1954, Amis praised 'Church Going': 'I sympathize with you for having a shot at saying what you feel' (*Letters*, p. 399). He was nevertheless convinced that 'Philip was in no serious sense a Christian, and resented 'the attempts since his death [in 1985] to rescue or hijack him for one church or another' (*Letters*, p. 1039).

[7] Amis was intolerant of the efforts of characters in Powell's novel-sequence *A Dance to the Music of Time* to rationalize existence by dabbling in the occult. See *Letters*, p. 1018.

[8] Amis was interested throughout his career in the more speculative forms of fiction, such as the ghost-story or Science Fiction. Such forms of writing, he points out in his *New Maps of Hell* (1960), are 'ready to treat as variables what are usually taken to be constants.'

[9] Amis discusses the reception of this story, 'Who or What Was It?' in the introduction to *Collected Short Stories* (1980; Harmondsworth: Penguin, 1983), pp. 12-13.

[10] For Amis's review of Powell's novel, see *AC*, pp. 56-59; Larkin discusses 'Dockery and Son' on his recording of *The Whitsun Weddings*, Listen Cassettes, Marvell Press, 1965.

[11] Anthony Powell, *The Acceptance World* (1955; London: Fontana Paperbacks, 1983), p. 70.

[12] Bernard Bergonzi, *The Situation of the Novel* (London: Macmillan, 1970).

[13] 'On Christ's Nature', which first appeared in the *Sunday Telegraph* in 1962, is reprinted in *What Became of Jane Austen? and Other Questions* (London: Jonathan Cape, 1970), pp. 212-23; hereafter cited as *WBJA?*. The quotation appears on p. 216.

[14] William Empson, *Milton's God* (London: Chatto and Windus, 1961), p. 146.

[15] Robert Conquest, 'Profile: Robert Conquest discusses Kingsley Amis, whose latest novel is published this week,' *The Listener*, 9 October 1969, pp. 485-86; p. 485.

[16] Martin Amis, *Experience* (London: Jonathan Cape, 2000), p. 180; hereafter cited as *Experience*.

[17] Kingsley Amis (ed.), *The Faber Popular Reciter* (London: Faber and Faber, 1978), pp. 36, 39.

[18] Amis told Dale Salwak that in *The Anti-Death League* he was trying to portray the 'malicious, malevolent side' of God. See *Contemporary Literature* 16, Winter 1975, pp. 1-18.

[19] *Experience* makes clear that Kingsley's 'hatred' of God has a profound effect on Martin's theology. He quotes with approval Kingsley's poem on Housman, 'AEH', with its implication that 'God is absent, or immoral, or impotent' (*Experience*, p. 170). The murder of Martin's cousin – Kingsley's niece – Lucy Partington by the serial killer Fred West, three months after she had converted to Roman Catholicism, raises 'questions of theodicy' in Martin's mind, 'naïve of me, no doubt' (p. 170). Although Kingsley remained silent on the subject he is sure his father shared them: 'I knew exactly what Lucy's fate awakened in him: hatred of God' (p. 350).

[20] Kingsley Amis, Column, *Daily Express*, 23 April 1969, p. 10, col. 8.

[21] Kingsley Amis, *We Are All Guilty* (London: Reinhardt Books / Viking, 1991), p. 52.

[22] Lytton Strachey, 'Muggleton' in *The Shorter Strachey*, selected and introduced by Michael Holroyd and Paul Levy (Oxford: Oxford University Press, 1980), p. 219.

[23] Amis, *Letters*, p. 1030.

[24] Larkin discusses his views on Remembrance Sunday in his recording of *The Whitsun Weddings*.

[25] *FPR*, pp. 19, 40, 48, 49, 51, 59, 62, 86, 95, 98, 126, 166, 176, 183, 184, 185, 187, 188, 192 and 201.

[26] 'The Human Abstract', *The Poems of William Blake*, ed. W. H. Stevenson and David V. Erdman (London: Longman, 1971), p. 216.

[27] Nevertheless, Amis found 'Jack Xt' (or 'Jack of Christ'), from 'If I were tickled by the rub of love' one of the most distasteful instances of Dylan Thomas's religiosity. See *Letters*, p. 109.

10
'Bread and Circuses': Christian History According to the World of Star Trek

LARRY J. KREITZER

1. *Star Trek* and the history of early Christianity

One of the most interesting *Star Trek* episodes for issues of faith and culture, dealing as it does with the history of early Christianity, is 'Bread and Circuses'. The screenplay for this episode was written by Gene Roddenberry and Gene L. Coon and was based on a story by John Kneubuhl. The episode was originally aired on 15 March 1968 toward the end of the second season and the content has made it the occasional subject of comparison with Christianity ever since.

The title of the episode is taken from Juvenal's *Satires*, a humorous, but sharply penetrating criticism of the first-century Roman world by one of its most creative, and enigmatic, poets. Juvenal published his first satires sometime around 100 CE (the exact dates of his birth and death are unknown). He is described by several ancient sources as having been banished by the Emperor Domitian (81-96 CE), which may account for his biting criticism of the Roman political system. In any event, Juvenal was well-placed chronologically to observe some of the tensions between the practices of the established Roman state and those of the burgeoning Christian faith. In this sense it is entirely fitting that the *Star Trek* episode which most clearly deals with the historical milieu in which Christianity arose is the one bearing a phrase from Juvenal as its title.

My aim within this chapter is to explore the way in which early Christian history is portrayed within the world of *Star Trek*. I shall be concerned in particular with the way in which the presentation of that history compares with that contained in what is generally regarded as the most historical of the New Testament writings, the two-part effort known as Luke-Acts.

The phrase 'bread and circuses' (the Latin is *panis et circenses*) has become in modern parlance something of a by-word for unrestrained and ill-disciplined pleasure, an all-consuming desire to be entertained, usually at the expense and degradation of others. It is especially associated with barbaric displays of physical combat in the Roman amphitheatres, fights to the death between heavily-armoured gladiators or maulings of perse-cuted Christians and unfortunate slaves by wild beasts. One of the most famous descriptions of persecutions of Christians occurs in Tacitus' *Annals* 15:44:2-8. It describes the activities of the notoriously cruel Emperor Nero (54-68 CE):

> Their deaths were made farcical. Dressed in wild animals' skins, they were torn to pieces by dogs, or crucified, or made into torches to be ignited after dark as substitutes for daylight. Nero provided his Gardens for the spectacle, and exhibited displays in the Circus, at which he min-gled with the crowd – or stood in a chariot, dressed as a charioteer.[1]

The image is a familiar one to us, fostered by means of Hollywood block-buster films of the 1950s and 1960s. Films such as *The Sign of the Cross* (1932), *Quo Vadis* (1951), *Ben Hur* (1959), *Spartacus* (1960), *Barabbas* (1962), *Cleopatra* (1963), and especially *The Robe* (1953) and its sequel *Demetrius and the Gladiators* (1954), have all helped to form our mental picture of the clash between Christianity and the Roman Empire in those first formative years following the death and resurrection of Jesus Christ. Indeed, it should hardly come as a surprise that 'Bread and Circuses' used many of the props and costumes of some of these epic films. After all, Paramount Pictures was the studio responsible for several of them.

Yet we are not without our own contemporary versions of 'bread and circuses', particularly within the mass media. Perhaps the nearest modern equivalent is the Sky Television's *WWF Superstars of Wrestling* which is rapidly growing in popularity among less discriminating viewers. Others might point to the sporting gladiatorial contests of Channel 4's *American Football* as another example of popular thirst for the thrill of 'bread and circuses'. Little seems to have changed in human nature in this regard; we have kept the same blood-thirst but simply switched the field of battle to a gymnasium, a sporting ground or a football pitch.

Most people know the Roman roots of Juvenal's phrase, but not many know its source or original context. The original setting of the satire from which it is taken is, in itself, illuminating. It comes from *Satire* 10, which is an extended discourse on the folly of the unscrupulous pursuit of power and an appeal for the reader to pursue virtue as the only proper goal in life. The immediate context of the crucial phrase (which occurs in line 81), has Juvenal describing the apathy of the Roman people in the aftermath of the fall of Sejanus from a position of power. In the eloquent translation of Peter Green, Juvenal laments the attitude of the people:

> Time was when their plebiscite elected Generals, Heads of State, commanders of legions: but now they've pulled in their horns, and there's only two things that concern them: Bread and the Games.[2]

Sejanus was the Prefect of the Praetorian Guard at the ascension of Tiberius to Roman Emperor (14-37 CE), and it is here that we have the first solid, historical connection with Jesus of Nazareth, for it was during the reign of Tiberius that Jesus' public ministry was conducted and it was technically under his imperial authority that Jesus was executed as a political threat. Perhaps the most influential vehicle for a popular knowledge of such matters is the BBC production of Robert Graves' *I, Claudius*.[3] As faithful viewers of the series will recall, Sejanus was a very ambitious man and soon consolidated power to himself, especially after Tiberius' withdrawal from public life to his island retreat on Capri in the bay of Naples. Rumour of the day had it that Sejanus had an eye for the imperial throne, and it took a lengthy missive from Tiberius himself to the Senate in Rome to remove Sejanus from office. Tiberius had been warned about the conspiracy just in the nick of time by Antonia, the widow of his brother Drusus, and took swift action to have Sejanus arrested and tried before the Senate. Sejanus was eventually executed on 18 October 31; he goes down in history as one of the most self-possessed leaders of his time. Juvenal picks out Sejanus as a particularly apt illustration of the fickleness of fate, noting that had things taken a slightly different turn, Sejanus himself could have easily been Tiberius' successor to the imperial purple.

By a curious twist of circumstance, this character of Sejanus is also an interesting connection to the world of *Star Trek*, for those sharp-eyed enthusiasts of *I, Claudius* will also recall that the character of Sejanus was played by none other than the accomplished Shakespearean actor Patrick

Stewart, now better known as Captain Jean-Luc Picard of the *Star Trek: The Next Generation* TV series. A curious coincidence!

2. The plot of 'Bread and Circuses'

The episode begins with the *Enterprise* encountering space wreckage while on a routine patrol. It is quickly determined that the debris is from the *S. S. Beagle*, a survey vessel under the command of Captain R.M. Merik, who was at the Starfleet Academy with Captain Kirk. However, there are no bodies within the wreckage, which has been drifting for six years, and it is assumed that the crew somehow managed to escape before the ship was destroyed. The trajectory of the debris is plotted and course is set for the nearest inhabitable 'M class' planet, Planet #4 in System #892. The plan is to determine the fate of the Federation crew and ensure that the Prime Directive is still in force, assuming that the crew of forty seven from the *S. S. Beagle* were fortunate enough to have made it to the planet. In short, this is another of those *Star Trek* episodes which plays with the idea of intervention in other cultures and explores the limits of non-interference; the Prime Directive forbids any interference in the historical development of alien societies.

What Kirk and his colleagues discover is that planet #4 is remarkably like a twentieth-century version of ancient Rome. In the words of Kirk's log on board the *Enterprise*, it is:

> an amazing example of Hodgkin's law of parallel-planet development. But on this earth Rome never fell. A world ruled by Emperors who can trace their line back 2,000 years to their own Julius and Augustus Caesars.

What links the reference in Juvenal to the story is the fact that this modern Roman world is complete with televised gladiatorial contests which are used to appease the masses – what we have is a TV version of 'bread and circuses'. Unfortunately, Merik and his entire crew have become the unwitting pawns in the hands of the unscrupulous leader of the planet and forced to do battle in the arena. Merik himself has been given a position of power, 'First Citizen', in charge of the gladiatorial games, but he is really a dupe in the control of another sinister figure, the Proconsul. This power-mad ruler, Claudius Marcus, has his eye on making the crew of the *Enterprise* similar captives – a plot which Kirk must somehow foil without breaking the Prime Directive himself. This dilemma, how to succeed in rescuing survivors without compromise of principle, sets up the crisis at the heart of the drama in 'Bread and Circuses'. It is a drama which plays upon the fascinating question of what a modern-day Rome would be like and there are numerous connections with the ancient world built within the story. Let us note what some of these connections are.

First of all, the Latin-sounding names of the inhabitants of the planet point to parallels with ancient Rome. We have slaves by the name of Septimus and Flavius Maximus with prominent places within the story, a gladiator named Achilles, and Captain Merik is known by his Latinized name, Merikus. A slave-girl named Drusilla also appears as the obligatory love interest for Captain Kirk, soon to become one of his many conquests as he sleeps his way around the galaxy. Roman geographical terms are also the norm, including numerous references to a parallel-planet version of 'Rome' itself. The 'Forum Section' of the city is mentioned as the place where dissident slaves are rounded up by the police, recalling the fabled ruins of the (earthly) Eternal City of Rome. Kirk explains to the ex-gladiator Flavius at one point that he is from a distant 'province' – an allusion to the geo-political make-up of the ancient Roman Empire.

In addition, deliberate parallels to the formal titles of ancient Rome are taken up and used within the episode. Thus Merik (Merikus) is 'First Citizen', echoing the title 'Princeps' a term chosen by Augustus in 28/27 BCE to express his constitutional position of authority within the Roman world. In addition, the 'baddie' in the story is 'Proconsul' Claudius Maximus, another key title of ancient Rome adopted by a character within the episode. A Senate styled along the lines of the ancient Roman institution exists (at one point the character Septimus describes himself as a former member of it). The Imperial military legions even figure briefly, when Flavius assumes, upon first seeing the trio from the *Enterprise*, that their Starfleet uniforms are outfits for some sort of new Praetorian Guard unit. More central to our discussion is the presentation of religion within the episode.

3. 'Sun-worship' and the Brotherhood of Man

The most important religious theme in 'Bread and Circuses' involves those who 'worship the sun' and describe themselves as 'brothers of the sun'. In the story-line, such adherents are invariably slaves within the structures of the parallel Roman society, runaways who have forsaken the brutality of the arena for a different way of life. The first mention of 'sun-worship' occurs when Kirk, McCoy and Spock are captured by a slave Flavius Maximus, who takes them to meet the leader of the band of runaway slaves to which he belongs, the man named Septimus:

> Septimus: Are you children of the sun?

> McCoy: Well, if you are speaking of a worship of sorts, we represent many beliefs.

> Flavius: There is only one true belief!

Eventually Kirk persuades the slaves of his mission and they agree to have Flavius lead them into the nearby city in order to locate Captain Merik. As the group leave, Septimus blesses the *Enterprise* trio with a benediction, highlighting the religious theme once again: 'May the blessings of the sun be upon you'!

However, the group led by Flavius is caught by the Roman police and placed in a prison cell. There they await their fate, presuming their death to be orchestrated in the televised gladiatorial games. While in prison Kirk has a discussion with Flavius which is important for establishing not only the time scale being suggested in the episode, but the nature of the 'sun-worship' which the former gladiator follows.

> Kirk: When the slaves began to worship the sun, they became discontent again. When did all this happen?

> Flavius Maximus: Long ago. Perhaps as long ago as the beginning of the Empire. The message of the sun that all men are brothers was kept from us. Perhaps I am a fool to believe it. It does often seem that man must fight to live.

Kirk: You go on believing it, Flavius. All men are brothers.

There is a strong pacifist streak within this 'Brotherhood of Sun-Worshippers'; they are peaceful and non-violent people. Flavius Maximus illustrates this when he refuses to enter the arena to fight in a gladiatorial contest (very reminiscent of Victor Mature's title character in the film *Demetrius and the Gladiators* mentioned above). At one point Flavius openly declares his commitment to non-violence. The Roman centurion guarding the four prisoners unlocks the cell door and the following exchange takes place:

Centurion: Flavius! Your friends are waiting for you. You've already been matched for the morning games. Come!

Flavius: I will not fight. I am a brother of the sun.

Centurion: Put a sword in your hand and you'll fight! I know you, Flavius! You're as peaceful as a bull.

It is clear up to this point that sun-worship is something quite special within this society. However, we eventually discover within the last moments of the episode (presuming that we had not been able to guess it beforehand) that all of this talk of 'sun-worship' has been deliberately leading us astray. It is up to Lieutenant Uhura to set the trio (and us!) right on this score:

McCoy: Captain, I see on your report Flavius was killed. I am sorry. I liked that huge sun-worshipper.

Spock: I wish I could have examined that belief more closely. It seems illogical for a sun-worshipper to develop a philosophy of total brother-hood. Sun-worship is usually a primitive, superstition-religion.

Uhura: I am afraid you have it wrong, Mr. Spock – all of you. I've been monitoring some of their old-style radio waves. The Empire spokesman is trying to ridicule their religion – but he couldn't. Don't you understand? It's not the sun up in the sky. It's the Son of God.

Kirk: Caesar and Christ! They had them both. And the Word is spreading only now.

McCoy: A philosophy of total love and total brotherhood.

Spock: It will replace their Imperial Rome, but it will happen in their twentieth century.

Kirk: Wouldn't it be something to watch, to be a part of? To see it happen all over again?

In fact, the essential core of the episode is built upon this play on words – the ambiguity of the spoken word 'sun/son'. I have no doubt it never occurs to many first-time viewers of the episode that it is really about 'Son-worship' from the beginning. Indeed, the director of the episode, Ralph Senensky, has deliberately reinforced our association of 'sun-worship' with what is being said by the actors throughout. The best illustration of this occurs when Septimus pronounces his benediction on the group as they leave the slaves' cave and travel toward the city. Here Senensky deliberately cuts to a shot of the sun shining brightly overhead at the precise point that Septimus says the crucial (ambiguous!) word. We may feel, as viewers, that we have been taken for something of a ride on this one, but the surprising revelation of the true nature of the 'Son' worship certainly makes for dramatic irony and a pleasant 'twist in the tale'. True, we are provided one hint that things might not be as they first appear in an early exchange between Spock and McCoy on the matter. Speaking of the Roman slaves, they say:

McCoy: Odd that these people should worship the sun.

Spock: Why, Doctor?

McCoy: Because, my dear Spock, it is illogical. Rome had no sun worshippers. Why would they parallel Rome in every way except one?

Yet even this is slightly misleading, for ancient Rome did have 'sun-worship', not least because she embodied the religious beliefs and traditions of her subject peoples, including the Egyptians – and, as everyone knows, their religious beliefs included a prominent place for worship of the sun-god Ra. In addition, there is good evidence supporting the worship of a minor sun-god, named Sol, amongst Roman peoples themselves. Augustan calendars even set an official date for sacrifice to the god Sol, on August 9. Nor should we forget the identification of Apollo with Helios early in the ancient Roman world, as witnessed by Horace's *Centennial Hymn*, composed for Augustus' reinstitution of the Saecular Games in 17 BCE. Line 9 of the *Hymn* explicitly addresses Apollo as 'Kind Sun'. Even more striking is the fact that the Roman Emperor Elagabalus (218-222 CE) attempted a reformation of the Roman pantheon with his own local god Sol taking central place (Elagabalus was from Syria, a province renowned for its cultic worship of Sol). A similar move was taken by another Roman Emperor, Aurelian (270-275), a generation later. So keen was Elagabalus to promote the worship of Sol, that he identified himself with the god and minted coins bearing inscriptions to that effect. Aurelian did the same and even had a Temple of the Sun built, probably on the Quirinal Hill in Rome. Thus, 'sun-worship' flourished in the Roman Empire up until Constantinian times when it was superseded by Christianity following the Emperor Constantine's conversion to the true faith. Indeed, just to highlight this, it is worth noting that in the year 321 Sunday was declared to be an official day of rest precisely because it was Sun-day.[4]

The point is that it would be a brave historian indeed who would categorically assert (as McCoy does) that 'Rome had no sun-worshippers.' Still, the exchange serves its purpose as far as the drama of the *Star Trek* episode is concerned, even if it is historically inaccurate. Clearly the aim is to juxtapose 'sun-worship' and 'Son-worship' within the story.

One final, curious fact is worth remembering here that succeeds in driving home this essential point of contrast ('sun' versus 'son'), but not at the expense of historical inaccuracy. It seems that Aurelian's 'Temple of the Sun' was originally dedicated on 25 December, at the winter solstice, as a symbol of the unconquerable sun coming forth once again to increase light. So widespread was the pagan festival associated with Sol and the winter solstice, that early in the fourth century the Christian church spiritualized it and transformed it into the Feast of the Nativity of the Sun of Righteousness. The first tentative steps were thus taken to that festival we now all know as Christmas.

In short, 'Bread and Circuses' sets out the relationship between 'sun-worship' and 'Son-worship' as a straightforward clash between pagan Rome and the truth of Christianity – and it leaves the impression that Christianity will eventually prevail over the more primitive Roman world. In this sense the episode is very reminiscent of the confrontation between pagan Rome and the Christian church which we see culminate in the legendary words of Emperor Julian II (known as Julian the Apostate) (361-363 CE), who, following his unsuccessful attempt to revive pagan religion at the expense of Christianity, was driven to utter on his deathbed: 'You have conquered, O Galilean!'

However, things are rarely so simplistic and it is probably nearer the truth to say that historically Christianity prevailed by absorbing, rather than confronting, pagan sun-worship. Let us now turn to consider the way in which the rise of Christianity is explained within both Luke-Acts and 'Bread and Circuses'.

4. The historical framing of the story

It has long been recognized that Luke's Gospel has a special concern with setting the story of Jesus of Nazareth against its historical background. Indeed, the author (traditionally known as Luke the physician) declares his intention along these lines in the opening paragraph of the work (Luke 1:1-4):

> Inasmuch as many have undertaken to compile a narrative of the things which have been accomplished among us, just as they were delivered to us by those who from the beginning were eyewitnesses and ministers of the word, it seemed good to me also, having followed all things closely for some time past, to write an orderly account for you, most excellent Theophilus, that you may know the truth concerning the things of which you have been informed.

This same attention to historical detail is echoed throughout Acts, which also opens with a similar declaration made to Luke's patron Theophilus about the life of Jesus (Acts 1:1):

> In the first book, O Theophilus, I have dealt with all that Jesus began to do and teach.

At several other points in the gospel narrative the writer provides historical anchors to his account of the life of Jesus of Nazareth. Thus we read in 2:1-2:

> In those days a decree went out from Emperor Augustus that all the world should be registered. This was the first registration and was taken while Quirinius was governor of Syria.

Or, again in 3:1-2, Luke's version of the story of John the Baptist, the herald of Jesus' messianic ministry, is opened with these words, filled as they are with references to historical personages:

> In the fifteenth year of the reign of Emperor Tiberius, when Pontius Pilate was governor of Judea, and Herod was ruler of Galilee, and his brother Philip ruler of the region of Ituraea and Trachonitis, and Lysanias ruler of Abilene, during the high priesthood of Annas and Caiaphas, the word of God came to John the son of Zechariah in the wilderness.

The central point here is that Luke clearly sets the story of Jesus of Nazareth within an historical context, firmly placing the portrait he wishes to paint within an historical framework. That is not to say that the other Gospel accounts do not contain references to important historical persons or events – they certainly do. However, these are generally incidental to the story of Jesus Christ as they present it and do not have the same theological significance as they do in Luke. When one compares Luke to the Gospel of Matthew, for instance, on this point the difference quickly becomes clear. Matthew opens his account of the life of Jesus with a genealogy (1:1-17), firmly setting forth the Jewish credentials of the Christ with no reference to the historical facts of the contemporary Roman world at all. Indeed, the Roman world is only hinted at in the body of Matthew's Gospel (a Roman military centurion figures in a healing story in 8:5-13 and a version of the debate between Jesus and the Pharisees about paying taxes to Caesar appears in 22:15-22). We have to wait until the trial and crucifixion of Jesus (in Matthew 27) before we have any detailed mention of Roman citizens, namely Pilate, at all. This stands in stark contrast to Luke, who is making a specific point about Roman history throughout. It is hardly surprising that all four references to the name 'Augustus' contained in the New Testament appear in Luke-Acts (Luke 2:1; Acts 25:21, 25; 27:1), as does the single New Testament reference to 'Tiberius' (Luke 3:1), and the two New Testament references to 'Claudius' (Acts 11:28; 18:2). It is as if Luke continually 'drops anchors' into secular Roman history, a style which helps characterize his work. As one New Testament scholar, Donald Juel, says: 'It is significant that Luke chose history as the medium through which to address his generation'.[5]

Effectively, the *Star Trek* episode does exactly the same thing, spinning out its tale of non-interference in another culture within the context of a defined historical period, that of ancient Rome. Yet, what makes 'Bread and Circuses' so effective is that it does not attempt to proceed as a straightforward story about ancient Rome itself. Instead, it up-dates the story, suggestively setting the whole thing within a futuristic context, bringing into play features of the modern world of the 1960s and making us as an audience imagine what a difference such features might make in shaping this fictitious Rome. But the key point of contact between Luke's effort and 'Bread and Circuses' should not be overlooked – the placing of the story within a concrete historical period, that of Imperial Rome.

5. Three distinctive Lukan echoes in the story

At three particular points, features of Luke's distinctive way of telling the gospel story appear in 'Bread and Circuses'. None of them is immediately obvious (Luke's work is nowhere explicitly quoted, for instance), but when the episode is examined closely they readily appear. Taken together they might be said to demonstrate how much 'Bread and Circuses' relies, perhaps even unconsciously, upon Luke's special contribution to the New Testament.

First, Luke's account of the annunciation of the birth of Jesus is alluded to in a curious way early in the episode. Shortly after Kirk, McCoy and Spock beam down to the planet in order to search for their lost comrades from the *S. S. Beagle*, Dr. McCoy remarks: 'Once, just once, I would like to be able to land someplace and say, 'Behold, I am the archangel Gabriel.' This is a fascinating parallel to Luke 1-2, where the archangel Gabriel is instrumental in announcing the births of John the Baptist and Jesus. In fact, Gabriel is mentioned by name only twice in the New Testament, both instances in connection with these annunciations (Luke 1:19, 26).[6]

Second, Luke's distinctive description of Jesus' ascension seems to underlie a comment made by Septimus to Captain Kirk while the two are in the confines of the slaves' hideaway cave. Kirk, seeking information concerning the whereabouts of the crew of the *S. S. Beagle*, yet conscious of the need to obey the Prime Directive and maintain secrecy, puts a suitably-phrased question of the slave leader who replies:

Septimus: No, Captain. I am sure I would have heard of the arrival of other men like you.

Kirk: Perhaps you have heard, let's say, an impossible story, or a rumour, of men who came from the sky? Or from other worlds?

Septimus: There are no other worlds.

Kirk: The stars...

Septimus: Lights shining through from heaven. It is where the sun is. Blessed be the sun.

It all seems innocent enough – until we remember that it is only in the writings of Luke that we encounter within the New Testament any description of Jesus' ascension from earth into the heavens following his resurrection from the dead. Luke explicitly gives us two declarations of this (Luke 24:51 and Acts 1:9-11) and alludes to a third (Luke 9:51), while the rest of the New Testament documents leave Jesus' present heavenly residence an inference at best. The crucial point is, that it is only in Luke that Jesus is explicitly said to have ascended into heaven – it is only in Luke's writings that the Son's movement to heaven is described in any detail. The comment of Septimus in 'Bread and Circuses' – 'heaven… is where the sun/Son is' – presumes precisely what Luke describes to us. As Leslie Houlden, commenting on the ascension theme within this New Testament document, has rightly noted:

> This occasion is then the watershed of Luke-Acts and makes sense of the conception of that novel work as a whole, with its wide historical and geographical sweep. In the New Testament it is a unique conception.[7]

In point of fact, we could legitimately say that the reason why we so often read ascension-theology into such descriptions as '(Christ) seated at the right hand of God' (Colossians 3:1 – drawing upon the Messianic passage in Psalm 110:1) when they occur in the New Testament, is precisely because Luke at this point has theologically won the day. His description of Jesus Christ's ascension is taken to be normative, setting the tone for our reading of the rest of the New Testament.

Third, there is an explicit polemic against what are perceived as false gods (by the followers of the Son) within the episode. At one point Spock shows Kirk a magazine entitled *The Gallian* which contains advertisements for a number of consumer goods all being marketed with the names of Roman deities. We have a Jupiter [8] automobile, Mars toothpaste, and Neptune bath salts all mentioned. Septimus explains at this point that the products are all:

> Taken from the names of false gods. When I was a Senator, I worshipped them too. But I heard the words of the Son. I became a brother. For that, they made me a slave.

The second part of Luke's effort, the Acts of the Apostles, describes in several key episodes how the truth of Christianity stands over against pagan belief in false gods. This is especially true in connection with the ministry of the apostle Paul, as he helps spread the message of salvation to the Greek-speaking world. A good example of this occurs in Acts 17:16-33 where Paul confronts the cultured men of Athens about their superstitious belief in false gods. In verses 22-23 we read these words:

> So Paul, standing up in the middle of the Areopagus, said: 'Men of Athens, I perceive that in every way you are very religious. For as I passed along, and observed the objects of your worship, I found also an altar with this inscription, "To an unknown god." What therefore you worship as unknown, this I proclaim to you.'

This recalls Peter's sermon recorded earlier in Acts in which the particularism of Christian redemption is declared in no uncertain terms. Note the closing words of the sermon (4:12), where, speaking of Jesus Christ, Peter says: 'And there is salvation in no one else, for there is no other name under heaven given among men by which we must be saved'. Again, it is the implied clash between Roman religion and Christian faith in Jesus Christ which underlies Luke's account. It is precisely this same clash which generates the conflict essential to the dramatic plot of 'Bread and Circuses'. 'Sun-worship' and 'Son-worship' are presented as mutually incompatible and irreconcilably opposed. Remember Flavius Maximus's declaration in the face of McCoy's espousal of religious pluralism (mentioned above): 'There is only one true belief!'

Perhaps it is because Luke, more than any other New Testament writer, addresses the Gentile world that this contrast shows up so readily. This is not to say that there is no theological tension within Luke-Acts over the matter; the fact that Luke even discusses the existence or not of other gods mitigates against such a simplistic suggestion. But it is to say that for Luke-Acts the final resolution of the matter is in no doubt – Jesus Christ is the sole source of truth and life and the claims of Christianity as a religious faith are absolute. In any event, the attitude expressed by Luke within his work about the pagan religions of the Greco-Roman world is remarkably similar to that of the Son-worshippers on Planet #4 and constitutes another point of contact between 'Bread and Circuses' and Luke-Acts. Interestingly, this particularistic attitude also stands in stark contrast to that of the crew members of the *Enterprise*, who are markedly more open and pluralistic in their approach to such religious matters.

5. Theological hope or misplaced optimism?

Before we get too carried away and make it sound as if 'Bread and Circuses' is nothing more than a popularized version of Luke's account of Christianity dressed up in science fiction garb, there is one further point of comparison between the two which must not be overlooked. It has to do with the impression left about the future of history. Will Christianity triumph or not? Will the effects of this new religion known as Christianity (or 'Son-worship') be positive or negative? There is little doubt that in 'Bread and Circuses' the viewer is left with a vision of eventual triumph, even over the less desirable aspects of slavery. Spock notes this at one point, remarking on how slavery has evolved into a social institution within this galactic Rome. In short, the story ends on a very optimistic note; some would even say that it crosses the border into naïveté. Joyce Tullock hits the nail on the head when, commenting on the world the *Enterprise* crew leaves behind, she says:

> Whether or not that world is all that different from ours today, or whether the growth of the worship of 'the Son' will improve conditions in that brutal society, is, in fact, an open question. The 'Son' worshippers are certainly benevolent and morally superior to the decadent Romanlike establishment, so the implication is that the planet's civilization is bound to improve. Let's hope it will. The *Enterprise* leaves it a growing, changing civilization, in accordance with the Prime Directive. But there seems to be something rather naïve in the attitude of the crew as they leave the planet. It's as though none of them have ever heard of the Crusades, the Dark Ages, or the witch trials.[8]

However much we may agree with Tullock in her assessment of Christian history (and it is difficult to dismiss it completely), that is not the end of the matter. In one sense this overstated optimism in 'Bread and Circuses' perfectly matches Luke's presentation of Christianity. Luke clearly presents the Christian faith as ultimately triumphant and eventually moving to embrace the whole of the world, spreading to the ends of the earth.

Many New Testament scholars have remarked upon the apologetic interest underlying Luke's work, the fact that he wishes to present Christianity in a favourable light to the Roman world of his day, to emphasize its positive features and to downplay the suggestion that the new religion was in any way a threat to the political stability of the Roman world. Others have fastened upon Luke's desire to address the needs of the believing Christian community itself as the motivation for the work. Regardless of what precisely we feel Luke's motivation to have been, it is hard to deny that his work is one of irrepressible hope – Christianity will triumph in the end.

Perhaps *Star Trek's* vision of the future in 'Bread and Circuses' is, as Joyce Tullock suggests, naïve in the extreme; but then so was Luke's vision of the progress of Christianity. We could go so far as to say that such optimism is necessary in a rapidly changing world filled with social problems and uncertainty – it is part of the mythic power of both stories. As Donald Juel notes in the conclusion of his helpful little book on Luke-Acts:

> Luke's optimism may be naïve. Yet in our time, in a society where Christians have real power or access to power, abandoning creation to the forces of darkness would be a premature surrender. The apocalyptic mentality is more dangerous, perhaps than naïve optimism. It is willing to consider the possibility of nuclear holocaust, and its preoccupation with crises of cosmic proportion can conceal the small wounds we regularly inflict upon creation. And even if we possess power, sensing genuine possibilities in our future requires confidence that life makes sense, that the past contains resources for the present, that we can believe in a God who is dependable and can be trusted with our destiny.[9]

Notes to Chapter 10

[1] Tacitus, *The Annals of Imperial Rome*, translated by Michael Grant (Harmondsworth: Penguin Classics, 1956), pp. 365-6.

[2] Juvenal, *The Sixteen Satires*, translated by Peter Green (Harmondsworth: Penguin Classics, 1974), p. 207.

[3] The TV production was based on Robert Graves' novels *I, Claudius* (1934) and *Claudius the God* (1935) and has been shown in America as part of *Masterpiece Theatre* hosted by Alistair Cooke on the Public Broadcasting System (PBS). The British Broadcasting Corporation (BBC) released the complete series on videocassette in September 1991.

[4] This matter of 'Sun-worship' is discussed in some detail in John Ferguson, *The Religions of the Roman Empire* (Ithaca, New York: Cornell University Press, 1970), pp. 52-56. Ferguson also briefly discusses (p. 237) a Christian mosaic found under St. Peter's in Rome which depicts Christ as the Sun-god driving his chariot across the sky.

[5] Donald Juel, *Luke-Acts* (London: SCM Press, 1983), p. 121.

[6] The other Gospel account of the annunciation of Jesus' birth, Matthew 1:18-25, does not mention the angel Gabriel by name.

[7] Leslie Houlden, 'Beyond Belief: Preaching the Ascension: (II)', *Theology* 94 (1991), p. 178.

[8] Joyce Tullock, 'Bridging the Gap: The Promethean Star Trek', in Walter Irwin and G. B. Love (eds), *The Best of Trek Number 3* (New York: Signet Books, 1980), p. 96.

[9] Juel, *Luke-Acts*, p. 123.

11
God around Us: Art within Us

JEAN LAMB

1. Introduction: reflecting visually on a way of being

A lecture I gave in October 1999 at Regent's Park College, Oxford, under the same title as this chapter, consisted mainly of a list of photographic slides.[1] Thus, the prospect of creating a consistent argument in a written form out of this list rather filled me with dread. The original request by the Centre for the Study of Christianity and Culture was to demonstrate through images and words the way in which the kinds of forms used in my art reflect patterns of Christian ministry, and how my art aids my ministry. This is an important area of research since – in a large part of the Christian church[2] – we are the first or second generation of ordained women ministers, and if we are serious that God has called us to serve as Christian priests we need to be able to reflect visually on how we have been changed and invigorated by this new way of being.

Our womanliness is going to have an impact on how we envisage the acting out of Christ's priesthood within us and for the world around us. It will mean that the priesthood given to men for nearly 2000 years is going to look different as our vision of God is included in partnership with men's vision. The priesthood of women helps to rectify the curse of Adam's sin and acts out the salvation which Jesus won for us on the cross. It is logical that it should exist, but miraculous that it should happen in our time.

A male ministry has both brought about a repression of forms used naturally by women and has also appropriated them in male hierarchies. We now have the task of understanding the art of woman and the forms she finds within herself, and how these natural forms and patterns of behaviour enable us to express the priesthood of Christ in a way which brings wholeness to the gospel. Jesus worked both with men and women to share in the fullness of his salvation. The choosing of the twelve male disciples or apostles fulfils the obligation to succeed the old order of the twelve patriarchs. Our waiting for nearly 2000 years marks the beginning of wholeness in the relationship between men, women and God in a way in which only Christ's short life was a forerunner.

2. The offering of human burdens as artist and minister

I was called to priesthood whilst I was painting a Lenten canvas on the passion and death of Christ in 1981. It was called *The Scourging of the Church* and it consisted quite simply of newspaper cuttings of people who had died that year for their beliefs or who were making a stand for their beliefs. I happened to include the pictures of religious sisters killed for their work in Chile and El Salvador, the South African township killings and the famous image of Bobby Sands in the Maze Prison. On top of these I threw a pot of red oil paint mixed with crystal dammer varnish in order to make the paint shine. Then I wrote the last words of Jesus at the top of the picture. Jesus died to save the whole world – to save those rejected and forgotten by society – he died for me.

In this picture-making process I realized that what I was doing was priestly, since I was offering the burdens of the people to Christ upon the cross and asking that his blood transform the brokenness of the world. Certainly in this I shared the priesthood of all believers, as many argued in opposition to my ever becoming an ordained priest, but I knew I had not only tapped into the secret of art as a transformer and lifebringer, but that I was being asked to become a key player in this process as a priest in Christ's church. Within two months I had been accepted for ministerial training by the Anglican Church and in September of that year I began a new life in St Stephen's House, Oxford. With one other woman I broke the tradition of exclusive maleness in a college dedicated to training for the priesthood in the Catholic tradition.

My call, since I became a Christian in 1976, has been to combine my faith with my art. In 1979 I had felt I was being called to be an artist in the Church and so throughout these last twenty years I have worked with this tension of either creating much art when not having a ministerial post, or else my art being squeezed to the minimum endeavour when ministry overrides. Always I have lectured and given art workshops, counselled through art and exhibited my pieces in churches and cathedrals. At the beginning it was extremely hard going.

After college, I had a studio for two years in an enormous Victorian vicarage in Reading. Being with the priest, Canon Maurice Brunsden, who had been exiled after being tortured in South Africa for supporting the liberation of his people through prayer and pastoral oversight, demonstrated to me how Jesus calls us to work for his kingdom. It simply means sacrifice. No other English priest had been able to inspire me to follow Christ – no amount of endless church services as a child would have encouraged me to go forward for ministerial training. This man did. He was broken, depressed, frightened (by the South African police spying on him in Reading), self-indulgent and a sinner, but he loved Christ and he demonstrated his love by laying down his life for Christ's holy church in South Africa. It is sacrifices such as his which have made South Africa free today. His encouragement given to Steve Biko, Desmond Tutu, Trevor Huddleston and Nelson Mandela formed the backdrop to renewal there and the beginning of my ministry in spiritually depressed England.

From that studio in Reading I went to St. Stephen's House and begged the Principal, now Archbishop of York, David Hope, for a studio space in the House. The House had recently been converted from a monastery for the Cowley Fathers and the Victorian architect had provided lofts. In one portion of the loft I painted for three years. There was not much time but the little I did became the foundation for a lot of new work later in Leicester. Some of the themes and forms I discovered at that time continue to be worked through my sculpture today.

3. Many 'found forms' in nature make up the whole body

Jesus calls on our faith and asks us to harness it in order to set in motion a new system or structure through which to live. In 1976 my call to become a Christian was through looking at the beauty of creation and acknowledging God's power to speak in it and through it. When I reproduced it on canvas his Presence flooded in unstoppable, giving such joy. What I have always done as an artist is to find a geometric or natural shape through which to channel the energies of God. So for earth I used the diamond, for the meeting of heaven and earth the semi-circle or a half-ellipse at the top of the picture; for Christ in Judgement I used a vertical eye shape, and the arch for Christ's presence in God's holy church. Later in the midst of intellectual debate in Oxford I used a multidimensional circle held in space in order to denote Being and Becoming.

The first set of slides I showed at Regent's Park College were not dis-similar to those early watercolours produced whilst at St Stephen's House. What I was trying to do visually in the lecture was to place down visual sounds, key notes, basic structures, before launching into complex narrative cycles. The sketches could be seen like a simple act of picking a flower in summer and seeing in it the world. I wanted to speak about the wholeness of the component part and the way in which everything acts together to build up the body of Christ whilst at the same time breathing life into the image of Christ within us.

The thirteen slides in this block were all of watercolour sketches, descriptive of land masses or sectional details of creation. One could compare that breadth of images to that of a liturgy of perspective and product which is the liturgy of the Mass, and to that of the individual peti-tionary prayer within such a liturgy. We stand before God's creation and try to unpick it or reweave it – but in vain. An artist but imitates the Creator God from the given materials with forms found both within and outside ourselves.

4. The redeeming of broken forms

The refashioning of the found form in nature is epitomized in the sacrifice of Jesus on the cross. Jesus' Godlikeness cannot accept the given in nature since it is flawed after the fall. In seeking to redeem humanity, Jesus also seeks to redeem nature. Jesus' found form as it were, is the Tree of the Cross which through sin is cut down to bear his body but which enjoys the resurrection of Jesus. The medieval artists told of this mystery in the flowering rod of Moses, the precursor of Christ's wood. I used that tradi-tion in my woodcarving *The Crucifixion of a Child* where the upper part of the cross becomes a living tree again.

My last major 2D project before I began woodcarving was a large woodcut made in 1988 called Sparamos Cross. I cut five pieces of block-board and formed them into a cross. Into each block I cut a section of Christ's body – his hands, his head, his heart and his feet. The image was the summation of suffering in the Church structure as a woman. There is no doubt about this, for the attacks had come on every side: three years in a male stronghold theological college and three years under a bishop who opposed the ordination of women to the priesthood. I felt my body had been cut up and thrown away; yet through the suffering and brokenness I made an image which when completed spoke of this universal condition. Here I realized that I had made an image of the eucharistic mystery even without planning it as such. I had followed my original mentor whose imitation of Christ in South Africa had so inspired me. I had followed Christ in this country to change and invigorate the church here and this poor broken cross was to be the pattern of my work.

The five parts of the cross, which could also be seen as the five wounds of Christ, I could print up differently, say upside-down to parallel St Peter's death, or repeated three times to imitate the Trinity, and so on. The last piece using these blocks was based on the theme of the Dance of the Sacrifice where all those elements of earth and spirituality come together. The black print of the block is superimposed over alternating red and green squares and rectangles denoting equality between the red of sacrifice and the green of given earth. For me this goes to the heart of the Christian message of the incarnation of God in our forms which he made, but which he needs to revivify if we are to perfectly act out his will.

My journey began in 1976 with seeing God in the beauty of created form in nature. Twelve years later I saw God's beauty in the incarnation with the suffering Christ and the eucharistic sacrifice through the brokenness of form. In the last twelve years since 1988 I have taken this brokenness in the literal form of wood, and tried from this to create personalities and narratives that tell the story of this eucharistic redemption.

5. The 'found form' as the basis for life-stories

As an artist I remake from the creation itself. I am not an inventor, however original my design, because I believe the pattern for all things comes from God. Some artists sketch the signs they see of creation but what I have always tried to do is to imbue God's Spirit into whatever form I find to work with.

A piece of wood is a found form which has already had its own life within the lifecycle of the tree. A piece of wood is often rejected, found by the roadside, begged from tree fellers or given by friends. I like to take these forms and change them into something beautiful which speaks of the way we need to redeem all of fallen creation. The first images I made were of heads, strange creatures reflecting damage from our society. Afterwards I turned my attention to the maternity project, which lasted for seven years between 1989-96. In this time I painted abstracts in water-colours and oils whilst being very figurative in my woodcarvings. The woodcarvings spoke of parents, gestation, journeying with children and finally the recognition of tragedy at the loss of a child and the suffering which parents undergo in holding a child in his vocation and purpose. These dark thoughts on parenthood led me naturally into explicitly Christian subject matter, seeing in the archetypal Mary the suffering borne by all mothers and in the archetypal Christ the suffering borne as a result of the sin of the world.

In a commissioned piece called *Our Lady of Sorrows*, 1995, Our Lady holds an empty womb before her. It is as though her heart has sunk into the pit of her body after the death of her son. The shape is both remi-niscent of a well, a well of tears but also of new life which is fulfilled in baptism, and reminiscent of the world; Mary held the seed of the new world within her and her empty womb describes its departure into a life of its own. My next piece, *Christus*, actually placed the broken Christ back into this baptismal womb, this time of Mother Earth rather than of Mary. Mother Earth cared for our broken dead Lord for three days. In that time Jesus' soul visited other souls in hell and brought them to life again after his resurrection on the third day. Both *Our Lady of Sorrows* and *Christus* are sculpted in the round but much of my more recent work has been carved from flat blocks of wood with deep relief.

I discovered the beauty of working in elm long after it has disap-peared from the landscape. It is easy to work, light in colour with few knots. The fibres seem to matt and interweave together diagonally as well as horizontally, thus providing a firm base for both deep cuts and detail. The first serious piece was called *The Crucifixion of a Child* which spoke of both the anguish of God and of the mother at the violent death of her child. In one sense I was continuing to live the Passion of Mary in that she had lost her most beautiful son the world had ever known. On the other hand I was bringing the argument right up to all of us about the way we treat our children by exposing them to unnecessary risk and by neglecting them spiritually, emotionally and physically. The image was a call to give up blind, selfish parenting and to help children become well integrated so that they can give love and not just receive love.

The problems of parenting led me, I believe, to consider ancestral sins and how they continue to belie all the good we try to do today. The twentieth century was one of the bloodiest in all history and yet somehow millions of people have survived, though utterly broken mentally by their ordeals. The way Jesus the Jew was treated was repeated in the Nazi atrocities throughout their term of office from 1933-45. In 1997 then, I began planning a new set of Stations of the Cross in elm and based on the themes of the Holocaust. To date only two pieces have been completed, Station I *Jesus condemned to death* (1999), which depicts Jesus before his accusers whilst the Jewish people are condemned to slavery in the camps, and Station II *Jesus takes up his cross* (2000), where we see Jesus carrying his cross just as the Jewish slaves in the labour camps haul trucks of the dead to the self-dug pits. Each Station is 32 inches x 36 inches with a depth of 2.5 inches, coloured with professional oil colour paints. The guilt of humanity towards Jews in particular, can only be expurgated through the blood of Jesus on the cross. Humanity is at a loss to explain its self-hatred – for all war against another is war against the self. We are silent apparently before the enormous tower of evil our parents have lived through and we continue to witness throughout the world today. Jesus teaches us that the only way to triumph is to submit to the will of God and to allow God to work out the image of salvation for us in the world today.

6. Artistic submission to the Creator

Christ submitted himself to the world initially in the incarnation as a child; he grew to manhood and took up a mission in ministry and finally died a most painful death on the cross, which is a man-made perversion of the structure of the tree. In using found form I am trying to imitate this godly submission to the art of the Creator God. The ego of the Renaissance artist, whose will over creation even twentieth-century artists inherited, has been stripped away in order to join with Christ in his work of redeeming flesh which is on its journey to heaven.

Both Renaissance and modernist art glorified the self-made achievements of human beings without paying due regard to the work of the

Creator. Post-modern art is at the beginning of its schooling; its influence may well last as long as Renaissance art; it is secular, rebellious, distant, disruptive, imitative of materialist culture, sarcastic and unilateral. It is flat and non-redemptive and cannot see beyond its own material borders. It sees no hope and conveys no hope to those who deal in the materialist hegemony. I could compare it to the funerals I take where neither the deceased nor the family have paid much attention to worshipping God in life and then find themselves in a state of shock when death creeps in upon them. Here there is real sorrow for there is no knowledge of life beyond death, no companionship apart from ageing flesh. Post-modern art wants to convey the shock of the material and its decay without helping us to recognize our hope, which is set in Christ alone. Christ did not rebel against the fallen world nor was he repulsed by what he saw. He came to experience and redeem, touch and save; in him was invested so much power from the Spirit of God that he could heal and transform the world's brokenness without simply reverting to anger and sarcasm (though all that was used on occasion).

Our tasks as Christian artists is then to pray that the Spirit of the living God falls on us and rests upon us as we approach our work of art. It is to turn aside from the distractions of this man-made world, into the world which God has created and in this we find true peace and renewal in the imitation of the art of heaven. So if we return to the title and purpose of this chapter which is to find God around us and art within us, we shall only be able to achieve this after having walked through the journey of renewal and grace and by shedding the scales of anger and retribution misplaced against a fallen world.

7. Remaking the earth and the place of the church

The Incarnation of God in our flesh tells us that we are not to accept fallenness as a given but to powder it with the glitter of heaven. We are to teach fallen people about the new way of life they could lead in the community of Christ, the church which counters the individualism of secularism and fear. We are to begin each day with prayer and end it in the same way in thanksgiving to God; we are to take nothing for granted but enter into the will of God for the renewal of the earth. Whatever gifts we have been given are to be used for this purpose.

The last set of slides which I showed in my lecture told the story of Christ's church in Sneinton, Nottingham, where I live and work. God has taken our family and placed us in an area of great deprivation. It is an area much neglected for a century until the last decade and we have recently heard that its renewal will continue through European funding. The way in which the comfortable and wealthy have built citadels of poverty for workers, never quite giving people enough to live on in terms of wages and space, has brought untold misery to generations. It brings about mental sickness, stress with poor diets and drug habits, in which I include medical medications and excessive drinking habits, and the abuse of children that is especially prevalent when men have a low internal self worth which is exacerbated by unemployment and debt. Violence and crime is rife amongst teenagers who are controlled by peer pressure to engage against their common enemy, the law-abiding citizen. In this wild place stands Christ's church, somewhat isolated and insulated against the needs of those around it. A crucifix outside reminds the passer by of Jesus' rejection by the wealthy and lawyers of his day. The beauty within amazes all that enter this volcanic looking outcrop which is our Church. Its structure is a mystery to all who see it and use it, for it truly reflects the art of God who is both with us and hidden from us. God demands that we look for him carefully and humbly and only then will he reveal himself to us.

Set within this building is a piece of sculpture called *Our Lady and Child Jesus*. It was commissioned for a church and she awaits a final destination. Made with green oak at least 600 years old, Mary holds the broken Christ child in an open vulnerable womb-well. She stands before our font offering her child to anyone who chooses to be renewed in baptism. In the last two years of work in the parish I have brought at least 50 people to baptism – adults, children and babies. Everyone is keen to make a new start in their lives by asking Jesus to be their friend and redeemer.

The last slide I showed in my lecture was of a work in progress called *The Visitation*, a piece about Mary and Elizabeth. When I showed it at that time it was not much more than a lump of wood that had just had its bark removed. It was a piece of 150 year old damson taken from my sister-in-law's garden in Cottingham. The piece was a commission for a priest who had been through a cycle of sorrow and renewal. The meeting of the old order with the new as reflected in Elizabeth and Mary, tells of the way in which God does not reject the old but chooses to build on it with new ideas which bring life to traditional structures. Mary both fulfils the Old Covenant and is the matriatrix for the new Covenant which includes all peoples. I included this slide because I was really excited by not quite knowing where the sculpture was going, what holes or fault lines I had yet to encounter and to integrate in the final piece.

The excitement I feel about my art in using God's creation is what I find challenging and invigorating about my work as a Christian minister. My work as a minister is to discover and extract rotten wood set in the heart of church life; it is to see the beauty in ugliness and to allow truth to pervade beyond the distortions of selfishness and enclosure. My work with material form has trained my spiritual eye to endure, to have patience, and to trust that God's work will be accomplished with joy and grace so that people may be themselves formed into a beautiful work of art.

Notes to Chapter 11

[1] This chapter is a written retrospective of a spoken lecture with photographic slides given at Regent's Park College, Oxford, in October 1999, as part of a series of lectures called 'Women in the House: The Art of Women Priests'.

[2] *Editor's note*: the author writes from within the Catholic tradition of the Church of England. The Free Churches in Britain have ordained women to ministry for longer; the Baptist Union, for example, approved the ordination of women pastors in 1920. However, this does not invalidate the author's argument that there has been male suppression of the finding of 'natural forms' by women in ministry.

12
Inculturating Christianity in Postmodern Britain

NICHOLAS WOOD

1. Positive engagement with culture

No human enterprise is conducted in a vacuum. Human beings are concrete and particular creatures, shaped by our genetic inheritance, conditioned by our physical environment, and born into a location in history and geography. So we are also born into a particular cultural tradition, into which we are socialized by our primary 'significant others' – traditionally by parents, teachers and peers, and now more than ever by the mass media.

Through these various processes we acquire language, and as George Lindbeck has shown[1], language requires a grammar, which carries within it a framework of interpretation of the cultural world we all inhabit. The American sociologist Peter Berger has characterized these as 'plausibility structures'[2]. All talk of God is rooted ultimately in concrete human experience. The point is that both the original experience, and any subsequent reflection and rationalization of that experience, take place within at least one, and often several, social and cultural settings. So the questions and solutions offered by any theological tradition reflect a particular social group. For example if we consider the English Reformation, it quickly becomes apparent that this was born not solely from high-flown theological conviction, but reflected a question of power and identity for the rulers of these islands vis-à-vis the rest of Europe – a legacy with which we still live and wrestle. Or if we consider the progress of Nonconformity in nineteenth-century England we shall find that it reflects the development of a newly wealthy industrial and mercantile group who were able to make powerful statements about their wealth and prestige through the building of bigger and better chapels. Even the timing of services, at the once hallowed hours of 11.00 a.m. and 6.30 p.m., reflected a social order in which the prosperous classes fitted divine worship between breakfast and lunch while their servants' spiritual needs had to be accommodated between afternoon tea and dinner!

There is sometimes a tendency within academic theology to ignore this wider socio-economic context and see theological development in terms of the history of ideas alone. But this is to give inadequate weight to the significance of the concrete and particular and the physical and material factors which shape human existence. Theology is the product of a community of faith whose lives must be lived in time and space, inhabiting not only a geographical location, but also a linguistic and cultural tradition and a way of life shaped by patterns of climate and land-use, work and leisure, and interaction with other groups whose lives are shared to greater or lesser degrees.

When we reflect on all of this the most obvious theological model to use in the interpretation of such a pattern is that of the incarnation. The heart of the Christian theological vision is the God who becomes incarnate in Christ. In Tim Gorringe's pithy aphorism: 'God engages'.[3] The incarnation is the ultimate expression of this characteristic of the divine nature. Christianity shares the divine nature to the extent that it is willing and able to become engaged with what the prologue to the Fourth Gospel describes as the 'flesh'[4]. This is of course shorthand for the whole reality of the human experience: the physical, social, cultural and all the other dimensions of human life. A theological tradition which is based on an incarnational understanding of God cannot do other than take the reality of the human social and cultural context very seriously. It might even suggest that human culture and society, however limited and flawed they may be, are things through which the divine can communicate. In fact Christianity argues that God does not simply communicate, but is able to be positively and creatively, indeed redeemingly, expressed. God, in Christian tradition, is not afraid of the flesh, however problematic we may find it.

Such positive engagement with the reality of human life and culture is at the root of Christianity's amazing success. From the very beginning it has proved to be an inherently translatable phenomenon[5]. Translation is the means by which Christianity makes itself universally accessible. It is a plant which has been able to take root in numerous cultural contexts; it is tolerant of a wide variety of conditions, and shows an almost infinite capacity to adapt to fresh settings and new circumstances.

In saying this one should not underestimate the difficulties of translation. Equivalence of terminology, let alone of concept, is rarely easy. Louis Luzbetak, in his significant work on church and cultures[6], recognizes three layers of inculturation. Using an anthropological method Luzbetak identifies three levels of culture: on the surface is the level of forms, that is, the shape of cultural norms in various societies; beneath the surface is the level of functions, which refers to the meanings and purposes of such norms; and beneath this is the level of social psychology in which are uncovered the fundamental assumptions and values of a culture. This third level is roughly equivalent to Berger's plausibility structure and lies deepest within the subconscious of a community. It is rarely questioned by its members, but Luzbetak argues that only when the Christian gospel is integrated at this level of culture is true contextualization achieved.

There is a complex dynamic at work here. The receiving culture is challenged and expanded by the new understanding which the gospel brings; the delivering culture is also challenged as its own narrow formulations and culture-specific practices are exposed; and, arguably, the gospel itself is expanded and deepened as new inculturations bring fresh varieties and expressions of the meaning of Christ to life.

At the heart of this dynamic is a tension. For the Christian community has constantly wrestled with the issue of how to discern authentic cultural expressions of the gospel. What some have seen as a process of inculturation, others might see as dangerous syncretism. In syncretism the gospel is too easily assimilated to a new cultural setting and loses its radical and prophetic edge. Another way of expressing too ready an accommodation with a particular cultural tradition might be to use the language of 'domestication'. Where a society has had long exposure to Christianity there is the possibility that the gospel is tamed and domesticated. This poses a double danger. In the first place the gospel loses its power to speak prophetically to such a society, and its challenge to radical discipleship can no longer be heard. Christianity becomes equated with conventional piety and moral respectability. Secondly such domestication threatens the translatability of the Christian gospel into other cultures. Where Christianity has become so closely identified with one society, one cultural norm, one social psychology, it seems utterly alien to other societies and cultures.

2. Christianity and European culture

This 'domestication' is a particular problem for Christianity in its wider
European context as well as for Britain which is our main concern here.
One aspect of this problem is that Christianity and European culture have
developed so closely through the centuries as to become virtually synony-
mous, at least until the eighteenth century. This means that Christianity
finds it hard to address its own cultural situation as the late Lesslie
Newbigin has forcefully reminded us in recent years[7]. It has also meant
that Christianity is so closely identified with Europe, or at least with a
certain type of European culture, that it may seem irrelevant to other cultural traditions. This has been a problem which has dogged the missionary
movement since the expansion of Europe in the days of colonial and
imperial endeavour. Christianity still struggles to free itself from what has
been termed its 'Latin captivity'[8] and to find appropriate ways of being
truly inculturated in non-European cultural traditions.

In recent years, the processes whereby Christianity became inculturated in Europe have been explored by the Dutch missiologist Anton
Wessels. In his volume *Europe: Was it ever really Christian?*,[9] Wessels
questions the depth and extent of the genuine Christianization of Europe
before the Protestant and Catholic Reformations. We often have too simple a picture of what we imagine Christendom was like. He quotes the
French scholar Delumeau who put it like this: 'the God of Christians was
much less alive in the past than has been thought and today he is much
less dead than is claimed'![10]

Despite this, Wessels notes the genuine success of the inculturation
process of Christianity in previous European cultural settings and attrib-
utes this to the way in which existing symbols were taken over by the new
religion and Christianized. He gives a detailed account of the way the
process developed in Graeco-Roman, Celtic and Germanic cultures. In
this process there is always a tension in the relationship between the local
context and the dominant or great tradition, reflecting the tension between
inculturation and syncretism.

One of the early questions faced by Christian mission in Europe was
that of replacement or transformation, represented respectively by
Boniface in Germany and Augustine in England. Does the Christian

Gospel come as a complete cultural package which simply replaces an existing cultural tradition, or is a more subtle process at work whereby the Christian message takes root in a new cultural setting and thereby develops new habits and forms? Wessels convincingly argues that where the new succeeds it does so because it does not simply replace but also preserves elements of the old in a new guise. This is not to doubt the fierce battles waged by the saints and heroes of early Christianity in Europe, but it was never total rejection: aspects of the old were incorporated into the new. In Ireland especially, the church adapted as much as possible to local tradition, in terms of the calendar, sacred space and great figures such as Brigid, the pagan goddess, who found a new life as a Christian saint. In Germany, many of the traditions relating to Odin are reworked in the cults of St Nicholas and St Martin. Similarly, in Britain it was Augustine's express policy to build churches on sites of former pagan worship. Our calendar is now so fully inculturated that we no longer even notice the pagan deities hidden in our days of the week – Wednesday is after all Odin's Day and Thursday is Thor's day. Even the greatest festival of the Christian year, Easter, takes its English name from a pagan goddess (Oestre)!

According to Wessels, successful assimilation requires both the abolition of that which is contrary to the gospel, and also the elevation of that which is capable of transformation to a new and higher plane. This leads to what he terms a reciprocal fertilization: the Christianizing of existing elements of culture, and the expansion of the horizons of the gospel itself. In other words, it is never simply isolated individuals who are baptized into the church of Christ, but communities, cultures and whole societies are also 'baptized'. The danger of syncretism always lurks and the proper defence of cultural and national identities must not be allowed to threaten the ecumenical, that is the global or universal, dimension of Christian faith. But not every connection between Christianity and new forms of cultural life needs to be dismissed as 'temptation, betrayal or syncretism'[11]. Lesslie Newbigin argues that the process of conversion in the European context produced a successful inculturation of Christianity, in that public truth, as it was understood and accepted in Europe, was shaped by the Christian story[12]. A whole culture was Christianized in the process of translation from a Judaic to a Hellenistic context. What Wessels presents to us is a reworked version of fulfilment theology, and I would like to return to this model at the end of the chapter.

3. The context of postmodernity

In the past, then, Christianity has inculturated successfully into a range of European cultures, but contemporary western culture is changing so fast that Christianity is finding it very difficult to keep up. The fathers of the church wrestled with the question of 'Jerusalem or Athens', but in the modern world we have to face the culture of other cities too. As Wessels puts it: 'The church in Europe on the eve of the new millennium must associate with other cities than Athens, without denying its own identity – "Jerusalem".'[13]

Many churches are still struggling to come to terms with modernity and wrestling with issues rooted in the nineteenth century, when in many ways popular culture has already moved into what is being termed a post-modern phase. Of course the notion of postmodernity is itself not uncontroversial, yet much of the current debate about the relationship of religion and culture centres on the issue of modernism and postmodernism. In the sociological disciplines, modernism refers to life in advanced industrial societies and the contrast is drawn with pre-modern existence. This is a development of the original talk of modernity in the seventeenth century as a word of contrast for all that was feudal or medieval. In contemporary philosophical usage, modernity and modernism have acquired a moral dimension with reference to the problems and tensions of life in the industrialized world. Andrew Walker has characterized it thus:

> Modernity is a historical process that began in the eighteenth century with the philosophical Enlightenment. It accelerated in the nineteenth century as industrialisation took place, and increased even more rapidly in the twentieth century under the impact of advanced technology and science. Modernity is a radical break, both socially and philosophically, with feudalism.[14]

Modernity and postmodernity are the outcome of a whole series of revolutions in European and world history and society. Not simply intellectual, these radical movements took scientific, political, industrial, socio-economic and cultural forms. A number of writers in this field refer to Peter Berger's notion of the 'sacred canopy',[15] by which he refers to the sense of a shared culture or shared roots, both spiritual and social. The combination of socio-economic, technological and intellectual processes have destroyed the pre-modern cultural consensus, resulting in a world where there is no appeal to common tradition[16]. Many aspects of communal life, family, marriage, the place of the elderly, have been radically reshaped (Walker suggests destroyed[17]) by the privatization inherent in these processes. David Harvey refers to the impossibility of universals, 'of any global project'[18] as typical of the postmodern society in which many now find themselves. The French philosopher Jean-François Lyotard famously characterizes this as 'incredulity towards meta-narratives'[19].

Since the oil crisis of 1973, the early twentieth-century modernist economics of 'Fordism' have given way to a new version of capitalism which Harvey calls 'flexible accumulation'. This has required a radical restructuring of the labour market (especially for women), industrial reorganization, accelerating turnover and consumption, rapid access to accurate and up-to-date information and co-ordination of the global financial system[20]. Following the shrinking of the world in the nineteenth century this has meant a second round of 'space-time compression'. Postmodernity is, for Harvey, a crisis in human experience of space and time[21]. Its prevailing mood, reflected in architecture and urban design, is that of 'fiction, fragmentation, collage and eclecticism, all suffused with a sense of ephemerality and chaos'[22]. For Walker too, the pluralism characteristic of postmodernity has to do with the culmination of this historical process in the arrival of mass communication, travel, new patterns of emigration and immigration and wider access to education[23], in sum, in the jargon of the age, with the arrival of 'the global village'.

Even a village is diverse. The point is that different communities live together cheek by jowl. In postmodern thought there is widespread recognition of many communities and cultures which co-exist within the same time-space continuum, many worlds in one world. Postmodernity shows a willingness to recognize their 'otherness' and difference, and an acceptance of the need of the voices from these worlds to find their authentic self-expression as part of the legitimate pluralism of our culture. But Harvey argues that by its willingness, in some forms, to ally itself with neoconservative entrepreneurialism, by its ignoring of the realities of global economic forces, and by its deconstruction of all forms of argument and meta-narrative, postmodernity destroys not only itself, but also disempowers the very minority voices it claims to acknowledge[24].

The ever-changing and short-lived images of television are seen by many as the ultimate expression of postmodern culture, a culture which posits history as 'an endless reserve of equal events'. This is paralleled by the growth of the 'museum culture' and the so-called 'heritage industry'[25], in which different worlds may be entered vicariously and with little danger of genuine encounter. If modernism (with its emphasis on planning) may be characterized by the notion of the house as a 'machine for living in', the postmodernist house (with a design emphasis) is 'an antique for living in'![26] The last three decades, since 1973, have been an intense period of space-time compression. In almost any city in the world:

'The whole world's cuisine is now assembled in one place in almost exactly the same way that the world's geographical complexity is reduced to a series of images on a static television screen ... The general implication is that through the experience of everything from food, to culinary habits, music, television, entertainment and cinema, it is now possible to experience the world's geography vicariously, as a simulacrum. The interweaving of simulacra in daily life brings together different worlds in the same space and time.'[27]

The throwaway society engendered and required by the consumer culture of late capitalism, has engendered also the throwing away of values, lifestyles, stable relationships and all manner of attachments[28]. While Charles Darwin might be seen as a symbol of the processes of modernism (or so Henry Chadwick suggests),[29] President Ronald Reagan symbolizes for Harvey the postmodern triumph of image over substance, aesthetics over ethics[30]. We are, in David Tracy's words, self-consciously 'linguistic, historical, social beings struggling for some new interpretations of ourselves, our language, history, society and culture'[31].

Some would see postmodernism as an entirely new phase in western cultural development, but David Harvey, out of his exhaustive and comprehensive analysis, suggests that it is a particular stage within the evolving modernism of the last two hundred years:

> '... there is much more continuity than difference between the broad history of modernism and the movement called postmodernism. It seems more sensible to me to see the latter as a particular kind of crisis within the former...'[32]

Seen as a whole movement in history, modernism 'explored the dialectic of place versus space, of present versus past,' and offered multiple possibilities in which the many 'other' worlds can flourish together[33]. This is surely the key feature of the contemporary experience. For pre-modern consciousness there was, at best, a sense of two worlds, the material and the spiritual. For the modern and the postmodern, with the space-time 'compression' of which Harvey speaks, within our global village there is consciousness of incredible diversity and therefore of choice, in every area of life, including that of religion. With this diversity of experience has come the recognition of the limitations on human knowledge. This is perhaps the crucial feature distinguishing the *post*-modern condition. Modernity was characterized by a confidence that humanity would discern and comprehend the meta-narrative joining the many worlds of our experience together and thereby master the cosmos. Postmodernity is much less optimistic and all meta-narratives are treated with the same incredulity. This is not to deny any possibility of truth, but simply to acknowledge that we know with *relative* adequacy, within the boundaries of language, history and society [34]. Any coherence within postmodern culture 'will be a rough coherence: interrupted, obscure, often confused, self-conscious of its own language use and, above all, aware of the ambiguities of all histories and traditions'[35].

4. Religion in Britain Since 1945

So the issue at stake is how Christianity can again address its own historic cultural setting, and for us in particular to ask how the Gospel might be inculturated in postmodern, and, for some at least, post-Christian Britain as we stand on the threshold of a new millennium[36].

If we examine the history of our society since the end of the second world war we see that the church finds itself in a radically new situation. Over the last fifty years there have been massive changes in our social and economic life which are reflected in the change from manufacturing to service industries, the reduction of the working week from over fifty to under forty hours, and the commensurate growth of the leisure industry. The changes in working life have inevitably brought changes to patterns of family life. The economy is based on the assumption of double-income families; most women work for much of their adult life and many more than some men; we have a high rate of divorce and single parent families; and we face challenges over the care of the elderly in our mobile society, in which few of us will continue to live and work where we were brought up.

A parallel phenomenon during this post-war period of rapid change has been the decline of institutions, whether we think of political parties, trades unions, or the Churches. For example while the population of Britain expanded from 32 to 50 million in the period 1900-84, the numbers of Anglican clergy halved from 20,000 to 10,000. In the 1940s religious life was still principally identified with the mainstream denominations and the churches had a somewhat protected position in education, broadcasting and many areas of national and local life. Now, even some within the Church of England have begun seriously to debate the possible advantages of disestablishment, and all recognize that denominational loyalty is hard to maintain in a post-institutional and consumerist culture.

However, we should not delude ourselves that decline has been only short-term and rapid, and therefore might be easily reversed. Robin Gill[37] makes a strong case for long term decline in the influence of the church in Britain for over a century. Anglican attendances declined from the 1851 census onwards, and even Free Church-going declined from the1880s onwards. Because of population changes both groups continued to build churches and chapels, and despite the growth of towns and cities Gill demonstrates that in many areas church capacity exceeded population both in rural and urban areas. The result was too many churches and chapels with small congregations and enormous debts. There were too few clergy to meet demands, which led to a pattern of shared ministry still in existence, and not many years later church and chapel closures. This created an impression of decline, with small congregations in large, empty buildings which was discouraging to those who did attend and was a strong disincentive to marginal or occasional church-goers.

Grace Davie has to some extent countered this argument with her well-known thesis of 'believing but not belonging'[38]. She argues that most people want to use churches for rites of passage, and most people claim to believe in God. Implicit religion is clearly an important factor, but both of these indicators are declining, however, and we have to ask searching questions about the nature of this supposed belief. At best it seems to indicate a vague theism, but a marked scepticism among many about an after-life. It is also true that private prayer persists with some, but the evidence suggests that this is mainly with the middle-aged to older generations, most of whom will have had some semblance of school religion and many will have attended Sunday School. In the second half of the nineteenth and the first half of the twentieth centuries, most children went to Sunday School, but their parents did not on the whole go to church; in the second half of the twentieth century, most children did not go to Sunday School and their parents did not go to church: 'In the absence of both churchgoing and Sunday Schools, a broad spectrum of Christian beliefs in any recognisable form is unlikely to persist in the general population.'[39]

The other and very considerable factor in assessing the progress of religion in Britain during the second half of this century is the greatly increased significance of religious minorities, whether we think of traditional religions or newer sects and cults. There has been a sometimes tolerated, often persecuted minority of Jews in Britain since the middle ages. During the late nineteenth and early twentieth centuries immigration meant that between 1881 and 1905 the Jewish population increased from about 60,000 to more than 160,000. In the 1950s Jewish numbers peaked at around 450,000. The current population is around 300,000 of whom about one third live in north west London. Part of the recent decline is due to emigration following the founding of the state of Israel after the Second World War, but about one third currently marry outside their faith tradition.

There are between one and a half and two million Muslims in the UK – about half of these in and around London, and two-thirds of the remainder in the West Midlands, Yorkshire, and Manchester. Most major centres of population will have at least one mosque and there are a growing number of Muslim schools, two of which have recently achieved state recognition and support in the same way that Christian and Jewish schools have done for many years.

Britain also has a sizable Hindu minority of some 400,000, with about 130 temples. The Midlands city of Leicester, for example has the second largest Hindu population of any other city in the world outside India. Similarly the Sikhs, who also number about 400,000, are the largest population outside India, living mainly in the East and West Midlands, Cardiff, Bradford and Southall. Nor should we forget an influential Buddhist minority, many of whom are western converts.

The reality of these diverse ethnic and religious populations is another expression of Harvey's 'space-time' compression and reinforces the diversity and range of choices in a postmodern culture. This has led some to adopt the so-called 'supermarket' approach to faith in which aspects of many traditions are combined in a kaleidoscope of cults and sects which we might file in the category of New Religions and New Age. Steve Bruce expresses the situation well in his comment that: 'The New Age exemplifies in stark relief assumptions which in dilute form are widespread'[40].

5. Inculturating the Gospel in Postmodern Britain

Our survey thus far suggests that over a period of several centuries the church was successfully inculturated into European culture in its pre-modern versions of Graeco-Roman, Celtic and Germanic tradition. This reciprocal fertilization produced the Renaissance, the Reformation and the Enlightenment resulting in the modern world of the last two centuries. The Church has been adapting to this recent reality perhaps less successfully than its first encounter with European culture. In many ways it continues to wrestle with the modernist agenda, even when culture is moving on into new post-modern forms. Just as the domestication of Christianity into European life and thought has meant that the modern missionary movement and the churches to which it gave birth have sometimes struggled to find appropriate non-European expressions for Christianity, we now find that for many people of the new Europe, Christianity is buried in the culture of the old Europe. How is a fresh inculturation of Christianity to be achieved?

There is a remarkable convergence of opinion from many quarters that this will depend upon the active engagement of local congregations of Christians with their own social and cultural context. This has been most influentially put by the late Bishop Lesslie Newbigin in his telling phrase, 'the congregation as the hermeneutic of the gospel'[41]. For Newbigin, effective Christian communities will have six characteristics. They will be communities of praise with worship at the very heart of all that they are and all that they do; they will be communities of truth, testing all things by the truth as revealed in Christ; they will be communities which exist for the wider community, not existing simply for their own ends but truly fulfilling William Temple's famous vision of the 'church which is on behalf of others'. Fourthly, within these communities people will be adequately prepared and sustained in their priestly ministry in the world, and fifthly the church will model a new social order of mutual accountability. Finally such congregations will be communities of hope.

Many of these notes find echoes in other writers. For example, Andrew Kirk of the Selly Oak Colleges writes of his vision for a Christian community which is characterized by its service of neighbours, its witness to truth, its search for righteousness and justice for all, and its focus on a genuinely caring community[42]. His first characteristic is that of care for the created order. While not noted or stressed by Newbigin, this is also the first characteristic of mission for a postmodern world embraced by the other great missiologist of recent years, the late David Bosch[43]. For Bosch, as well as being ecological, contemporary mission will be counter-cultural, ecumenical, and contextual. It will be the life of the church pursued by the laity and not left to a clerical élite. Above all it will be rooted in the local worshipping community. Similarly, if we listen to an

Orthodox scholar such as Andrew Walker,[44] he too sees the renewal of the liturgy and worship as one of the key notes of contemporary mission, along with churches which are prepared to wrestle with issues of plausibility structure – once again here we notice the concern for truth – and which are committed to be a holy people, living a distinctive community life-style. He even argues for the strength offered to mission, in post- or late-modernity, by the gathered church model. We find similar sentiments being expressed by Anglicans too, for example the evangelism officer Canon Robert Warren with his plea for 'missionary congregations', and Bishop John Finney with his recent discussion of Celtic and Roman models of mission[45].

From Ecumenical and Reformed, from Orthodox and Anglican sources we see a remarkable convergence of thought as to the character and mission of the church in a post-modern period. Where is this convergence coming from? Clearly one root is the common context of western secular society, that contextual and experiential dimension which we argued at the start is vital to the whole theological enterprise. But it also stems from a willingness to re-examine the tradition and learn again some lessons from the past in previous experiences and experiments with inculturation in Europe.

In particular, I want to suggest that there are three tributaries contributing to this stream of thought. Finney gives the lead here with his advocacy of a Celtic style of mission rather than what he describes as the Roman pattern. Of course we cannot but be aware of the vogue for all things Celtic at the present time and that might make us cautious. But both Finney, and Anton Wessels in the careful study I referred to earlier, see in Celtic patterns of mission vital clues for the re-evangelization of contemporary Europe. Certainly the focus on creation and mission which takes seriously the ecological crises which the whole planet faces, has plenty of support from what we know of the Celtic tradition. Celtic tradition also focuses more on process than event, and this too chimes well with Finney's earlier research on *Finding Faith Today*[46] where he demonstrated that people usually come to faith through a journey which takes on average four years. Celtic mission adopts as its motif the road to Emmaus, with its accompanying and slow dawning of faith, rather than the more familiar and dramatic Damascus road model so beloved of evangelical tradition. Finney also argues that the Celtic model which focuses on the monastery is a particular version of the gathered community. Not that he is advocating a return to monasticism, although contemplative spirituality is also increasingly recognized as an attractive option not simply within Christianity but also within the so-called New Age movement.

The significance of a committed and gathered community is being rediscovered, not simply in its Celtic version, but also through the revival of Baptist and Anabaptist studies. This provides us with the second tributary that is contributing to the river of thought I have just outlined, and I suspect that much of that is due to the gracious and patient advocacy of my friends and colleagues Alan and Eleanor Kreider during their influential ministry in these islands over recent decades, especially in their fostering of the 'Baptist and Anabaptist Network' of study. This rediscovery of (Ana-)Baptist tradition contributes a radical dimension to the missionary church for the twenty-first century based as it is on a community that is committed to truth and holiness, that is willing to be counter-cultural and to pay the price for that choice.

The third stream in this increasingly mighty river is provided by the western rediscovery of the riches of the Orthodox tradition, centred as it is on the worshipping congregation, in particular the eucharistic community, which roots the church at the heart of the gospel tradition, in Christological truth. Orthodoxy also provides a strong trinitarian basis for pastoral practice and missionary outreach.[47]

This coming together of three streams of tradition produces some rapids and eddies within the flow; it is by no means all smooth and calm. The Celtic and Orthodox models seems to be generally positive towards culture, whereas the (Ana-) Baptist tradition offers a more critical perspective. In trying to learn from all three perhaps what we require is a new form of critical engagement which brings us back to the tension with which we began between inculturation and syncretism. How can this tension best be held and explored creatively? I suggested earlier that Wessels' thesis was a form of 'fulfilment theology' and I want to conclude by suggesting that this too might be a theological insight which it is worth revisiting.

6. Inculturation and fulfilment

It is about a century ago that fulfilment theologies came into vogue, particularly in relation to the issue of mission among people of other faiths and cultures. At the turn of the last century it was linked especially with the name of John Nichol Farquhar, a Scot who spent many years as a missionary in India and who wrote an influential book explaining how Christianity might be seen as *The Crown of Hinduism*[48]. Within a couple of decades such theologies came to be seen as both imperialistic in their recruitment of other systems into the Christian camp, and as fundamentally mistaken in the light of Barth's powerful case for the discontinuity of God's revelation in Christ from all human belief systems. These criticisms must be heeded. However, as I began by arguing, Christianity is a religion of engagement. It centres on the story of God's commitment to the world, his willingness to engage with it in a radically new way, and this means that Christianity is inherently translatable, however difficult that process might sometimes be. In other words there is within our theological mainstream a recognition of continuity as well as discontinuity, a tension which is actually contained within the biblical doctrine of fulfilment if properly understood.

Fulfilment language evolved in the specific context of the relationship of Christian faith to its Judaic roots and we must always be sensitive to the uniqueness of that relationship. However, first century Judaism was already a faith in dialogue with Hellenism, and as Christianity expanded into the Roman world beyond Palestine, its engagement with Graeco-Roman culture became increasingly significant. A key issue for the first Christians was the question of the relationship between their new-found faith in Jesus and the Jewish heritage in which it was so clearly rooted. Recent studies have emphasized the significance of the group of *plēroō* words (in New Testament Greek) for this discussion, and these have played a vital role in the development of missiological thinking in the late nineteenth and early twentieth centuries. A brief examination of recent biblical scholarship raises the question as to how far this earlier application of the term 'fulfilment' was true to its New Testament range of meaning.

Walther Zimmerli, in an influential contribution to the understanding of the fulfilment theme, has suggested that it is the core of the New Testament preaching[49] and Richard T. France agrees that it is in some sense the theme of the whole New Testament and the bone of contention between the early church and Judaism[50]. Later generations look back to discern the pattern of God's dealings with his people and to discover the promises given within the covenant relationship. In their own time they look to the affairs of the nation and the wider world in anticipation of the pattern being repeated and the divine pledges being redeemed. This detection of pattern assumes that God is at work to fulfil his purposes and achieve his goals. However, fulfilment can take unexpected forms. According to James Dunn, in the end:

> The experience of Christ, the freedom brought by Christ, called for such a radical interpretation of the Old Testament that some of its revelatory functions had to be consigned to an era dead and gone.[51]

The significant point is that the use of *plēroō* words seems able to embrace this discontinuous element within the notion of fulfilment. It must not be assumed that fulfilment implies only continuity, an unbroken line of development from promise to completion. As Zimmerli has hinted, it is important to recognize that 'fulfilment' is not an unbroken or steady development. For example the use of the fulfilment motif in Matthew's Gospel includes the typological chapter 12; here it is affirmed that in Jesus there is present that which is *greater* than David or Solomon or Jonah. Fulfilment for Matthew evidently includes a strong element of transcendence or excess. Such fulfilment language embraces both continuity and discontinuity and it is difficult to establish where the emphasis lies. This may be because it varies from place to place, including perhaps the difference between the struggles of Jesus' own day and those of the Matthean communities. What *is* clear is that this fulfilment theology is stretching language in order to contain both the continuous and discontinuous elements of the Christ-event. God is faithful in bringing his pattern to completion and fruition, but he is also free to innovate and surprise his people by the manner of the fulfilment which he offers. The reality of the redemption exceeds the promise of the pledge, and that which is found in Christ transcends the imagination, even of Moses and the prophets.

Similarly, in what most scholars would regard as the late Pauline (or deutero-Pauline) letters of Colossians and Ephesians the cognate noun *plērōma* or 'fullness' appears, and here the Christological content of the term is at its most developed point within the New Testament. Scholars generally suggest that the writer of Ephesians, whether Paul or another, further extends the application of the *plērōma*-language in ecclesiological terms. The whole movement of thought reaches its climax in the notoriously obscure verses: 'he (God) has put all things under his (Christ's) feet and has made him the head over all things for the church, which is his body, *the fullness of him who fills all things*' (Ephesians 1:22-23 RSV). The Greek is capable of a number of constructions, but the piling up of such all-comprehending terms is highly significant. It points to the role of the church as that which fulfils both the purposes of God and the destiny of human culture and history. Clearly this was hardly written with a postmodern, multicultural, multi-faith world in mind, but Ephesians does have a particular interest in the relationship of Jew and Gentile within the Christian community, which is symbolic and representative of the new humanity God is creating in Christ. This process will eventually embrace the entire universe and God's purposes in creation and redemption will be complete:

> In Christ is already seen the full character of God, and that fullness is now being imparted to the Church as the first decisive step in the process by which it is to be imparted to the universe at large.[52]

Even at this early, New Testament, stage we can see emerging some of the later characteristics of fulfilment theology. It is highly Christological in character, and experientially rooted in the life of the Christian community as it wrestles with the question of religious faith and secular culture outside of Christ. The theme of fulfilment relates both to the purposes of God in creation and redemption, and to the spiritual aspirations of humanity for salvation and liberation. In Christ meet both dimensions of fulfilment. What perhaps was not sufficiently emphasized in the late nineteenth and early twentieth-century interpretations of this

doctrine, is that fulfilment is as much about discontinuity and radical transcendence as it is about continuity and completion. The cross of Christ
contradicted many expectations of how God would fulfil his ancient
promises, and a doctrine of fulfilment which is true to the New Testament
will include this less comfortable aspect. It is just such a creative tension
of which this whole area stands in greatest need according to David
Bosch, who criticizes all the current approaches for simply being too neat,
with no loose ends:

> The various models seem to leave no room for embracing the abiding
> paradox of asserting both ultimate commitment to one's own religion
> and genuine openness to another's, of constantly vacillating between
> certainty and doubt.[53]

Like Kenneth Cragg, Bosch sees the need for poetry more than theory, for a meeting of hearts as much as of minds. In recent decades
Bishop Kenneth Cragg has demonstrated how a new and refined fulfilment theology might work in a world of many faiths[54], and now Anton
Wessels has shown how it proved very effective in the initial engagement
with European life and thought. Perhaps the task ahead of us is to see how
such an approach might work in the complexities of contemporary British
and western culture. It will be an inculturation which does not always
look to condemn or abolish and replace, but also to transform and elevate
that which is capable of carrying gospel for a new generation, and to
expand the horizons of the old. There is no inherent reason why this cannot be done amid the complexities of contemporary postmodernity as it
was done in the ferment of religions and cultures of the first century
Hellenistic world.

A significant question must be how far such inculturation was a deliberate missiological policy, and how far it was an unconscious process
which simply happened. Even if we conclude it was more likely the latter
that does not mean we may not now use such awareness in a more strategic missiological encounter. Like the (Ana-)Baptists this will be a critical
engagement, in which, in Newbigin's phrase, the congregation must
become the hermeneutic of the gospel. Such a congregational basis will
ensure its contextual relevance in a postmodern culture, but it will learn

from the Orthodox in being centred on vital eucharistic worship which
will keep it in fellowship with the whole company of Christ's people and
the living tradition of the gospel. There will be no room for narrow
parochialism, since like the Celtic Christians such congregations will be
committed equally to the communities within which they live and work or
socialize. Indeed their commitment will embrace the whole planet. After
all they will share the biblical vision for the mission of God: a new
heaven and a new earth, the whole of creation renewed and restored in
Christ[55].

Notes to Chapter 12

[1] George Lindbeck, *The Nature of Doctrine* (London: SPCK, 1984).

[2] Peter Berger, *The Social Construction of Reality* (New York: Doubleday, 1966).

[3] T. Gorringe, 'Sacraments' in Robert Morgan (ed.), *The Religion of the Incarnation* (Bristol: Bristol Classical Press), p. 158.

[4] John 1:14

[5] See Lamin O. Sanneh, *Translating the Message* (Maryknoll, New York: Orbis, 1989).

[6] Louis J. Luzbetak, *The Church and Cultures* (Maryknoll, New York: Orbis, 1988).

[7] e.g. Lesslie Newbigin, *Foolishness to the Greeks* (London: SPCK, 1986).

[8] See for example Robin H.S. Boyd, *India and the Latin Captivity of the Church* (Cambridge: Cambridge University Press, 1974).

[9] Anton Wessels, *Europe: Was it ever really Christian?* (London: SCM Press, 1994).

[10] Jean Delumeau, *Le Christianisme, Va-t'il Mourir?* (Paris: Hachette, 1977), p. 139; cit. Wessels, *Europe*, p.5.

[11] Wessels, *Europe*, p. 167.

[12] Lesslie Newbigin, *The Gospel in a Pluralist Society* (London: SPCK, 1989), p. 222.

[13] Wessels, *Europe*, p. 171.

[14] Andrew Walker, *Enemy Territory - The Christian Struggle for the Modern World* (London: Hodder & Stoughton, 1987), p. 71.

[15] Peter Berger, *The Sacred Canopy: Elements of a Sociological Theory of Religion* (New York: Doubleday, 1967).

[16] Walker, *Enemy Territory*, p. 188.

[17] Ibid., pp.120-130.

[18] David Harvey, *The Condition of Postmodernity*, (Oxford: Blackwell, 1989), p. 52.

[19] Jean-François Lyotard, *The Postmodern Condition* (Manchester: Manchester University Press, 1986), p. xxiv.

[20] Harvey, *Postmodernity*, pp. 141-71.

[21] Ibid., p. 201.

[22] Ibid., p. 98.

[23] Ibid., p. 136.

[24] Ibid., pp. 116-118.

[25] Ibid., pp. 61-2.

[26] Ibid., pp. 63-5.

[27] Ibid., p. 300.

[28] Ibid., p. 286.

[29] Henry Chadwick, *The Secularisation of the European Mind in the Nineteenth Century* (Cambridge: Cambridge University Press, Canto Paperback, 1990), p. 174.

[30] Harvey, *Postmodernity*, pp. 329-30.

[31] David Tracy, *Plurality and Ambiguity* (London: SCM Press, 1987), p. 50.

[32] Harvey, *Postmodernity*, p. 116.

[33] Ibid., p. 127.

[34] cf . Tracy, *Plurality and Ambiguity,* pp. 61ff.

[35] Ibid., p. 83.

[36] Key texts for this section to which I am greatly indebted are: Steve Bruce, *Religion in Modern Britain* (Oxford: Oxford University Press, 1995); Grace Davie, *Religion in Britain since 1945* (Oxford: Blackwell, 1994).

[37] Robin Gill, *The Myth of the Empty Church* (London: SCM Press, 1993).

[38] Davie, *Religion in Britain*: see note 36.

[39] Gill, *The Myth of the Empty Church*, p. 206.

[40] Bruce, *Religion in Modern Britain,* p.120.

[41] Newbigin, *The Gospel in a Pluralist Society*, ch. 18.

[42] Andrew Kirk, 'Missio Dei; Missio Ecclesiae' in Kirk (ed.), *Contemporary Issues in Mission* (Birmingham: Selly Oak Colleges, 1994).

[43] David Bosch, *Believing in the Future* (Leominster: TPI/Gracewing, 1995).

[44] Andrew Walker, *Telling the Story* (London: SPCK, 1996)

[45] John Finney, *Recovering the Past* (London: Darton, Longman and Todd, 1996)

[46] John Finney, *Finding Faith Today* (Swindon: The Bible Society, 1992).

[47] Here also see Paul S. Fiddes, *Participating in God. A Pastoral Doctrine of the Trinity* (London: Darton, Longman and Todd, 2000).

[48] John N. Farquhar, *The Crown of Hinduism* (Oxford: Oxford University Press, 1913).

[49] Walther Zimmerli, 'Promise and Fulfilment' in Claus Westermann (ed.), *Essays on Old Testament Interpretation*, transl. J. L. Mays (London: SCM Press, 1963), p. 113.

[50] Richard T. France, *Matthew: Evangelist and Teacher* (Exeter: Paternoster Press, 1989), p. 166.

[51] James D. G. Dunn, *Unity and Diversity in the New Testament* (London: SCM Press, 1977), pp. 94-99.

[52] G. B. Caird, *Paul's Letters from Prison* (Oxford: Oxford University Press, 1976), p. 43.

[53] Bosch, *Transforming Mission*, p. 483.

[54] See for example, Kenneth Cragg, *The Christ and the Faiths* (London: SPCK, 1986).

[55] e.g. Romans 8:18-39

Index